Clear as Glass

A Mother's Journey
of Letting Go

Karen Sobanek Cioffi

ISBN 978-1-64492-847-9 (paperback)
ISBN 978-1-64492-848-6 (digital)

Christian Faith Publishing, Inc.
832 Park Avenue
Meadville, PA 16335
www.christianfaithpublishing.com

Scriptures taken from the Holy Bible, New International Version®. NIV®. Copyright © 1973, 1978, 1984 by International Bible Society. Used by permission of Zondervan. All rights reserved.

The events in this memoir are true, but some names have been changed.

Printed in the United States of America

To my beloved Savior Jesus Christ, my beloved son Jason, and my beloved brother Jamie. The three Js in my life, who I will always greet in the morning and wish a peaceful night. Thank you all for loving me.

ACKNOWLEDGEMENTS

I'd like to thank my editor Janet Ruth Young for her support writing this book. You have given me your compassion, love and insight that allowed me to give more of my heart to my story. Thank you Melissa for listening to your instincts directing me to Janet.

Also, to Jack Minor who put his "art" as he calls it of editing this book.

To my friends and family that have been there for me. To the members of Alcoholics Anonymous and Al-Anon for sharing your truth.

To Laurie Estey for your expertise in your field.

To Compassionate Friends for helping parents through the ultimate pain of losing a child.

To my husband Greg for demonstrating the consistent love you have shown me I didn't think existed.

To my heavenly Father who has always loved me and been there for me. Forgive me for looking for it elsewhere. Thank you for not letting me go.

Most of all to Jason who taught me about tolerance of the human condition of imperfection. I can only wish to have his sense of always being grateful for the simple things in life.

PREFACE

"You don't want to be here," the psychiatrist told me.

I glanced through the open door and into the waiting room of the schizophrenia support clinic at the Erich Lindemann Mental Health Center in Boston. An older man in his forties sat beside his mother as they waited for his appointment. His mother was in her seventies. Although I was only in my thirties and my son was still a teenager, I realized this woman and I were in the same boat. I knew exactly what the doctor was telling me: that although both of us had sons with a mental illness, I should not bring my son to his appointments for the rest of his life. I would have to stop coddling Jason and help him learn to live independently.

I didn't ask to become a single mom at age nineteen, and I certainly didn't want to have a son with schizoaffective disorder. Having grown up in a neglectful, alcoholic home with a narcissistic mother who cared only about what I looked like instead of how I felt, I had no idea how to be a good parent. Nothing in my upbringing prepared me for the challenge of parenting a son with a mental illness. I was still struggling to accept Jason's diagnosis.

While I knew Jason needed to be here for treatment, I also wanted to believe that he was different from the other patients we saw gathered around the front entrance.

Men and women were standing in a line outside, rocking from side to side as they smoked cigarettes that burned down to their fingers stained yellow with nicotine. Most of them had poor hygiene because of their illnesses and potbellies from the medication.

The psychiatrist was right. More than once I thought, "Is this what's going to happen to my son? Ten years from now, will he be standing around, oblivious to everything around him like those people?" They looked dead. As I looked into their eyes, I was terrified, thinking I could be looking at Jason's future.

I wanted him to be happy and vibrant. I knew I had shortcomings as a mother, but Jason was still a young man, and we still had a chance to turn things around.

To help my son, I would have to accept his illness much like I had to accept my own untreated alcoholism. I understood life would be a challenge for me as I had to navigate the sometimes-infuriating mental health system, support Jason without living his life for him, and be willing to give up my fear and control, putting him in God's hands.

I would also have to recognize and unlearn the narcissistic traits I learned from my mother that had become a part of my life. I would have to change the way I had always been and become the kind of mother to Jason that I never had.

This is our story.

INTRODUCTION

Clear As Glass: A Mother's Journey of Letting Go is the memoir of a mother tested by three crises—teenage pregnancy, her son's mental illness, and her son's early death—and how she learned both to love and to let go of her son.

I wrote this book to help other parents who are raising a child with mental illness. My story is one working mother's experience of navigating through the mental health system and doing what needed to be done to help her son. Those of you in this situation will witness another parent struggling to accept a child's strengths and limitations and deciding when to advocate or intervene. You will see the steps I took and the tools I used to keep Jason safe from hurting himself or others and learn what not to do when your child is in an institution calling every day and crying to come home.

Maybe, like me, you've had a traumatic childhood but have still become a success in the world. I was successful in business, but you'll learn that I was not as put together as I appeared. How successful are you really when you go home at the end of the day and scream at your children for being children? If you are living this fraudulent life, know that you are not alone. May my truth help other parents see their own shortcomings and possibly change their behavior early on, as it powerfully affects children's lives.

My story would have turned out very differently had it not been for Alcoholics Anonymous and Al-Anon. For readers in recovery, this book offers an illustration of how the twelve steps are executed in accordance with the book *Alcoholics Anonymous* (a process known as big book step study) and the clarity a person can receive from doing the steps. I suffered major losses in my life, including the death of my son. But thanks to the twelve steps, my sponsor, and God, along with reading my Bible and accepting professional help, I did not have to return to drinking or drugging or even prescription medication to relieve that pain. God healed me, but so did my opportunity to help others.

Raised to believe in a harsh and punishing God, my journey led me to a different God, one who loves me unconditionally. The greatest accomplishment of my life was raising my son to know God. Spending time with your children and directing them to God and his love is the most important gift you can give to them and to yourself. And as much as I miss my son, because he gave his life to Christ, I am not concerned where his soul will be eternally.

I hope that this book will inspire you to treasure your child. Jason was a gift from God, and although I didn't always treasure that gift, I learned through God's grace how to cherish him. Love those that God has given you because you don't know when he will take them home. Please take care of one another, and at the end of the day, ask yourself who is it that loves you. You'll know the answer by the life you've lived.

Chapter 1

"Stay still," my mother said, pulling on my hair.

Ma curled my hair a few nights a week, and I dreaded it. Holding a bobby pin in her mouth, she grabbed at my hair, formed a curl, and then jabbed the sharp pin through to hold it. The whole ritual took about forty-five minutes. Curl, flatten, jab. Curl, flatten, jab. Then I had to try and sleep with the pins digging into my head.

I have pictures sitting on my tricycle with my Shirley Temple curls on a rooftop porch beside my brother Todd. I was cute, with big beautiful green eyes, a round face, and those curls my mother worked so hard to maintain. However, my expression showed that I felt miserable. My face betrayed my inner turmoil, displaying a fierce scowl as I stared into the camera. Even at a very tender age, I knew I was living in an unsafe home.

My mother, Mary Arlene Derome, was born in 1934. Ma was French Canadian, Irish, and Scottish, growing up in East Boston. She had dark wavy hair and brown eyes and was blessed with a petite attractive figure. Her childhood was something she never liked talking about, and even when she did, what she said was telling.

Whenever she mentioned her parents, it was always to tell us how great they were. She never said anything negative about them, but I sensed there was more going on than what she was telling us. She praised my grandfather's Boston baked beans. She'd tell us how impeccably dressed and strict he was. None of her brothers were permitted to come to the table without a shirt on. She told us Grandpa would be very angry if anyone talked back to him.

She said, "Oh, you didn't speak up to Grandpa in his house."

Whenever we visited Ma's parents on Saturday mornings, I felt like I couldn't move or Grandpa would get upset. I believe my mother was still trying to seek his approval. She'd make baked beans for her parents and take them on the bus from Chelsea to East Boston, then walk three blocks carrying the hot beans.

My parents told me contradictory things regarding Grandpa's employment. My father told me he lost his job due to his drinking. Ma said Grandpa used to be a fireman, but he quit because of some of the things he had seen. Perhaps he saw a child burned or something like that. My mother wasn't sure, but she said he later got a job working in a greenhouse.

One of Ma's famous lines was that she was a "change of life baby." What I heard her saying was that she was an unwanted pregnancy. She was the youngest of eleven children, and I suspect at that point my grandparents were tired of raising kids. My uncle and aunt said that Ma was spoiled when she was young, but I believe no one paid attention to what she was doing. She told my brothers and me how, when she was sixteen, she used to take the train to the Hillbilly Ranch, a country music bar in Boston.

I asked her, "Where were your parents, Ma?"

She didn't have an answer. She was probably wondering the same thing.

Ma met a man at the Hillbilly Ranch named Andrew Andersen. His friends called him Andy. He was in the navy, stationed at the historical Charlestown Navy Yard. Ma and Andy dated for a few months. She told me that whenever Andy visited, my grandmother would hide Andy's shoes so my strict grandfather wouldn't see them when he came home.

Eventually, Ma and Andy had a misunderstanding and broke up. A year later, my mother met my father. Eugene August Sobanek was born in 1933 in the small Wisconsin town of Krakow. He was handsome and had olive skin, hazel eyes, a dimple in his chin, and small sharp features. His parents were both German and Polish. My dad grew up in a strict home, and my grandparents wanted him to be a farmer.

A girl he fell in love with dated him for a year before dumping him when her boyfriend got out of the service. Not wanting to stick around the farm, my dad joined the coast guard and was stationed in Boston.

Both my parents still had feelings for other people, but within a few months, they were married. They were both good-looking, and I suppose they were brought together by lust. They had no money, so a justice of the peace performed the ceremony. Over the years, my mother continued to talk about Andy—how handsome he was and how much fun they had together. He was the one that got away, and she never quite got over him.

When I was three, my parents moved to Chelsea, a small city of two point five square miles just over the Tobin Bridge from Boston. During the time I grew up there, the streets were lined with many two- and three-family houses, along with many barrooms.

There were three of us kids: eleven, eight, and three. My oldest brother, Wayne, was quiet and kept to himself, and I didn't get much attention from him. He kept a small green turtle in a fish tank on his dresser, and he liked Mike Nesmith of the Monkees. Todd was tall for his age, and the kids eventually named him Big Bird. He had an explosive temper, and even at that early age, I felt there was some-thing not quite right with him. But he was talented in that he drew very well.

Dad was a machinist, and my mom was a homemaker. She dropped out of school in ninth grade. I never asked why, thinking the question wouldn't have been received well. Her talk about religion was limited. If something bad happened, like one of us falling off our bike, she said it was because God was punishing us. What power I thought I had as a child to think that I could get God to move in even small areas to intervene in my life since whenever something bad happened it must have been my fault.

Ma viewed the world as a dark and frightening place. She was afraid of traveling, especially flying. She constantly talked about death and told me scary things that happened many years ago, for no reason other than to frighten me. One time, she told me in graphic detail about a child murder that took place in nearby Revere a couple of miles away. She also related a story about someone who fell asleep on a couch that caught fire. Often, the "moral of the story" was not to leave the immediate neighborhood, the box that we lived our lives in.

I also remember being across the street from our house and under the porch when a boy in the neighborhood took a stick and put it near my vagina. The sad part was that my brother Todd, someone I thought would protect me, just watched, thinking it was funny.

After a couple of years, my parents lost the house on Congress Avenue. My mother told me it was due to Dad's drinking and not paying the bills. We moved to Watts Street, about a five-minute walk up over the hill. Shurtleff School was three blocks away, near the downtown area. Each day, I had to walk by a very old cemetery surrounded by a black wrought iron fence and a Jewish butchery that always had freshly killed chickens hanging in the window. On my first day of kindergarten, my mother just left me on the landing. Terrified at being abandoned, all I could do was cry. I remember chasing a little boy around in class, trying to get his attention. Even at this young age, I was already trying to attach myself to a male. I had a fear of being alone and abandoned that I would carry with me throughout my life, and that eventually catapulted me into alcoholism.

The friends I made in school and in the neighborhood helped me find some relief from the anxiety. A girl named Lisa asked me to walk home with her and her sister. Lisa was a bubbly brown-haired Jewish girl with a cluster of dimples on one side of her mouth. We were always giggling with each other. Her mom was a nurse at Chelsea Memorial Hospital, and Lisa would ask me to keep her company after school until her mom came home. We'd play "puddle" in front of her house—a game where we avoided stepping on the lines between the bricks in the stairs. Her house was peaceful, and I felt safe there.

Unfortunately, when you have alcoholic parents, nearly no one was allowed to play at my house. Lisa came over once a year, on Christmas Day, because I wanted her to experience Christmas. We had an artificial tree with lots of silver tinsel. My parents hid the gifts in their bedroom closet, and when they went out, Todd would rip a piece of the wrapping paper to see inside. On Christmas Day, my brothers and father would set up their Mattel racetracks on the floor and play together. I took my gifts into my bedroom and piled them up on my bed. I wanted to create my own space to play in with Lisa.

Other than that, my mother didn't like to talk to most people, and she didn't want kids in our house. She'd tell us constantly not to tell our business to people out on the street. She lived with a lot of shame from secrets she had from childhood and in her own life. This made me feel at an early age that I was always doing something wrong.

When my father was at the bars after work, my mother would tell us over and over he was out drinking. I got anxious hearing that because I knew when he got home there would be yelling and physical fighting. I'd stay and hide in my bedroom, which had a door that opened to the hallway, so I could hear everyone coming up and down the stairs.

The bar was only a few streets away, so Dad would walk home. Sometimes he banged loudly to have someone open the door; other times, I'd hear him in the hallway trying to find his key, already sounding angry. What made his coming home even more anxious and terrifying was we never knew what was going to happen when my father came home after a night of drinking. I'd lie there, trembling in my bedroom, terrified of what would take place when he opened the door. Each time he was out drinking, I would pray to God that when he came home he'd go right to sleep and not beat up my mother. There were times when it seemed like he was going to do just that until my mother made a comment. This spark was all it took to light the fuse; then they'd start yelling at each other. Wayne would get out of bed and pull my father off my mother while we all screamed for Dad to stop. I was so grateful Wayne was there because he was older and tried to get things under control. This happened a few times a week. The unpredictability made it especially scary for a child.

The insanity of my father coming home drunk and Todd's explosive temper, if he was disciplined or criticized in the slightest way, was too much to leave to chance. It was an unpredictable house to live in, and I wouldn't have wanted to be embarrassed if I brought a friend home.

Although my mother didn't like school, I did well in school and always wanted to be a good little girl. When you feel powerless as a child, being good is one way to feel like you have control. I had childhood dreams of becoming an archeologist. I loved research into learning how our past can give us clues as to why things are the way they are now. Who lived many years ago, and how did they live? Where did God play a part in the world?

I also had dreams of becoming a professional ice skater. I loved the freedom of skating on the ice and how pretty the skaters looked with their leotard outfits. My father took us skating sometimes and tried to teach me how to skate backward. But whenever I asked my parents for things like dance school or skating, I was told no, they couldn't afford it. What made it so painful was it seemed as if I was the only one they didn't have money for. Todd was able to go to Boy Scouts, which cost money, but I never said anything. I always felt I was asking too much. I was fortunate to have friends like Marla who took dance lessons and skating lessons that would teach me what they learned.

My dreams slowly became unreachable due to the increasing neglect and lack of safety at home. Like most children felt during those years, I wanted the ideal family, like the Brady Bunch. Although they had a blended family of boys and girls, they were respectful of one another's boundaries, unlike what I was experiencing at my house with Todd. Their parents were always home and took an interest in all of them. The Waltons were another favorite of mine. They were poor, but they loved one another.

My youngest brother, Jamie, was born in the summer of 1968. He looked a lot like me, with a round face, but he had brown eyes. The night he was born, I was sent to my cousin Cinnia's house in Winthrop to spend the night. Winthrop is a seaside town ten minutes from Chelsea. I was only five, but all I could think of while I was there was to be on my best behavior since I should feel grateful they let me stay. I was impressed with Winthrop and decided that I wanted to live on the water. Cinnia's mother, my aunt Ethel, dressed well and wore her makeup beautifully when she came to our house on Friday nights. And in my little mind, I thought that must make Winthrop a nice place.

I always felt closer to my dad than my mother, probably because, despite his alcoholic rages, Dad spent some time teaching me things. We enjoyed watching *The French Chef* and Mutual of Omaha's *Wild Kingdom* together. He'd help at times with my homework while Mom never did anything with us but take us to the beach.

Ma loved the beach. She took us to Revere Beach as far back as I can remember. We took a bus that stopped around the corner from our house. My mother wore a housecoat over her bathing suit and a kerchief over her hair. One kerchief was powder blue with round sequins like fish scales that blew in the wind. We sat across from the old bathhouse, next to what used to be the Metropolitan District Commission police station. Ma used Vaseline to get a tan, and I'd look at her toenails, which were always painted a frosted pink. She sat on the lounge chair she carried faithfully each time we went. My toenails look the same. They're not flat; they have a heightened curve to them that detaches from my skin. Even today, when I lie on the couch, I find myself crossing my legs like she always did, and I see my mother on her bed watching television. We stopped going to the beach when we left Watts Street.

Through the years, Ma always threw in our faces the fact that she took us all to the beach. For years, I just agreed, saying, "I know, Ma, you did." More recently, I said, "Ma, you're the one who loved going to the beach. You say it like I owe you something for taking us. Taking kids to the beach, that's what mothers do." Whatever she did, she exaggerated it, as if she was doing special things no other mother in the world would do.

Growing up, Jamie and I were the closest as siblings. We watched World Wrestling Federation matches on Saturday mornings and played with his Mattel Matchbox cars. Jamie was a funny kid. He loved adventure and cars. He also loved Snoopy, and one time, he ironed a Snoopy decal onto his underwear.

My mother would tell you a different story. She'd tell you that Todd was in every picture with me and was protective of me. But in reality, I was in constant anxiety around Todd because he peeked at me while I got dressed or came into my room while I was sleeping. He also had an explosive temper. I developed an unhealthy bond with him, as most victims of abuse do. As a child, I didn't tell anyone about the sexual abuse and how he bullied me. I was terrified of him and did what I needed to do to survive. Both my parents must have known about his mental state, but they left me alone with him anyway. I felt physically unsafe with Todd, and I felt emotionally unsafe with Ma because she defended him.

Todd was always skipping school and lying to my parents. My mother admitted that he was a habitual liar, but she still stood by him. He always got in trouble for stealing. In school, he was bullied quite a bit due to his height, his awkwardness, and the fact that he spoke inappropriately at times. He'd ask private questions most people don't ask like, "How much did you pay for that car?" or "How much money do you make?" I was so embarrassed when he did things like this, but when he was bullied, I'd stand up for him if I could.

When we grew older, I buddied up to Todd because he had money from his addiction to stealing. We were walking to school one day when he was about twelve and he pulled out a wallet that wasn't his with bills in it. He told some story that I didn't believe about where he'd found the wallet. Later, he robbed houses, mostly for jewelry, Oriental rugs, or Hummel figurines.

While living on Congress Avenue, I met my longtime friend Susan, who was two years older. She was big-boned for her age and very motherly toward me. Susan's mom worked at the airport. So after school, Susan started supper, baked, washed, and hung out the laundry, along with caring for her siblings. Susan's back porch was straight across from our kitchen window on the second floor, so I could always see what was going on. Her brothers would hit her sometimes if she told them what to do.

Susan's family moved to Las Vegas in 1973. She wrote to me regularly, telling me about her new school and friends, but she also asked me not to hang around with my friends back in Massachusetts. I guess she was afraid of losing our friendship, and I felt that I better not tell her what I was doing with my friends because she might get mad at me. Even then, I was already developing the false persona of "people pleasing," which means doing what other people want instead of what you want for fear of not being liked or loved. My people pleasing started with Todd, whose temper was unpredictable when he didn't get his way, and my mother, whom I could never please. Now here I was, ten years old and afraid that someone living three thousand miles away might get mad at me.

On Friday nights, my mother had her family over, basically so she could drink, and my dad would stumble up the stairs drunk, with bagels from a place in Chelsea everyone loved. Bagels were cheap, and because the place was open until two o'clock in the morning, they were one of the few foods you could buy after the bars closed. On the nights my aunt and cousin visited, the insanity wasn't so bad.

As the child of two alcoholic parents, you learn at an early age that you're not as valuable as others. My parents consistently reinforced the lie that I wasn't good enough, and eventually, I started telling the same lie to myself. My mother bragged about my good grades to her family, even though in private she never encouraged me. My father could hold it together in front of extended family when he was drinking, but he didn't care when we were alone.

For instance, my father could somehow save money to buy a car, which was a luxury in our neighborhood during the early seventies. He and my mother would take us to Lincoln Park, a popular amusement park in southeastern Massachusetts where they'd sit in the pavilion all day and drink pitchers of beer while we went on the rides.

On one occasion, Ma's brother Uncle Buddy and my cousins from the South Shore joined us at the park. Throughout the day, I pretended that everything was fine. I was feeling "less than" my cousins Renée and Michelle, who wore Exersoles and designer jeans, clothes of far better quality than what I wore from Bradlees, the local department store. While running around the park, I was gripped with anxiety, worrying about my father driving us home after a day of heavy drinking. He had driven drunk on numerous occasions and one time bounced the car off the guardrail on the Southeast Expressway in Boston. At nine years old, I cowered in the back seat, trying to safely drive the car with my mind. I was so afraid we'd hit the guardrail again that I kept peeking between the seats to see if the road ahead was safe. It was one of many times when I felt powerless and thought if I just willed something with my mind maybe I could change things. I did that a lot as a child because the people who were supposed to protect me weren't.

One day, Aunt Ethel came with us to Lincoln Park. My father didn't drink that day, knowing he'd have to drive home and wanted to appear responsible. What a message to give your children: you can be at ease playing on the rides today because your aunt is with us. I had some peace that day, knowing someone else more important than my brothers and me was with us so we'd get home safely.

Academically, I continued to be competitive. Although I had stress at home, I wanted to do well in school, and I did. God had given me perseverance, and I needed it, coming from a home like ours. In many ways, that perseverance would help me with my son, Jason, later in life. Although my mother dropped out, my father was intelligent and encouraged education, but his bouts with drinking overshadowed that. After graduating from high school, my brother Wayne got married and left home. Prior to his departure, he spent many nights rescuing my mother from my dad's beatings. The night before his wedding day, he held my father in a bear hug to refrain him from beating my mother. Of course, the next day we all went to the wedding like nothing happened.

Wayne's apartment was robbed right after he got married. It turned out Todd had broken in and pawned Wayne's valuables. When Wayne found out about it, he made Todd take him to the pawnshop. Todd was only about fourteen years old then. Wayne was pissed, and who could blame him?

In addition to friends' houses, there were only two places I felt safe: the library and church. Both were quiet and had structure, which is what we so desperately needed in our home. You can't feel safe as a child when your parents are out of control. I don't recall my parents taking us to church, but they held us responsible to go and make the sacraments. I loved attending CCD (Confraternity of Christian Doctrine) classes at St. Rose Church on Broadway. The entrance had three wooden doors and three flights of stairs. Although my home life was violent and uncertain, I continued hoping that God was there and could help me. At this point, as a child, I considered becoming a nun. I liked the idea of the church taking care of me.

I still have my dress and veil from my First Communion. I understood the purpose of Holy Communion was the confession of sin. Having an abusive father, going into the confessional box and sliding a window open to talk with a man I didn't know was frightening to me. I never understood why the priest had the authority to tell me what my penance was. What made one sin different from another? Nothing. It was just the priest's opinion.

I'm not sure why we left Watts Street. The landlord may have increased our rent to force us out since all my parents did was fight and yell at each other. Even today, I can almost smell the mildew-sweet odor from our next apartment that was downtown on Pearl Street. The putrid smell came from the constant use of chemicals to exterminate cockroaches. I was devastated. I felt like I walked into a new life, a life I didn't want and didn't need. We lived on the second floor of a six-family brick house.

Now that we were close to where the bars were, my mother started drinking daily. We didn't have much money. My father got paid on Thursday night, and we would take a green Checker cab right away to Stop & Shop to buy groceries. By Tuesday, Ma would send me to Leo's grocery on the corner with a list of things to buy "on the cuff"—bologna, cheese, bread—and a note: "Leo, do you mind giving me these few things until Thursday?" Lots of families in the neighborhood lived that way.

Despite having little money, Ma was intent on looking good. She would buy clothes in the cheaper department stores and put nice outfits together. Pantsuits were in style, and she'd dress up in her favorite institutional-green leisure suit. She set her hair with bobby pins, the same way she did mine. She'd put on her makeup, curl her eyelashes, and be out the door before school ended. This marked the beginning of my coming home from school to the reality that my mother was choosing to drink at a bar instead of being home for her children.

Seventh and eighth grade were difficult. I was no longer in touch with my elementary school friends and feeling lost in the world, but I continued to make the honor roll through seventh grade. I was doing my best to hold on to that bright little girl. Smoking cigarettes became a part of my life now. Although I experimented with them years before, I now became a daily smoker just for the relief the nicotine brought.

While we were living on Pearl Street, a man about sixty years old that my mother knew from the bar began driving past my house in a silver AMC Rambler, waving for me to go into his car. I know there was a trade-off with him, but I'm still foggy as to what it was. I think I let him touch my leg so he'd give me money while he asked how I was doing and told me not to tell my mother he was coming by. If I tried to talk with him outside the car, he'd say, "Get in the car" in an angry voice like my father's and Todd's. After I stopped accepting his invitations when he motioned me into his car, he finally left me alone.

When I was twelve and Todd was fifteen, he told me how a baby is created. He explained intercourse to me, and I wanted to puke. I would learn much more than I wanted to know after we moved from Pearl Street.

At thirteen, I was barely getting to CCD classes because our house was becoming more and more neglectful. I felt like I had to be home all the time because my parents weren't there. I asked my mom's brother Billy, a witty man with silver hair, to sponsor me for my confirmation. He was the only person I felt comfortable asking. He lived a few towns over in Saugus, and we'd see him off and on growing up. After my confirmation, I took my first hit of THC, which I got from someone at the corner we hung out on, where the Richdale store was.

I was trying to hold on to the world with God, but I was slowly spiraling into a world without him. I was angry with him because I wasn't getting what I wanted, which was for him to make things better for my family. It was becoming harder to go to school and even harder to believe I was worth anything. We had no hot water to take a bath regularly or wash our hair. I owned very little clothing, and many times, there was no laundry detergent in the house. My parents were losing interest in being a family or taking care of us. They both went out drinking—she in one bar, he in another. He'd work all day and then go straight to the bar. When my parents weren't home, I felt I had to be there for Jamie. I was starting to believe, as my mother told us, that God was a punishing God. As time went on, I developed a constant fear that he was out to get me.

After living on Pearl Street for about a year, we moved again. A man at the bar where my father drank told him he had an apartment to rent. My father said he'd take it, and off we went. This apartment was on the other side of town, closer to our old house on Watts Street. It was a two-family with green aluminum siding and was probably a nice home at one time. When we moved into the house, we had almost no furniture. I was fourteen years old now. My parents' lives were becoming more and more unmanageable. I was hoping my mother would stop drinking now that we were farther from the downtown area since she didn't drive. No such luck; she walked to the bar daily. I was also hoping she'd step up and leave my father, but she dealt with the abuse by drinking even more.

Jimmy's, where my mother was now drinking, was on Broadway. She drank there regularly for the next ten years. It had a front and rear entrance and was shaped like a bowling alley. It had a bar with no table or chairs, only the barstools. The empty beer bottles were stored in cardboard cases along the wall by the back entrance where the jukebox was. When I walked in, I could smell the stale beer from the empty bottles. I'd occasionally indulge in the pickled eggs and pig's feet on the bar shelf.

Ma's spot was at the rear entrance, the last stool next to the pay phone, so she could see who came through the front door. When someone wanted to use the phone, she'd give them a dirty look, like the one she gave me when she didn't approve of something. They weren't doing anything wrong; she just didn't like people near her unless they had something she needed, like a drink.

When I sat with my mother, she'd tell people in the bar how smart I was.

"This is my daughter Karen. She gets straight As in school. She's smart, like her father. Not like me, I'm stupid. I dropped out of school in ninth grade."

She drank Miller Lite from the bottle. I would watch her raise and lower the bottle, the clear liquid flowing toward her red lipstick and then spilling back down.

Then she'd usually comment on my appearance in a negative way that made me question my decisions and my taste as opposed to what she liked or wanted.

"Don't you think red would go better with that scarf?"

Then she would remind me how prettily she dressed me when I was a small child and how nice she curled my hair.

"People complimented me on your hair all the time," she said. Her concern was all about how I looked and how that made her look to others. She pointed out what she did for me in an attempt to make me feel I owed her something. Behind closed doors, of course, there were no more compliments. Only when my aunt visited on Friday nights could I expect any positive attention.

When my mother and I talked, she regularly reminded me how I always stood up for my dad. "You're all for your father," she'd say. When I was twelve or thirteen, she began telling me that my dad had beaten Wayne and locked him in a closet. I think she told me so I wouldn't think better of him than I did of her.

I did stand up for Dad. They were both terrible parents, but although my father came home drunk, he still worked every day as a machinist. So I guess I felt this made him more responsible than she was. He had a job in Woburn but was let go when he wrecked a truck because of his drinking. Now he worked across from my middle school in Chelsea while my mother drank at the bar.

The reality was neither of them cared. I needed to hold on to a lie to protect myself from the devastation that was taking place in front of me. If I didn't hold on to the lie that he cared, I would be left with no parents at all.

* * *

I would have liked to be reacquainted with my old friend Lisa, but that didn't happen. I didn't feel comfortable reaching out to my former friends. The tapes in my head were playing, "You're not good enough," and my self-esteem was in the gutter. My parents' absence was taking its toll on me, causing me to seek out attention from boys and men. I didn't necessarily like them as boyfriends; I just liked the attention I got, the same way I liked the attention from the people at the bar when my mother bragged about me.

I started to skip school, and my grades began slipping. Once again, we had no heat or hot water, so I couldn't bathe or shower, only take a sponge bath. I had beautiful long brown hair at one time. Now I went to school wearing a bandanna on my head because I couldn't wash my hair, and some of the boys in my homeroom would make fun of me. I had been a pretty little girl, when inside I was suffering. Now, as a teenager, all I could feel was shame and guilt.

Todd was stealing more and more. He gave me some of the money from his thefts to get food, which I used to buy alcohol and mescaline. Giving me money was his way of manipulating me. He'd introduce me to the older men he sold his stolen goods to. I went with him because I felt I owed him something for the money. Older men liked talking to an attractive teenage girl. Sometimes he'd take me to the combat zone in Boston to chat with an older guy who worked in a store that had peep shows.

School was no longer a priority; partying and surviving were. Todd, Jamie, and I were pretty much left to fend for ourselves. We had no lock on the back door, and the front of the house had a broken window. Todd robbed houses and used the money to remodel the garage in the backyard. He added a fake Oriental rug and a couple of couches with a table. Nothing fancy, but it gave us a place to be in the summer that was comfortable. It became a hangout for the neighborhood. I had a sense of security when people were around, but deep down, I knew it wasn't a safe place. Kids from the neighborhood only came by because my brother had alcohol and weed, which he was always generous with. I think it was his way of making friends since kids always made fun of him earlier in life. I participated in the underage smoking and drinking that went on from late afternoon into the night. I remember taking crossroads (a form of speed) and sniffing "locker room"—a liquid in a small bottle that gave a quick high.

Todd was still unpredictable. One minute, he was nice to me, and then the next, he flew into a rage. He was very suspicious and sometimes paranoid. If I spoke against my mother or made a comment about her, he'd take it as personal criticism toward him. If I said, "Ma, why are you out drinking every night? Jamie's here alone," Todd would say, "Shut up, Karen. Don't tell Ma what to do." If I tried to correct him by saying, "Todd, you're lying. That's not what happened," he'd say, "Yes, it is, Karen. Shut up and mind your own business."

Unfortunately, I felt I had no one else to turn to.

* * *

Drinking was more important for my parents than household essentials. My parents, Jamie, and I slept in the same room for shared warmth because we had no heat, except for what came from the kitchen stove. The rest of the apartment was blocked off to enclose the areas close to the stove. We had only one towel in the house for five people. One night, my father came home and started fighting with my mother. He pushed her into a loose storm window resting under the windowsill. Ma fell into the window, smashing the glass, and Dad fell headfirst, slashing his forehead on the broken glass. I ran to the bathroom to get the one and only towel for him to use to stop the bleeding.

Later that night, as I lay on the fold-out single bed where Jamie and I slept, I could hear my parents having sex in the same room. I think Jamie had fallen asleep, but the bed wasn't comfortable, and I found it difficult to fall asleep after a fight like that. I lay there, angry that our parents had just put us through witnessing all that violence, and now they were taking care of their sexual needs with us nearby as if nothing had happened. I was sickened by it and wanted to scream.

Poor Jamie. When my parents fought, he'd yell for them to stop. One night, a neighbor called the police to have Jamie removed from the house for neglect. My father had to go to the police station to pick him up. I was five years older than he was, and I always felt responsible for him, but more than once, I stayed at a friend's house in order to get away. As I was walking home that night, I could hear my parents fighting and Jamie screaming. I didn't want to deal with it, so I arranged to stay at my friend Mary's house.

I met Mary in the neighborhood a few years before. She was one of nine children. Her family was burnt out in the Great Chelsea fire in 1973, so they bought a small one-family house around the corner from us. The fire burned and completely destroyed eighteen blocks of the city, causing over one thousand people to evacuate the area. Like Susan, she was older than me and didn't take any crap from anyone. I liked being around her because I felt she looked out for me, something I felt I couldn't do myself. Her family often provided me shelter. When I slept on the top bunk in her room, her cat would make her way up and sleep between my legs. Mary's mother cooked every night, and I often ate breakfast or dinner with them.

I also sometimes spent the night at the home of another friend, Sandy, who lived alone with her mom. Her dad died before I met her. Sandy was quick-witted and liked to tease me, but not in a hurtful way. We had so much fun together laughing and giggling over nothing. Her mother, Sophie, was a former burlesque dancer. Sandy and her mother fought a lot, but it was funny to witness. Her mother was gracious, feeding me and providing a warm place to stay.

I'm grateful for Mary's and Sandy's friendships during these difficult years. It was hard to be a friend since I felt like I was in survival mode every day. How could I be a friend and feel like I could give anything back to them when I felt like I had nothing to give to myself? Years later, Sandy reminded me how much I worried about Jamie when I stayed at her house. She said sometimes she'd ask her mother why I couldn't stay over, and Sophie explained, "Karen's got her little brother to look out for." At the time, I felt guilty for not wanting to go home to an insane house. I always felt like I was doing something wrong.

A part of me wanted someone to step in and take us from our parents, but another part wanted to protect my parents in case the authorities wanted to take us away from them. I didn't want them to get in trouble for neglecting us. I guess the devil you know is better than the devil you don't know. I think I was afraid that Jamie and

I would be split up in foster care. After all, I was only a child, but I bathed and fed him. When he was nine years old and out on the streets late at night, I'd look for him to make sure he was okay. We didn't have a phone, so finding him was the only way I could make sure he was safe. I was a child left with the responsibility of taking care of another child while everything was out of control. I was trying to be his mother.

As Jamie got older, my parents' alcoholism got worse. He never had any stability that he could remember. I know he felt unloved. He was basically an afterthought with my parents.

We left Maverick Street and moved back to a six-family house with gray aluminum siding on Congress Avenue. The kitchen floor was plywood. My mother put the washing machine against the sink to hang the black hose over it so the water could drain. Outside, the house smelled like burnt rubber because there was a tire company a few doors down from us. The smell lingered through the neighborhood, particularly on those hot summer days.

Again, we had little furniture and no heat, and unless I did the food shopping, we went hungry. At this point, my dad decided to stop giving money to my mother. He worked at a machine shop across the street from the middle school I was attending, so I'd stop there on Fridays and he'd give me sixty dollars to go to the local supermarket. His shop was located near an on ramp that led to the Tobin Bridge. When you walked in, it brought you to a counter with shelves of machinist parts behind it. The supermarket delivered, which helped tremendously. I bought basics like potatoes, bread, milk, hamburger, and pork chops. I cooked very simple meals. Todd also cooked occasionally because he was older. My father sometimes ate at home when he came home drunk late at night.

I thought it was good of Dad to give me money for groceries until my husband asked me recently, "Karen, why didn't he *take you* food shopping? Don't you think that would have been better?" It never crossed my mind that he could have done that. I thought everything else was my responsibility, so why not food shopping too. Dad wanted to feel better knowing I did the food shopping so he could go out drinking after work with a clean conscience. I guess, in his mind, it justified him being at the bar. I, on the other hand, wanted to help and please him, hoping he wouldn't leave us. This was another lie I told myself: I had to earn his love. I had to give up being a child to save the family.

It was during this time that my parents chose to stop parenting their children. They were hardly ever home. My mother started going to the bar early in the morning. On Pearl Street, she didn't leave until midafternoon; now it was nine thirty, and she'd be out the door. We were unaware my father was no longer paying the rent. One night, my father sat at our table drinking while the two of us snorted cocaine with Todd.

I started keeping five dollars from the money he'd give me for groceries so I could buy a fifth of Old Thompson whiskey for two dollars and get drunk. I'd use the rest of the money to buy candy bars and what little food I could afford on the street. I'd sit at Jimmy's after school; when I did go in, it was to try and connect with my mother. I was putting myself in her world, which is another form of adapting to the circumstances I was in, in an attempt to get love from her. Jamie, now nine, would come to the back entrance of the bar on his Big Wheel to ask my mother for a few dollars to buy a sandwich. I'd try to coax my mother to go home, but she refused. She'd give me a look of disdain, which she always did if I said something she didn't like. It was the same look she gave me when she'd ask me what Todd and I were doing in the bedroom when he was molesting me. If I asked for something I needed, I got the look.

Even the barmaid, Alice, told Ma to go home and be with her kids, but my mother just snapped back and said, "They're fine."

When my mother introduced me to guys at the bar, I thrived on the attention, but she was just manipulating them so someone would buy her a drink. I was being victimized and didn't even know it. How could I? I was only fourteen years old. She once told me her father brought her to the bar when she was the same age. Did he bring her because she was pretty and maybe her looks got him free drinks? Oh, how we mirror each other and don't even know it.

There is absolutely no good reason to leave your children every day and night to drink in a bar. But I denied that for many years to protect myself from the anger and grief I attempted to suppress. Instead, I watched Ma use her looks to manipulate men, and I learned that behavior from her. I began using it to get what I wanted. Nobody at home cared what I was doing, so why not?

After an hour or so with my mother, I'd go across the street into a back alley off Fifth Street and drink with the older guys on the stairs. Eighteen was the legal drinking age at the time. I was under-age, so I'd ask an eighteen-year-old to buy me alcohol. Most men on the street were more than happy to help.

At fifteen, I lost my virginity to a man I didn't know. He was about forty and lived off the parkway in Revere. Todd left me there one day after introducing me to him at the guy's apartment door. He told me he'd be right back and then left. The man was tall with gray wavy hair, and I felt intimidated when I walked into his apartment.

He fed me raviolis from his glass kitchen set. Next thing I knew, I was getting off his bed to go into the bathroom because I was bleeding. He only had white towels, and I was afraid to clean myself with one, in case I stained it. Imagine that. Here, I've just been raped by a stranger old enough to be my father, and I'm worried about dirtying his towels. It's amazing what a girl will do to feel loved or wanted.

I didn't receive any money from this encounter, but Todd may have. I denied the truth and convinced myself that I could trust him to take care of me despite all he had shown me growing up. My brother was exploiting me by selling me off to older men, and I was letting him do it. I was abandoning myself to get attention. How had I gone from being a straight-A student to this? How does this happen? It happens when you feel like trash because this is how you have been treated by the two people who should have loved you the most.

We lived on Congress Avenue during the famous Great Blizzard of 1978. For two days, the storm battered the northeast, including New York City. Massachusetts, Connecticut, and Rhode Island were hit especially hard. We received over twenty-seven inches of snow in less than forty-eight hours. Having no heat or hot water again, we used the stove to keep warm. I don't know what my parents did about bathing because they weren't home much. Jamie was running around on the streets, staying out until late at night. I was mostly alone in a cold house, worrying about him and what was going to happen to our family. We had a very small television with poor reception, and the storm didn't help. I needed to do something with myself, so I began cleaning. Since we didn't have much furniture, I started to clean the kitchen and sweep and mop the floors. Compulsive cleaning gave me a sense of having control. This habit was one I would fall back on throughout my life.

I desperately tried to hold on by spending time alone in my own room until one morning I got up and my feet were so cold I couldn't stand. I had to sleep in Todd's bedroom off the kitchen, which had two beds. A couple of times, I woke up, and Todd was half asleep on the floor next to my bed.

I said, "Todd, what are you doing?"

He said, "Nothing, Karen."

I let it go because if I pursued the issue, he'd just get angry. I always felt like he was pushing my boundaries by not respecting my space.

Sometimes he'd come home, and sometimes he didn't, but he continued to steal and got in trouble regularly with the law. Eventually, he was put in jail.

If I wanted to bathe, I'd boil water on the stove to fill the bathtub. We only had a couple of small pots, so it took quite a while to fill it just a few inches. By the time the next pots were boiling, the water I just put in would be cold. I'd take a quick bath and then put Jamie in after me. He'd be dirty from running the streets on his bike, just being a kid. I can see him now while I'm writing this.

At one point, my oldest brother Wayne, who was married at the time, thought it would be a good idea to remove Jamie from the house because he was being neglected. Wayne brought Jamie to his home in Saugus, where he lived with his new wife. That was a disaster. I know he meant well, but his wife wasn't having any part of it. Jamie told me how he'd hear them fighting about him. Jamie felt like he was in another place where he wasn't wanted. Despite neglecting Jamie, my dad was furious and demanded that Wayne bring him back.

These were rough years for us. They would be the final stretch in my parents' marriage. I know other people have lived in poorer conditions than we did, but they made it through because they had love within their families. It's one thing to be poor, but it's another thing altogether to be poor because your parents chose to not take care of you. My parents' selfish desires took precedence over their children.

While playing outside one winter, I had to go home because my fake Earth Shoes were soaking wet. Earth Shoes with rubber soles were a popular brand in the seventies. Mine were artificial suede; I couldn't afford the real ones. I went home to put them on the stove door to dry, not realizing the rubber would melt from the heat. Now I couldn't go out at all because they were the only pair of shoes I owned.

I was so embarrassed, but what I could I do? I was with Andrea at the time. She was a friend I knew from Watts Street during my elementary school years. I wanted so badly to hold on to that time of my life before things got really bad with my parents. Andrea was great with fashion and had a tendency to walk on her toes. Later, I punched or pushed her to prove to some tough girls I wasn't a wimp. It pained me to do it since we grew up together. It was sad that I treated a childhood friend that way in order to survive in the neighborhood. I did it because of me losing Karen and who I truly was.

* * *

Before long we were evicted from Congress Avenue because of nonpayment. A deputy from the sheriff's office came with a constable to have us removed from our home. For my father, this was the final straw, and he decided to leave us. He didn't tell anyone. He just made the decision to abandon his family, and on the day of the eviction, he was nowhere to be found.

The constable and the landlord threw our belongings off the third-story porch. I grabbed a few bags of pictures, remembering that my mother once said they were something you couldn't replace. I knew they were important to keep. Rather than assume a leadership role after Dad left, my mother wanted to stay at the house of a man she met at the bar rather than worry about us. Todd did whatever my mother wanted to make sure she was happy, whether the situation was safe or not. Wayne was living his own life with his wife, and I don't think he wanted to get involved again. All I knew was I had Jamie to take care of.

I arranged for Jamie and me to stay at a friend's house until my mother got an apartment. I was fifteen at the time and very stressed about the future, wondering how I was going to hold it all together. I now believe I shut down after my father left. I didn't realize how scared I was until later in life. I was afraid because he was the only provider we had, and now he was gone. I also felt an emotional connection to him, and now that he's gone, I felt empty and used. To cope, I created a story that my father had a good reason to leave us instead of accepting that he didn't love us. I defended him for years, using that justification to hide from the pain of knowing he had abandoned us. I denied those feelings as the years went on, masking them in many ways.

I focused much more on drinking after my father left. I worried that if I didn't have money from Todd or left over from food shopping, I couldn't buy alcohol.

Although my mother was staying at the house of the man she met at Jimmy's, she met Chris, her future boyfriend, at another bar, Burke's Pub, on Fifth Street. I was there the day she met him. Chris was a local man who made his living as a bookie. He was short, very quick on his feet, and very well-liked. He had a glass eye from a trucking accident years before, but you couldn't really notice it until he took off his glasses. I took a liking to him, I think, because he had money and wasn't a drinker himself. Ma wanted to borrow money from Sam, the owner of the bar, but he wasn't in that day. Chris offered to lend her some money, and that was the beginning of a twenty-three-year relationship. Chris was married at the time, but his children were grown and out of the house. He fell in love with my mother and took good care of her. I thought having Chris might keep Ma out of the bars. Not quite.

After Chris began dating my mother, he found her an apartment. It was on the third floor of a three-decker in the Mill Hill area of Chelsea. Jamie and I reunited with her and Todd. This would be the last house I lived in with my mother.

When I moved back with her, my drinking was going on day and night. My room was at the front of the house, which faced Broadway. When I woke up late for school from drinking the night before, I'd see people waiting for the bus to take them to work, wishing I could have a normal life like them. That year, I was held back in ninth grade homeroom but had tenth grade classes. I needed to make up some credits to officially get into tenth grade. I was used to getting good grades, so it felt humiliating to be held back. My fear of people's opinions and my pride got in the way of doing what I needed to do to progress. Because of the insecurities that were developing due to my dad leaving and not having a family unit anymore, I had a fear of leaving the house. Everything seemed to have happened so fast. I was sixteen now, and my mother said, "If you're not going to go to school, you need to find a job or leave."

At this time, Chris told me that Todd was not my father's child. I can't recall why this came up, but I believed Chris since Todd didn't look anything like my father. Todd had bad acne and a nose like a beak; my father had a button nose. Todd was also much taller than my father. My father looks Polish and German; Todd looks Italian. Chris explained that Todd's father was a man named Ronnie, Uncle Buddy's best friend. I heard the name growing up and sensed my mother might have had a thing for him.

The infidelity was one of many secrets my mother held inside and one I would one day mirror myself.

Chapter 2

Entering my late teen years, Todd was still introducing me to older men in East Boston. I was sixteen and a half when I met Rob Dolan. He was a house painter by trade and recently bought a two-family home on Paris Street just outside of Maverick Square. Rob was forty-three with silver hair and looked a little like Jerry Vale, a pop crooner from the fifties and sixties known for his velvety voice and classic love songs. Rob had children by his wife and another woman before he met me. He had no relationship with the three children from his marriage, but the nine-year-old daughter he had with an ex-girlfriend came to stay with him on weekends.

Rob was a gambling addict. Being self-employed, he could cut out and go to the track whenever he wanted. After painting on the weekdays, he spent the afternoons and evenings at the horse track at Suffolk Downs.

My role was to entertain Rob's daughter while he went to the track. I recall that I was the one who decided not to let her go to the track. I told him he shouldn't take her because there was nothing for her to do. Most likely, that scenario reminded me of sitting with my parents over the years, feeling bored and trapped while they drank. Also, I think she liked being with me. I'd try to encourage her to do well in school. I wasn't going, and I knew school was important.

My relationship with Rob quickly became another situation where I found myself taking responsibility for someone else and putting my needs and desires last. One more person with an addiction being selfish while I thought I had to pick up the pieces. I had no feelings for Rob whatsoever. I needed to feel wanted and have a stable home. Any place other than my mother's house was a good place for me.

After hanging out with Rob and his friends for a while, I eventually moved in with him. I now realize I was looking for a father figure since my real father was nowhere to be found. A few months later, we learned he was living in Sandown, New Hampshire.

At this point, I left school for good. I met with a guidance counselor, and he tried to talk me out of it, but I just dropped out. Jamie seemed to be getting more acclimated with a couple of new friends he met in the neighborhood. I didn't feel the need to look out for him since Chris was living with my mother and Jamie liked him. Chris took care of Jamie's needs.

Jamie had graduated from his Big Wheel to a bike, and he was always out with his friends riding around. In 1979 or 1980, Jamie met a boy named TJ. Every day Jamie did a wheelie on his bicycle past TJ's house on Broadway in Chelsea. TJ said to himself, "I want to meet that kid," and one day when Jamie came by riding the rear wheel of his bike, TJ joined him, and they rode three blocks together on one wheel. When they finally stopped, TJ introduced himself to Jamie, and they became friends.

One day, the two of them were out with another kid from the neighborhood, pushing trash barrels over on their bikes. Jamie had a stick and somehow picked up a soiled diaper on it. When he tried to fling the diaper off, it wrapped around the neck of the other boy they were riding with, and TJ and Jamie laughed their heads off. TJ was a couple of years older than Jamie. They developed a longtime friendship based on their love for BMX bikes, dirt bikes, and motorcycles—-anything with two wheels and speed.

* * *

I found a job at a curtain factory not too far from Rob's house, and I'd walk to work. I can remember the women sitting at their sewing machines and playing their Italian music. After sewing the curtains, they'd drop them into a cardboard box, and I'd separate them by cutting the threads. I was thinking at the time, "This is not something I want to do for the rest of my life." For the next year, I worked as a cashier at the local convenience store in Maverick. During this time, Rob was doing less painting and more gambling. When Rob lost at the track and I was with him, he'd start kicking trash cans and swear and yell in front of everybody. He'd throw the phone when he was angry at someone he was talking with.

Rob didn't want me to have friends or a car. He discouraged me from seeing my old friend Mary. We shared the cost of a red four-door Lincoln Continental. Rob had me apply for the loan and a friend of his cosigned it, but Rob wouldn't let me drive the car. While I was working at Harbor Food Mart, he'd drive by, beep the horn, and say hello. East Boston was famous for car thefts in those days. Thieves would break in through the rear quarter window of the Lincoln and take it for a joy ride. The car ended up being stolen and stripped, but I was still liable for the payments.

Rob was trying to control me, and I was letting him. I felt like I was living with Todd. Both our lives were becoming more unmanageable. We had been using cocaine together, when at one point he decided to not only use cocaine but to start selling it. I continued going to work, many times not sleeping the night before due to my using. Life was becoming a blur, and I was getting by day to day.

As a teen, I used to want to be married to a wise guy, hang out with that crowd, and drive fancy cars. I got the idea from hanging around Todd. He sold his stolen goods to some people who ran in wise guy circles in East Boston and the North End. The truth is when you live that lifestyle, it's only a matter of time before things will collapse and you'll feel the loneliness of not having a relationship with God or any true friends. It is a dead end way to live and I too was on my way.

Soon Rob was in over his head and stopped paying the mortgage. I was still working, trying to have some stability in my life, but who was I fooling? I was constantly drinking and drugging myself to find relief. Rob regularly asked me to babysit his drugs so he could go to the track. I'd stay home, but I'd sneak as much cocaine as I could. If I could manage to get high and pay him back for the way he treated me, why not?

Because Rob was gambling and using drugs instead of selling them, he did not have the money to pay the dealers. Eventually, his life became so unmanageable he was forced to leave the area.

He asked me if I'd go with him to Florida, and I said I would. I had the option of asking my mother for help, but I felt certain she'd reject me. I had no contact with my father since he abandoned us, so his help was not an option. I could have gone to a shelter, but instead, I people pleased again, putting someone else's wants and needs before my own, and off to Florida we went. We drove down in a gold 1978 Gran Torino. I couldn't question Rob on anything. When I'd ask questions during the drive down to Florida, like what he thought we were going to do there, he treated me the same way Todd had. He wouldn't tell me why we had to leave East Boston. I knew he owed money for the drugs, but I felt there was something more that he wasn't telling me.

This was not what God wanted for me or what I wanted for myself. But if I told Rob no, that would have left me to face the reality that I was all alone with no one to turn to for help. That truth was a level of pain I didn't want to feel, so I tucked it away in my heart for many years. Looking ahead at an empty road while driving to Florida, I was scared, not knowing what my future would bring. I felt like a nobody, worthless. I was hiding from the pain of knowing no one was looking out for me because no one cared.

I only had my license for about a year. I'm seventeen, and here I am, driving in the wee hours of the morning on a highway heading someplace I know nothing about. I'm with a forty-four-year-old man who's angry and untrustworthy. In the quiet of the night driving, I'd see tractor trailer's headlights in the side mirror roaring toward me in the left lane. I couldn't wait for them to go by because their power frightened me so late at night on the dark highway. Rob told me if I drove directly behind them, it would save us gas because the draft could pull us. This memory would come back one day in a most interesting way.

We drove to St. Petersburg and rented an efficiency apartment—a furnished hotel room with a little kitchenette. While sunbathing in front of the hotel, I noticed a strange creature on the ground. It was a chameleon, and it scared the heck out of me. I was never this far from home, and I had no experience with such creatures.

Rob wanted to make sure I found a job. God forbid, he should look for work. I found an opening at Court Laboratories through an agency that helped young people get employment and training. The company was a government-contracted agency that plotted wetlands in the United States. I liked the job I was doing there, plotting wetlands from a map and outlining them from microfiche. The woman who trained me was an American Indian who unfortunately had a drinking problem. She was very nice, but there were times she wouldn't show up at work, and a coworker would go looking for her. Through her, I was seeing my own future.

After a few months, Court sent a group of us to Utah for a couple of weeks to do some research. The trip was exciting, but I had never been on an airplane before. The company gave me a travel budget that included traveler's checks. Rob had no money, so he asked me to leave him with three hundred dollars, and he'd reimburse me when I came back. I don't remember the amount I left, but I recall leaving myself without adequate travel funds so he could gamble. I didn't speak up to him because I was afraid. I also felt that without Rob, I'd have to face that I was alone.

Our flight was scheduled for August 3, 1981, the day of the air traffic controllers' strike. I didn't know what an air traffic controller did, but I knew it had something to do with the safety of the plane. The crew let Rob walk me on the plane because I was afraid. In the seat next to me was a man from our office I didn't really know. He was around my age, good-looking, with a tan. He dressed a little preppy, wearing a collared shirt and khaki pants. I tried to talk with him, but he wasn't that friendly. I felt more afraid because I couldn't emotionally attach myself to him to feel safe, the way I usually did with men.

While in Utah, I met many Mormons. I thought they were hypocrites because I felt anyone who was religious thought they were perfect. I smoked cigarettes then, and for the first time, I encountered a restaurant that didn't allow anyone to smoke in it. "Who the hell do they think they are?" I thought when I saw that. I think I felt threatened and ashamed because I wasn't living a godly life.

The company gave us a couple of government vehicles so we could go and explore. The mountains were breathtaking, and I loved seeing the clear clean water coming down from the top on a summer day. I was excited to be out there, but I had no idea what I was doing with my life.

After the trip, Rob picked me up at the airport. Of course, he didn't have the three hundred dollars he owed me. He told me to tell the company I lost the traveler's checks. I told my senior manager what happened, and they weren't happy about it, but they said we'd work something out. This situation was sad because God had his hand in my life, placing me at a job with a great opportunity, and I was letting Rob take all that away from me. I'd only be there a few more months before this nonsense would come to an end.

While I was working every day, Rob was doing odd painting jobs and hitting the track. I was the primary breadwinner, getting paid every two weeks, which I never experienced before. But the money was gone the day I received my paycheck. I'd meet Rob after work at McDonald's, and while he drank his coffee, he'd pontificate on how I should look into getting a part-time job there. Even then, I was thinking, "Are you kidding me? You're not even working."

I began to talk to Rob about leaving Florida. I was realizing I couldn't stay here much longer. He wanted to use me to pay the bills so he could gamble. He didn't want me to have one job; he wanted me to have two. One night, after being with him intimately, I told him, "I just got pregnant." He thought I was crazy, but it ended up being true. Two weeks later, we pulled up to our apartment complex, and two undercover police cruisers surrounded our car. The police pulled out their guns and asked us to get out of our vehicle. I was petrified. It turned out they were DEA agents. Rob had sold drugs to an undercover agent back in Boston, and they finally found him. I didn't know what I was going to do.

I visited Rob in jail in Tampa while staying at the efficiency apartment for a few more days. Before his arrest, we were in the process of moving into a place called Sun Catcher Apartments. They were full apartments with a bedroom, kitchen, and a living room. I moved in, but I had no furniture and not enough money to continue paying the rent. I don't know what I thought I was going to be able to do. I was a teenager, all alone and trying to figure things out. I didn't think there was any other way. Growing up the way I did, I learned to rely on myself because there was no one else to rely on. I didn't realize I had choices, so I was making really bad ones. I did what I could to survive. It was another traumatic period in my life.

I stayed at the Sun Catcher Apartments for only two weeks. The police eventually extradited Rob to Boston where he was held while facing federal charges. Rob's parents paid his flight back to Florida to get me, and then the feds paid for our gas back to Boston. At eighteen years old, even I knew that didn't sound right. Why would the government arrest you and then pay for your gas? It turned out Rob decided to rat out his friends. When he returned to Florida, he was out on bail. He eventually plea-bargained. Somehow, because of his testimony, the feds gave him money to drive from Florida to Boston.

While living in Florida, I began watching the evangelical Christians Jim and Tammy Bakker on TV. This was before Jim Bakker's fall from grace. I believed in God and knew he was there, but since my family broke apart, I was making decisions that led me away from him. Every day in Florida, there were many shows on TV about God. I needed to watch them, I thought, to have some hope that my life could someday get better. Although I didn't call it sin at the time, I was living in it, and it was hurting me. Because of my own decisions, I was brewing more and more with resentment that would explode. My anger toward my parents, particularly my father and how he left us, would lead me to act out in many unhealthy ways.

We made it back to Boston, and I still hadn't had my period. We had no money and nowhere to live. I know we stayed a short time at his brother's house in Winthrop and then at my mother's in Chelsea. Rob's brother and his wife had two daughters. They were kind, but I didn't feel they wanted us staying there, and I didn't blame them. Rob was a grown man. He needed to grow up, and I needed to find a better life for myself.

My mother, on the other hand, just didn't care. I think she let us stay at her house for a night or two, all the while telling me I had to find a place to live. It would have been nice to hear her say, "Karen, why don't you stay with us? We'll take care of you and the baby." That's what I would have loved to have heard, but my mother was not going to offer that option. After all, she and my father had abandoned us, so why would she offer to help me now that I'm carrying a baby? She was fine; she had Chris to take care of her. I knew I was the one who got pregnant, but love and support can go a long way in these situations.

She later said, "You know, Rob could have been arrested for statutory rape." I looked at her and thought, "Well then, why didn't you have him arrested?" I was underage when I met Rob and started sleeping with him when I was sixteen. My mother said that to me not because she cared but to let me know she had done me a favor by not getting Rob in trouble. If it were me, I would have chased down my daughter or at least told her she didn't have to live that way. That's what good parents do. They look after their children to make sure they're okay.

After about a month of staying in people's homes and sleeping in the car behind the Revere Police station, Rob was brought into custody to do federal time in Allenwood, Pennsylvania. The court gave him a month to square away his affairs. He spent most of that month at the track instead of taking care of his pregnant girlfriend.

I heard that my father moved back to Chelsea and was living at a friend's house. Although I was pretty sure I was pregnant, I was procrastinating on what I should do. I finally called the abortion clinic and found out what the procedure would cost. I didn't have enough to cover it, so I went to see my father to ask him for the additional money. A typical adult child of an alcoholic, I was concerned about his opinion of me. When I told him I was pregnant, he was disappointed, but he lent me two hundred dollars. By the time I went to the clinic for an exam, I was too far along. I was going to become a mother. I had stopped drinking and doing drugs, at least temporarily, as soon as I learned I was pregnant. I had some fear that my using these last five years could already have affected the baby, but I put those feelings aside.

When I went back to tell my father and give him back his two hundred dollars, he didn't offer to help me. In fact, he didn't even offer to let me keep the money. He had the funds; he was working. Deep down inside, I wanted my father to be someone he wasn't. I already told myself a false story about him, that he cared enough to get a place for the both of us and I could live with him while I was pregnant.

While visiting him one day, he told me he met a woman named Dottie who worked as a barmaid in Chelsea. She was a heavy woman I used to see in Jimmy's Café who didn't drink. She grew up in East Boston like my mother and was divorced. I was floored. I had never known my father to be with a woman other than my mother. My gut told me I was being pushed aside again.

I didn't think of talking with an adoption place or counseling center. I don't believe I could have lived with myself, knowing my child was out there somewhere without me. Being the true caretaker in this alcoholic family, I'd find a way to take care of him.

Rob had a friend, Fred, who allowed us to stay at his house in Revere for a short period of time. Fred was Italian with wavy salt-and-pepper hair and acne-scarred skin. Rob knew Fred through some of his "dealings." Rob was negative and envious about other people's successes and possessions. He told me he liked to fix up houses but not finish them.

Rob was shipped off to jail, and I landed back at Mary's house in Chelsea. Mary was the friend whose sister I stayed with when Jamie and I had nowhere to live; fortunately, I had kept up the friendship.

I landed a job as a cashier at Liberty Market in East Boston. I was miserable and filled with anxiety, worrying every day about what the future would bring. Shortly thereafter, I left work and applied for welfare. While I was at Mary's house, Rob called regularly from jail and reversed the charges. Rob never considered what the phone calls took out of the little money I had. It was all about him and when I was going to visit him. I was eighteen years old, pregnant, with no money and no permanent housing, and he wanted me to visit him in Allenwood, Pennsylvania. How selfish can you get?

But I was no better. I had used him also. I wanted out of this relationship. I had no confidence I could take care of myself, but I started blowing him off when he'd call. I couldn't pretend I cared about him; I had already moved on.

Rob's friend Fred and I were getting closer. I can now admit that I was manipulating him too. Fred broke up with the girl he was dating and loaned me his car for a while. Eventually, I moved into his house. Although Fred was in the process of renovating, it was still a beautiful home. The hearth in the living room had an indoor grill inside it. The living room had red crushed-velvet furniture with gold trim and black-and-white tile floors. The dining room had wicker chairs and a long mirror along the wall. I thought the house was exotic looking. Fred was fresh out of a divorce, from which he was still hurting. I think we needed to help each other. I lied to Rob that I was just living there, but in reality, the relationship was more than that. Fred's being in a relationship with his friend's girlfriend while the friend was in jail was not the best display of character. On the other hand, he did take in a pregnant woman who had nowhere to go. It wasn't the ideal situation, but at least, I was safe.

Fred developed a heart condition shortly before I moved in and needed to take nitroglycerin pills. He was a defendant in a court case that eventually landed him at the Concord state prison. For now, he was making sure I was okay. He told me my attitude, which was miserable most of the time, could negatively affect my pregnancy. I didn't pay much heed to it. There was a lot of pretending going on in my life. I needed to pretend to survive in my house. But now, being inauthentic was causing my resentment to build more and more. Even at this age, I knew this was not what I wanted. Pregnant, lying to my baby's father about what I was doing, having sex while pregnant with a man who is not my baby's father, and not being in the truth. I needed professional help, to talk to someone about my predicament. But at the time, my self-will wouldn't allow it.

Fred was supportive, but he also stayed in contact with his ex-wife since they had children together. I was emotionally unavailable to him, so it didn't bother me much. The truth was I was looking to another emotionally unavailable man like Rob to be someone he wasn't so I could feel safe. Every man I dated was my father over and over again. I hurt people repeatedly by falling into this trap.

Fred took me out with him every day. A few times a week, he took me for chocolate ice cream frappes at the Banana Boat on Revere Beach. We'd also visit his friend Dominic, who was married and had four sons. Dom raised finches in his basement. He also sang in different bands as the lead singer.

At one point, Fred drove me to see Rob. I pretended I came alone. In fact, Fred and I were on our way to Disney World. All this pretending was killing me inside. I often wanted to be honest but felt if I did, I'd be alone. I also didn't want to deal with Rob's temper. When I returned, Mary's parents got tired of covering for me with Rob. The next time he called, I said, "Rob, I moved in with Fred. I needed to have a place to stay, but we're only friends." He said, "Just friends?" as if he already knew, but at this point, I didn't care because I wanted to get away from him. From there on, I never heard from him again. I was free from him, and that felt great.

Jamie asked to come live with us, and Fred didn't mind. He had been living with my mother, stayed with us for a while, and then moved in with my father. One night, I was washing the kitchen floors, and I must have leaned forward too long because I started to bleed. I went into the bathroom, terrified that God was punishing me because I wanted to abort the pregnancy. Thoughts like this are the result of growing up with a mother who talked about a punishing God. First, I didn't want to be pregnant, and now I'm asking God not to take my child. Fred wasn't home. Jamie was worried and said, "Call an ambulance." I'm not sure how I got to the hospital. The doctor told me the baby had leaned on my placenta, which caused me to bleed. He recommended that I stay overnight. I said, "No, I want to go home." My mother didn't like hospitals, and I heard that over and over again growing up. To this day, I wonder if my child's future condition had anything to do with that incident. Only God knows the answer to that.

I was nineteen years old when Jason was born on June 1, 1982, at the Malden hospital. I couldn't lie down while in labor, so they sat me in a chair that resembled a potty and placed a mirror on the floor that allowed me to see the baby's head as it came out while I was pushing. I was so thirsty, but the nurses would only give me crushed ice. Fred was there, but he knew he had to leave because I was getting resentful. Rob was still in prison. I basically gave birth alone, with no one there but the hospital staff. I named my son Jason Michael Dolan. When my dad visited, he questioned why I gave Jason Rob's last name if I didn't plan on staying with him. I decided he was right and gave Jason my last name, Sobanek.

Neither of my parents asked me how I was doing. They didn't seem happy that Jason was born. I felt like I again did something to fail them. I was still hoping someone would step up to help me, and I started to feel angry that I had become a mother and wasn't supported by my family. What denial I had in my teenage mind, thinking that the parents who weren't there for me would possibly be there for my son.

My mother was in the early days of her relationship with Chris and enjoying her freedom, doing what she wanted. They both came to the hospital to see Jason. Typical of my mother, instead of asking "Are you okay?" she was more concerned about how I looked. She looked at me and immediately asked what was wrong with my eyes. I didn't know what she was talking about. I looked in the mirror, and the whites of my eyes were bloodshot from pushing so hard.

She asked, "How are you going to take care of the baby?" and then said, "I took care of you kids. I'm not taking care of some-one else's." I told her I'd take care of him myself, but deep down, I doubted that I could do it on my own. A little while into the visit, she told me that Chris hadn't eaten, and they'd have to get going. Basically, she was saying, "I want nothing to do with this."

Another baby in the nursery weighed ten pounds; he was a big boy. The parents and family were so elated for the new addition to their family. I didn't feel any connection to my baby. I was frightened beyond words, and I didn't know how to ask for help. Asking for help was not an option in childhood, so I developed a spirit of self-reliance and became prideful. In the years to come, my pride would hurt me many times and in many ways.

My friend Susan came to visit. She just had her son, Mathew, seven months before. The nurses brought Jason to my room to be with me, and I had no idea what to do with him. He had bags under his eyes, like he hadn't slept at all in my womb. He looked like he went through a lot coming through my canal. I told Susan not to make fun of the way he looked. I was acting like my mother and didn't realize it.

I stayed in the hospital for four days—a long stay compared to today. When I left, Jason didn't come home with me because he had jaundice from excessive levels of bilirubin in his blood. I brought him home the next day. I was confused and not ready to be a mom, but I didn't say a word to anyone. My attitude wasn't the best, and I'm sure Fred knew I wasn't happy.

At this stage in my life, I was feeling detached from God. He felt farther and farther away from me and the childlike faith I once had. My sins of living outside his will were weighing heavy on me. Soon I would resume my drinking to keep from feeling the pain of the past and from the loss of a father I thought would love me. I was confusing my earthly father with my heavenly Father.

Fortunately, Susan lived in the next town, and she was a godsend during this time. One day when Jason first came home, I boiled his clothes. I figured if you sterilize the bottles, you should sterilize the clothes too. Susan and I both had a good laugh that day. Fred was helpful too. Having children of his own, he played with Jason a lot. This was 1982, the time of the Claus Von Bulow trial. Every day I'd sit on the couch with Jason while Susan and I called each other, enmeshed in the case. Jason was a colicky baby, which added to my stress. I was starting to believe God was punishing me for having a baby out of wedlock. My mother's words about a punishing God still haunted me, and they couldn't have been farther from the truth.

There were times when I'd keep Jason in his swing for a couple of hours to quiet him or drive him around in the car to calm him down. I'd hold him and walk him up and down the kitchen, then stand in front of the glass door that overlooked the backyard and show him the birds in the trees. His crying only fueled my resentment of being a young mother and made me afraid to ask anyone to watch him. My friend Susan was a single mom herself, but she had her parents to help her. She lived with them when Mathew was born.

Fred went back to jail at the Massachusetts Correctional Institute in Concord, a state prison about twenty miles west of Boston. Before he left, we moved from the house Fred owned to an apartment off Shirley Avenue in Revere, not too far from the beach, in a neighborhood that used to be filled with Jewish delicatessens and shoe stores. We rented the first floor of a two-family house. The apartment had a foyer inside the front door, a long hallway with rooms on each side, and a kitchen at the end of the hall. I enjoyed this period of time when Jason was about six months old and we were safe in a new place where only the two of us lived. I was becoming more comfortable being his mother. I was receiving a monthly welfare check, and getting financial help took some of the stress from me. I can see Jason now, coming down the hallway in his walker, getting stuck on the threshold, and me helping him over it. Although I started drinking again six months after Jason was born, for the first time I felt like I had a home that I alone was taking care of. That's all I ever wanted really—a safe home.

While Fred was in prison, his friend Dominic called or stopped by periodically to check on me. He told me about growing up in Baltimore and wanting to become a professional singer. Instead, he fell in love, got married, and had four children. When Dom was near me, we felt a mutual attraction. He was the first man I was ever attracted to. One day, he leaned in and kissed me. Although he was still married, I was being needy, selfish, and manipulative to say the least. I had met Dominic's wife when we visited them during my pregnancy, and she was very kind. I just didn't know how to be alone.

One day, I took Jason and we went to visit Fred. On the way back, it started to rain. Jason was crying in the back seat, and I yelled at him to stop crying. I was a wreck because the windshield wipers didn't work. I looked in my pocketbook, and the only thing I had to wipe the windshield was a Kotex pad. Thank God, it worked. I've come to learn that babies cry, cars honk their horns, traffic happens, and it isn't because of me. I was self-centered and believed people acted a certain way because I had done something to cause their actions. I was being harassed and punished in my mind because of my childhood neglect and abuse.

Even though I was now an adult, I continued being stuck in the mind of the little girl who needed protection and love from her father. I sought men who were physically or emotionally unsafe, just like my father and Todd; Fred, being involved in crime and having to go to prison, was just one example. Dominic cheating on his wife. Rob making me stay home to babysit his drugs. My relationships with men were all about survival. I used Fred for a place to live, and now I was moving on with his friend because I wanted out of his life. It was a vicious pattern that prevented me from growing emotionally by trying to help myself. I didn't know I could do things differently.

Before Jason and I moved out of that apartment, two born-again Christians came to visit. I forget how I knew them, but I believe God sent them to get me on the right path. The Big Book of Alcoholics Anonymous says we alcoholics "bristle with antagonism" when we hear someone speak of God. That was me. I didn't want to hear anything about God and how he could help me and my son.

Fred returned from prison. I wanted to leave him and continue seeing Dominic, but where would I go? Being with Dom wasn't an option either. He was married and had his own family. Dom talked me into asking my father if I could stay at his house. I made the call at a pay phone down the street from my apartment, away from Fred. I told my father I wasn't happy where I was and asked if Jason and I could come live with him and Dottie in Chelsea. When I was growing up, Dad sometimes said yes but with a sense of disapproval. I heard that tone in his answer, but this time, I didn't care what he sounded like; he said yes, and I had a place to stay. I continued to bury my sense of hearing disapproval when I asked for help.

I went back to the apartment to tell Fred I was leaving. It was a scary confrontation. I told him I needed to take care of Jason and start over. I thanked him for his help with us and said I was sorry, but I couldn't stay. I don't believe I had the courage to tell him I was with Dominic, but he must have had an idea. Fred didn't say much.

He just walked up and down the hallway in his bathrobe. I was a mess and didn't know what I was doing. Although my behavior turns my stomach now, I didn't give much thought about how my actions affected other people. These men were forty to forty-five years old, and I had no business being with them, just like I had no business being with Jason's father.

I don't recall the first time Dom manhandled me, but it happened frequently. He would grab my arm or yell at me, and I didn't like it. Once I was outside my father's house, sitting in Dom's truck and telling him I didn't want to see him anymore. After I left his truck, I walked up my father's stairs when Dom pulled me down to get me outside to talk with him. Another time, he came to my job, hopped over the desk, and forced me into the bathroom to talk. Here was another man I let use or abuse me. Another angry guy I not only submitted to but sought protection from, just like my brother. I know intellectually that I had my own will to do what I wanted, but at that age, I didn't feel I did.

I was doing much more drinking during this time, mostly at home. I didn't have the means to pay for a babysitter. If I did, I'm sure I would have been out at a local bar. Cocaine was back in the picture, which I did when Jason went to bed. For a little while, I was even selling it. I wasn't good at it because I'd snort more than I sold.

I'd like to tell you my dad was happy I had moved in with him, but he wasn't. Dottie didn't seem to care too much. When I got there, she was more concerned about my father and what he was doing. Like me, Dottie had her own insecurities regarding my father. I was just grateful to have a place to stay.

They lived at 67 Clark Avenue, Chelsea, on the second floor of a six-family bedroom apartment, around the corner from where my mother lived with Chris when my father left us. Dottie and my father's bedroom was at the end of the hall. He sat on his recliner in their bedroom after supper and read *The Boston Globe*. Dottie's three youngest children lived there, along with Jamie, and now Jason and me. Debbie, at two, was the youngest, and Randy was four or five. Bobby was about seven, an easygoing and lighthearted kid. I loved him from the first time we met.

I was still on welfare, and I gave my father twenty-five dollars a week to live with them. I kept Jason's crib in one of the bedrooms while I slept on a twin mattress on the floor near him. Jason was about ten months old at the time, and I was feeling lost, even at my father's house. He never discussed what went on when he left a few years before, and we acted as if everything was fine. I wouldn't dare confront him about it, for that would put me in jeopardy of being alone.

Dottie and my father had a quick wedding in 1983. He divorced my mother so he could marry her. They invited a few people from the bar where Dottie worked and held the ceremony at the Winnisimett Club just outside Bellingham Square. Although I was only twenty at the time, I found ways to drink at the wedding and the rest of the night. I had mixed emotions about my dad getting married again. I guess I was feeling left behind. Dad was moving forward in his life and barely thought about how I was going to take care of Jason and me. His lack of concern was very hurtful, but I wasn't allowing myself to feel that pain. I was too busy numbing it.

One night, Dom chased me up the stairs of my father's apartment and started hitting me. My father came out into the hallway and asked what was going on. I said, "Nothing, Dad." He knew what was going on, but he didn't want to deal with Dom. After all, Dom was behaving the same way he had behaved with my mother. I stopped returning Dom's calls, so he left me alone for a while. I had had enough, and I needed to move on. I knew my father wasn't happy with how my life was turning out, but I hold him partially to blame for his daughter acting out and desperately looking for a father figure.

Chapter 3

While living with my father, I went to Employment Connections to get some job skills. I think they were teaching me how to type. A staff member told me after a few sessions that I didn't need to be there. Stunned, I said, "What do you mean I don't need to be here? I need help." The employment counselors thought my typing was good enough already, and when they learned I had been an honor roll student through seventh grade, they told me I was already qualified to get a job. I went home and told my father this exciting news. Shortly thereafter, he saw an ad in the paper for a receptionist at a local auto glass business in Chelsea. I knew he wanted me out, and I couldn't blame him since I was drinking more at the time.

Dad did me a favor because the glass company became a lucrative career for me in the years that followed. I took a cab to my job interview, never thinking about walking to the office. After all, it was August. The interview couldn't have been more intimidating for a twenty-year-old dropout, a single mother with untreated alcoholism and virtually no self-esteem.

The company's office was a one-story cinder block building, one of the few businesses in that part of town that survived the Chelsea fire. Dave, the general manager, wore a suit. He had silver hair and smoked a cigar. He asked, "Can you type?" I said, "I can, but not that fast." He then asked if I liked dealing with people, and I said I did. I hadn't prepared for the interview at all. I was clueless as to what business the company was in. Having been left to fend for myself for so many years, I was emotionally and educationally stuck. When the company brought me back for a second interview, I had the nerve to ask them to tell me right away if I was hired because I didn't want to have to pay for a taxi again.

I was hired for four dollars an hour. I would be working from eight to five at the front desk, scheduling appointments for customers to have their auto glass replaced. I began to learn some things about the company. The business had been established shortly after World War II, and when I was hired, they had fourteen locations. They eventually grew to become the largest auto glass company in New England, and I grew right along with them. I had no idea at this point how long I'd be there or the role I'd play on my journey with the company. In many ways, they became a second family to me.

I was in no condition, mentally or physically, to be working full-time, but I felt I had to prove to my father and myself that I could do it. I still sought after his approval, and I was also fearful my father, like my mother, might ask to me leave his house if I didn't go to work. I'd spend the next six years struggling behind the desk to stay sane while being a chronic alcoholic.

Around this time, I took Jason's father to court to seek child support, but it became too costly for me to chase him for it. Rob had been paying thirty dollars a week for a few months and then abruptly stopped. We have a backward system in this country when it comes to helping single mothers. Despite my limited income, I was making just enough that the judge said I had to hire my own attorney. If I were on welfare and Rob wasn't paying child support, the court would have paid for my lawyer. I was also taking time off from work to go to court. I didn't need the aggravation, so I gave up. I was grateful to be earning enough to take care of us, and I didn't need Rob's money.

While living with my father, I found a woman who could babysit Jason while I was at work. She charged me forty dollars for the week. After paying her and my father's room and board, I was left with about forty dollars for the week to cover diapers and food for Jason and me. I usually ate supper at my father's at night. In the morning, I'd walk to the sitter on the other side of town, drop off Jason, and then walk to work. One morning, I walked with Jason in his carriage to the armory near my dad's house to stand in line and apply for state-subsidized rental assistance called Section 8. Based upon my income, I'd pay a portion of the rent, and Section 8 would pay the rest. In six months, I received the certificate, and I could now find my own place to live.

During my stay at my father's, I was partying a lot in the evenings, leaving Jason home with a woman named Katherine, whom my stepmother took in off the street. She hung around the house most days, and I immediately sensed she had some mental health issues. I pretty much begged her to babysit so I could go out and drink. I'd pay her to watch Jason, but I also borrowed money from her to buy alcohol. She wasn't the safest person to leave my baby with, but I'd lie to myself that she was okay so I could go out drinking.

I found a quaint apartment on the other side of town that accepted Section 8 certificates. It was a two-bedroom on the third floor that was recently rehabbed by the state to a brand-new condition. Two men who lived above my father sold me a refrigerator and a kitchen set for a good price. The refrigerator had a freezer you had to defrost regularly by chipping away the ice, but I didn't care so long as it worked. I didn't have a living room set or a bed for Jason. He was still in his crib.

Jason was accepted into Kangaroo Pouch, a wonderful local daycare center in a three-story brick building right under the Tobin Bridge. When I left Jason there at fourteen months old, he'd cry and cry. Each morning, when I left, I'd wave to him through the basement window, feeling awful that I had to leave.

I didn't realize how attached he was to me since I felt detached from him and his love. I didn't have to go to work; I could have stayed on welfare, but I wanted a better life for us. This choice meant being away from my baby nine hours a day. He was already walking, but I missed potty training and just being with him in the moment as a baby. If I could go back in time, I would have stayed home.

Jason started daycare at a sliding-scale fee of sixteen dollars a week, and with each raise I'd receive, the fee would increase. The center was open at seven thirty in the morning to five thirty in the afternoon. Sometimes, after leaving the glass company at five o'clock, I'd stop at the bar a block down from the daycare and have a quick drink or two before picking Jason up. Once I ordered my drink, I'd become frustrated that the daycare was only open until five thirty. Sometimes I'd drive drunk with him in the car. I was starting to put alcohol before my son and his welfare. I was recreating the unsafe life I had grown up in and wanted to prevent Jason from having.

In 1986, my brother Jamie graduated from Chelsea High School. I was so proud of him, especially considering he had come a long way and went through so much with my parents' divorce. I believe if my father hadn't taken him in, he probably wouldn't have graduated. He needed the structure my father provided at this point in his life. Still, Jamie had a lot going for him. He had grown up to be a good-looking young man. He had thick brown hair that he combed back, stood about five feet eight, and was in good shape. He had a nice complexion with olive skin and round eyes like mine. Like my father, he was gifted in his hands. He could fix anything. He painted his own cars, took engines out on his own, and picked up quickly on anything mechanical.

I asked Jamie to apply at the glass company as an installer, and he started the day after graduation. He teased me that I took him right out of high school before he could take a break from school. Everyone who met Jamie loved him, including my coworkers and boss. He had a high-pitched giggle and used to make fun of the way the male Kennedys spoke with their heavy Boston accent. He'd say "Fenway Pauk," not pronouncing the r.

Jamie worked with us for ten years before leaving. He was a great auto glass installer, but as his drinking got worse, he'd isolate himself, and no one would hear from him. He ended up at another glass company nearby for a few years, but I was sad to see him go.

People wonder how a talented, good-looking kid like Jamie could eventually get involved in drinking or drugs. He kept a lot in, and it was only a matter of time until the pain would force its way out. He wanted relief from the childhood trauma he couldn't escape from. Heredity may also have made us susceptible to substance abuse. Either way, the chances of not looking for relief somehow were nil.

* * *

While living at the apartment, I continued to drink and go to work, calling in sick whenever I was too hungover to get out of bed. Some days, I didn't call in at all, which caused more insanity in my life. My stepbrother Bobby became my regular babysitter on the weekends so I could go out drinking. He witnessed the insanity as my alcoholism progressed but never judged me for it.

My boss also knew I had a problem but hung in there with me. I was still in contact with my ex-boyfriend Dominic. I learned he fathered a child with another woman he'd been seeing all along, who would later have another child with him. He was still trying to control me by coming to the glass company and abusing me verbally for leaving him. One day, he came in and tried to lock me in the bathroom. My manager was getting sick of the abuse and might have said something to Dom because that was the last incident with him at the office, and he finally faded out of my life. Unfortunately for me, allowing abuse from men didn't.

One day at work, I met Corey, an auto glass tech. He lived in Saugus in a one-family home with two sisters and his parents. I thought he was cute, with dark hair, brown eyes, and, like many of the men I dated, Italian looking. I felt comfortable conversing with him. For once, I was interested in someone my age who was not a father figure. The truth was I was still looking for someone to take care of me.

When I met his parents, I realized his father was an alcoholic. I felt sorry for him since I knew what it felt like to come from a home with an alcoholic father. We were cut from the same cloth. He held a lot of rage in since childhood, just as I did. The difference was that his family had a nice house and his parents were together. My eyes saw a home and family that Jason and I could be part of despite the alcohol.

When I drank, I was cocky with my mouth and angry at people I felt didn't care about me, but deep down, I didn't care about them or myself. My relationship with Corey quickly became rocky, with verbal and physical abuse from both of us. Sometimes I'd get drunk and not come home when I was supposed to, and he'd ask me where I was or give me a hard time. I responded by yelling at him or maybe

I'd push him. Other times, he'd punch the wall in my apartment, saying I provoked him. I took his car one night and was stopped by the police for drinking and driving. They didn't arrest me, but Corey had to come to the police station to bring me home. We had to walk because they impounded the car. He abused me by grabbing and yelling at me all the way home. He was pissed. The saying goes, "Like attracts like." I was picking men who were angry as I was. I was a long way from admitting the abuse I was putting up with and the abuse I was inflicting on those around me.

Jason was still enrolled at Kangaroo Pouch. One day, he showed the staff where Corey had slapped his bum the night before. The school called to let me know what happened. I wanted to kill Corey. I had hit Jason once on the back of his head, which forced his forehead to hit the corner of the sink in the apartment. This scared the wits out of me so bad that I never hit him again. I was a yeller, not a hitter. I wasn't good at setting limits with Jason, so I often yelled because I felt out of control. I have come to learn that both behaviors are abusive.

I called Corey's mother about the handprint. She was a nice woman and loved Jason, but she didn't want to get involved. What did I expect her to do? Naturally, she'd protect her son. I think I just wanted her to rescue us. I was a coward with men, making me afraid to confront someone who hurt my son because I was so afraid of being alone.

Just before I left Corey, I got involved with yet another guy. His name was Brad Stevens, and he was from Birmingham, England. Although I was still drinking, I continued working at the auto glass company and took Jason to as many places as I could for vacation. Fred had moved to Florida. Since we remained amicable, I'd bring Jason and my stepbrother Bobby to visit him, and we'd all go to Disney World. Fred let us stay at his house for free, no strings attached. Brad was also vacationing in Florida. He was blonde and light skinned with a muscular build and very kind. When he spoke, it reminded me of the British royal family.

At the time, I wasn't capable of being with someone who was kind to me. He was a good listener and validated my feelings. Brad talked with me about getting help with my drinking and becoming a better person. He gave me a feeling of being safe, which was foreign to me with a man.

I wasn't safe for him to be around emotionally. I was still involved with Corey and looking for a way out of the relationship. Latching onto the next guy was my standard solution. Whenever I was drunk and feeling lonely and unloved, I called Brad in England. The calls provided relief from my untreated alcoholism and the abusive, dishonest relationship with Corey. Brad later visited me in Boston, and I didn't know what to do with him. I recall telling Brad I was staying with Corey, and I didn't want a relationship with him after all. Poor guy, I couldn't be honest with him or anyone else. I was just wasting people's time.

I was using men as my source, putting the responsibility on them to make me feel whole. They could never live up to the task, and I'd just move on. I was doing whatever my head told me to do, which was to hurt people just as I was feeling hurt. Men were merely tools for me to survive instead of people to love.

The funny thing is that I was taking care of Jason and me, so I didn't need a man. Despite this, I was mirroring my mother, who had men take care of her because she wasn't capable of working. I didn't realize that since I was bringing in income, I didn't need to be the same way. I was so busy in survival mode that I was unable to love and enjoy anyone. The solution was there: stop drinking and give my life to God. I had quite a way to go before that would happen.

By this time, Jason had graduated from kindergarten at Kangaroo's Pouch and was attending St. Rose, a Catholic school in Chelsea. He was turning five during the summer of 1987. This birthday would be his last before I got sober. During my active alcoholic days, I did my best to keep him in good schools. St. Rose had also been my family's parish. I enrolled him there so he could learn about God. God was always in the back of my mind, even when I wasn't following him.

According to the comments written in his grammar school report cards, Jason struggled with organizing assignments and getting his homework done. He had a hard time following directions and could easily get upset and frustrated. I'd get frustrated too while helping him with his homework. I used to ask him if I was speaking gibberish, because he couldn't understand simple directions. I saw the problems as simple, but apparently, he didn't. I took his behavior as being defiant, never thinking that maybe he's incapable of understanding what I was explaining.

I feel now that the issue was my lack of soothing him when he was a child. Just letting a child know it's okay and that they're okay—something I didn't receive growing up—can do wonders. I was critical and had no patience, which didn't help Jason feel calm.

At other times, I spoiled him, which didn't do him or myself any favors. I wasn't good at being consistent with him or providing structure in the house. I'd buy him material things to make him happy to substitute for my being emotionally present. I'd buy Jason the best Air Jordan sneakers he wanted and would spend money eating out a few nights a week with him. I'd take him on vacation at least once a year, whether I could afford it or not.

Jason loved Nintendo games and anything that had to do with them. He was very competitive and had a hard time dealing with losing when playing against someone else. Playing games was a way to comfort himself from the crazy ups and downs that came from living with a mother suffering from untreated alcoholism. Games gave him a distraction from the anxiety he felt in my home, just as I found distraction in alcohol, men, and shopping. I made a lot of money, but I never learned how to budget it. I bought way too many things for myself, like clothes I didn't need. I shopped every week and maxed out my credit cards. What you fear, you make happen. I was afraid I'd have no money, like when I was a child, so whatever I made, I spent, which kept the cycle of fear going. The only savings I had was my pension plan and some diamond jewelry I bought over the years at the Jewelers Building in Boston. I felt I could sell it if I did run out of money.

I did my best to enable Jason to be connected to whatever opportunities he wanted to be a part of. Jason enjoyed playing Little League baseball for a few years and won a few trophies. He even did karate for a while and was good at it, but as soon as the teacher wanted to step him up a class, he didn't want to go anymore. I understood that I couldn't force him to continue if he didn't want to, but I struggled to be there emotionally, as my mind was usually somewhere else. Being a single mother from a crazy house and being thrown into motherhood and a full-time job wasn't easy. I bullied him to get what I wanted instead of communicating my disappointment when he didn't listen. Discipline and boundaries are important. They help children feel safe, but what did I know about that?

Jason had quite a few friends from school. Peter—an only child like Jason, quiet, and reserved—had spent years in daycare with my son and was one of his closest friends. The two of them would alternate staying at each other's houses on weekends. I used to ask Jason if Peter was mad because he didn't look happy, which made me feel uncomfortable. Jason said, "That's how he is. He's shy." I was always trying to make people happy. I thought that was my job.

Another friend, Jarrod, was from a Jewish family. He liked to be in his own house after school and on the weekends, so Jason stayed at his house a lot. I'd pick Jason up from Jarrod's and tell him how I had a close Jewish friend growing up too. I felt like he was mirroring my childhood by making a Jewish friend.

My stepbrother Nico's son, Jay, also spent quite of bit of time with us. He'd stay over, and I'd take the two of them to the movies, Bonkers, or to Chuck E. Cheese, the kid's indoor arcades. We also went bowling. I used to ask Jason, "What do I look like, the entertainment committee?" He'd laugh, but he liked that I thought of fun things to do with his friends. I felt like I didn't do enough. Growing up with alcoholism creates haunting thoughts that taunt you, saying you're never quite good enough.

After leaving Corey, I began dating a guy named Angelo, who was friends with a coworker I befriended. Angelo worked as a truck driver at a Boston cement company. He was looking to become an iron worker and bounced at a bar part-time. I wasn't even sure if I liked him, but of course, I chased him anyway. I'd bring cocaine to the apartment he shared with his brother, who wasn't too fond of me. I don't blame him. I wouldn't want someone in my home doing drugs either, especially with the drug forfeiture laws.

My use of drugs and alcohol was finally coming to an end. I was becoming sick of the life I was living. I wasn't getting to work, and I felt my life spinning out of control. I was afraid I'd lose Jason, and I knew there was no one in my family who would step up and take care of him if something happened to me.

The problem was I didn't know how to stop the insanity that preceded the first drink. I needed help, so in October or November of 1987, I finally made a call to a coworker who was in Alcoholics Anonymous. He directed me to a detox facility at Mount Pleasant Hospital in Lynn, a couple of towns over from where I lived. Either Jamie or Bobby gave me a ride. Some people can go many years chasing that high, which is really nothing more than looking for relief. I wanted to stop this madness and live a better life.

Chapter 4

When I arrived at the detox at Mount Pleasant, the staff asked me what drugs I used, took my blood pressure, asked the usual medical interview questions, then put me on lithium to relax me. I'd like to tell you I stayed there and completed the program on my first visit, but I wasn't quite done yet. I knew after the first day that I didn't want to stay. I wasn't ready. You need to have a hunger for sobriety where you are willing to do whatever it takes to get it, just like a starving person will eat shoe leather if nothing else is available. That desire cannot come from just feeling bad physically and emotionally and wanting a break from alcohol. You have to surrender to the fact you are an alcoholic and can never drink alcohol in safety again ever.

I went home against medical advice, went back to work, and didn't use alcohol or drugs until the insanity of the first drink came back. When you're an alcoholic, you're vulnerable to the lie in your head that tells you since a period of time has gone by, this proves you can handle it, so it's okay if you drink again. And so about six months after leaving Mount Pleasant, I found myself at the Caravan Club, a dance club behind Revere Beach frequented mostly by locals that usually had great dance bands. I sat at the large circular bar like a big shot, thinking I was better than everyone else. I didn't ask for a drink at first because I was under the delusion I wasn't there to drink.

I acted like I had it all together that night, being on the hunt for another guy who I thought would take care of me, looking for the emotional connection I thought I had with my father, but now as an adult via sex. After ordering a few sodas, I met two men at the bar, Bill S. and Jimmy L. Soon after, I gave in and ordered a Black Russian from the bartender.

The insanity of alcoholism is what the Big Book of Alcoholics Anonymous calls "the mental twist." The lie we tell ourselves is that it will be different this time when we drink. As an alcoholic, I need to realize that it is the first drink that gets me drunk because of my physical allergy to it. When I put it in my body, it sets up the compulsion for more alcohol, of which there's never enough.

I spent time talking and dancing with the two men. I didn't know them from a hole in the wall, but I had no problem going home with Bill. He was the one I had my eye on. Whenever I drink, I put myself in unsafe situations. I didn't think about my safety or what he could have done to me. I didn't use a condom nor was I on birth control pills, which was very irresponsible of me. I stopped taking them a few years ago because of my lack of sex drive. My brother Jamie was babysitting Jason, and I didn't even bother to call and tell him where I was.

I woke up the next morning in Bill's basement apartment in Revere, grateful that I wasn't dead and glad I went home with the guy wearing the blue shirt. Bill was the better looking of the two. How sad my thinking and my behaviors were.

Bill told me he was leaving for work. I fell back to sleep and then left him a note that read, in part, that I was an alcoholic. I needed to get help and was going into detox. I told him which detox it was, even though inside I still wasn't sure I was willing to go. My present boyfriend Angelo phoned my house in the morning, and Jamie told him I didn't come home last night. I called Angelo when I got home and tried to lie like I always did, but he was done. Who could blame him?

I got in touch with my longtime friend Susan, who came by the house and encouraged me to go back to detox. I was having second thoughts now. I didn't want to go. I was standing in my kitchen with Susan, wondering what I should do. She said, "You need to go back. You need help." I thought I could do it on my own, but I eventually submitted and went. That was one of the best decisions I ever made.

The staff evaluated me again, but this time, they didn't give me lithium to detox, possibly because I only drank for one night. My father, who lived around the corner from us, took care of Jason while I was there. During my stay, he asked when I'd be out. I told him, "I don't know. Whenever they decide to release me."

When he asked me that question, I recognized the familiar annoyance in his tone, which let me know indirectly that he didn't appreciate having to take care of Jason. I felt anxious, like I was doing something selfish and wrong again. I wanted to scream, thinking about how selfish he had been. He abandoned his children and is now remarried and taking care of someone else's children, yet here he is, putting pressure on me to "hurry it up" in detox. Very sad.

I was just trying to get some help. I went through most of my life not asking for what I needed, believing I should trust and rely on my own thinking, which wasn't always a good idea. Everyone needs help at some time in their life.

Jamie brought Jason to the detox to give me money or clothes, but because it was during a nonvisiting time, I couldn't touch my son. I had to see him through a glass window. He was six at the time. I recall him being on Jamie's lap, asking when I was coming home. I might have told him, "Mommy's sick, and I'm trying to get better." I felt like I was in prison. Not being able to hug your son is a terrible feeling.

Al-Anon is a program for people affected by someone else's drinking. One night, during an Al-Anon meeting at the detox, I had a spiritual experience. I don't recall what was being said by the man speaking at the table in the front of the room, but I was sitting in my chair listening when it finally hit me that I was an alcoholic. I was thinking to myself, "That's what's wrong with you. It's not your fault. You have a disease." The grace of God entered my heart that night and allowed me to understand that I was sick, not bad. I felt relieved, finally knowing what was wrong with me and there was something I could do about it. I will be forever grateful for his mercy.

The next day, I went to the doctor in the detox and explained to him how since attending last night's meeting I felt different and more at peace. I understood what was wrong; I had a disease. I told him I felt strange. He said, "Don't worry about it. I'm sure it's a good thing," which indeed it was. A few nights later, in my room, I heard God speak to me. He simply said, "Good night." The three other women sharing my room were not there at the time. I knew God was speaking. He knew I was ready to listen.

After ten days, I left Mount Pleasant, scared and feeling vulnerable. Thankfully, I learned what I needed to do to stay sober. I followed all the suggestions I received at the detox: to go to meetings, individual aftercare at the hospital, and group aftercare.

I remained close to Mount Pleasant for a couple of years. Of course, I picked up another guy there, Derek Bradford, who worked in the exercise trailer behind the detox. I dated him for a few months when I left. After all, I couldn't be without a guy. That was one crutch I truly wasn't willing to let go of. I think he had been sober for three years. He was a nice man, but he took a chance being with someone newly sober like me. He came by my house periodically, and we became friends. I wasn't able to be honest and tell him I didn't want to see him anymore. The relationship eventually fizzled out from lack of communication.

For now, I was running around to meetings, drinking iced coffee like a maniac, and feeling good for being sober. After about three months of sobriety, I took the test to get my GED (General Equivalency Development). I received a grade of B plus, and I was thrilled. I was twenty-five years old and had been out of school since I was sixteen. I only made it to the ninth grade, which I failed to repeat because I left my mother's house to live with Rob. I knew I wasn't stupid, but it felt good to do so well. My stepbrother Bobby had balloons as a celebration for me when I got home after taking the test. He was always so supportive of me.

I was back to work and feeling great, realizing I could probably do more than work as a receptionist at the glass company. I was grateful they held my job, and I expressed my appreciation to them. I will be forever grateful for their decision to keep my job open for me. I attempted to go on the road in sales a year before, but I wasn't ready. Now, after being sober for a year and still working behind the desk, I was at a crossroads of either making more money in another position or leaving the company. Although I didn't graduate high school or go to college, I knew I could better myself.

God had a plan, and the general manager who helped hire me was leaving to work with his son at a new glass company he recently opened. My own manager, Bob P., approached me about going on the road. When he asked if I'd be interested in giving it another chance, I said I would. The company gave me the prior general manager's territory in the greater Boston area along with a company car. I was assigned to visit about one hundred seventy auto insurance agencies once a month. My job was to represent the company and convey to each agency the value and benefits of using our company for their policyholders' glass needs. I was excited but also terrified I could fail.

My early days of selling were difficult, and I wasn't sure I made the right choice. I believed people I visited would send business, only to come back a month later and find that no auto glass jobs were being done for their policyholders. Some of these agencies were giving work to our competitors who offered rebates. I didn't know it then, but I was in the familiar cycle of letting people show me who they were but wanting to believe they were trustworthy, just like with my family.

So what did I do? I responded exactly like I did as a child. I tried harder to win agencies over by rewarding them with gifts they didn't quite deserve. I'd buy concert tickets and dinners at high-end restaurants, no matter the cost. I had and have many other clients who send a lot more business, and I took care of them too. But the ones that only threw me a bone I'd overcompensate for. I got caught up on the gerbil wheel of self-will by not asking for help from my company with the rebating problem. This led me to the insanity of not feeling good enough again. It was exhausting, and I wanted out, but I didn't know how to get there.

Eventually, I started to let go of the behaviors I needed to survive as a child. I became Karen, the outgoing sales rep my clients would come to know and trust, eventually being one of the company's top producers. I was beginning to realize I couldn't win everyone over or control who sent me business. I rewarded the clients who helped me and did my best with the ones who didn't. I was finally accepting I couldn't change people's character, but I could welcome people who connected with me. That was finally good enough. My sales numbers started to soar. This was the beginning of a new career that would allow me to take very good care of Jason. It was 1989, and it was time for new beginnings. I was still regularly going to AA and my aftercare groups to get the support I needed. I appreciated the opportunity to grow with the company and felt I was moving forward.

I also met another man. I was on the hunt for a guy again. I still believed the lie that I needed a man to take care of me to feel whole. I was always in God's care, but I didn't believe it.

I noticed a good-looking guy regularly walking by my office who dressed a little preppy for the area. He wore collared shirts with shorts and leather slip-on shoes. His style of dress made him look easygoing and smart. He was about five foot seven, thin, and had the Italian look I was attracted to. I thought he was gorgeous.

He worked next door from the glass company. I knew the woman who worked upstairs from his office, so I asked her about him. I was hoping she'd tell Jesse I inquired about him. That's how I operated; instead of letting God do the leading, I tried to open my own doors. I had to make things happen or not happen. I guess he was eyeing me too because one day I received a dozen red roses with a card asking if I'd have dinner with him. I was so excited. When I called the number on the card, he said, "What's up?" That's how young guys talked. Just the same, I was impressed and wanted to know him better.

Our first date was in May 1989. We had lunch across the street from our offices at Floramo's, a well-known Chelsea restaurant whose motto is "Where the meat falls off the bone." They make great baby back ribs, and you can smell the barbeque all over the neighborhood. We sat in a booth and both ordered the steak tips. I was trying to act confident but really feeling shy inside. I was scared to be with Jesse because I was so physically attracted to him. I loved everything about him or at least everything I could see. The truth was I wasn't feeling good enough to be with him.

On another date, we went for dinner in the north end of Boston at an Italian restaurant called Ristorante Saraceno, a quaint little place on Hanover Street with Italian art on the walls and the smell of tomato sauce cooking. The waiters all spoke with an Italian accent. I felt so special being with Jesse. What I liked about him was his free spirit and positive outlook on life. I wanted what I thought he had—a loving family, money, and intelligence. He was twenty-one and attended the Florida Institute of Technology for several years. He wanted to become a pilot and loved to surf and golf. These were activities I knew nothing about but found attractive in him.

I was newly sober and had no idea how to be in a healthy relationship with a guy. That night after dinner, we met his brother Tony, who was staying at a Boston hotel. While hanging out in Tony's room, we kissed a bit, and I noticed a raised scar on his cheek from a car accident. I didn't know Jesse well, but already I was comfortable touching a scar on his face. I was already trying to connect with him physically, which was all I knew.

Early in the relationship, I was impressed when Jesse picked me up for dinner in a Porsche that once belonged to Bruins Hall of Famer Phil Esposito. What I failed to do was allow myself the time to see if I really liked him and how I felt being with him. I was caught up in the flesh and didn't give myself enough time to get to know him. Although I was sober, I was not spiritually fit. I had "untreated alcoholism," which means I was spiritually sick and still unhealed from my past. I hadn't received the "psychic change" the Alcoholics Anonymous book talks about. Since I hadn't done the twelve steps, I was bringing this sickness into the relationship with all the baggage from years before. I had put the drink down, but I hadn't dealt with the underlying causes of why I drank. Since I had such low self-esteem, I didn't feel I had much to bring nor was I worthy enough to receive. I didn't know how to have healthy, honest relationships. I didn't even have one with myself.

While riding in Jesse's car one night, I was too timid to ask him to put the convertible top down. When I did, he made a remark about me being a baby. That set up the future for our relationship. I felt I couldn't be truthful because honesty wasn't received well. His remark was a reminder of the negative responses I received growing up. I shut down early on in the relationship for fear he'd leave me if

I was myself. The sad part was I loved everything about him on the outside, but my fear of being honest led me away from being emotionally intimate with him.

Today, I believe we were both emotionally unavailable to each other. I was a coward with my feelings because sharing them could cost me my survival growing up, but that wasn't serving me well now. I was hurting people, including myself. Being with someone closer to my age was a great feeling. Jesse wasn't like the older men I didn't want to look at when I was physical with them. I actually met someone I was attracted to, and the feeling was mutual. But because of the false self I developed growing up, my job at the glass company, along with Jesse, became my source instead of God. I was still going to meetings regularly but living a double life in sobriety. I was acting like this sober spiritual person in front of Jesse while doing the wrong thing behind his back.

During my years with Jesse, I took advantage of his trust in me. I didn't know how to live life sober. I did whatever felt good, without thinking of whom I was hurting or the consequences of my behavior. Whenever I felt sad or hurt, I'd act out sexually, looking for an emotional connection. It might have been just getting attention from a guy or actually sleeping with him.

When I worked behind the desk before going into sales, I met a customer Ken who owned a trucking company. He grew up in Winthrop, and I thought he was very handsome. He only came in the office a few times to fix his car, but I had an immediate attraction to him. Like Jesse, he was about five seven, my age, and had that Roman Italian look about him. At some point, I reached out and connected with him. I started having sex with Ken during those times when I didn't know how to talk with Jesse. I'd call him to relate my sob stories about my relationship with Jesse, when all I needed to do was allow myself to be emotionally intimate with my boyfriend. I'd tell Ken I had broken up with Jesse and then have sex with him at his office. This became a pattern until Ken called me on my behavior about contacting him only when I was fighting with Jesse. My behavior was absurd and really kept me from being loved or loving someone else. Sex became another way of escape from how I was feeling.

This behavior went on for years. I was running away from my past and myself, not realizing I was spiritually sick. I was hiding my double life behind the fact I was sober and going to meetings, retreats, and church daily. I was trying so hard to behave better, but I couldn't get out of my own way. Just going to meetings was not enough. I needed to do the twelve steps in AA.

Jesse was young, and at one point in our relationship, he wanted out. I told him I loved him, trying to manipulate him into staying. I say manipulate because I didn't even know if I loved him or not. I was afraid of being alone. That is not a reason to tell someone you love them or stay in a relationship with them. He stayed, and it would be a roller-coaster ride for the next seven years. I'm not blaming everything on myself; he was an adult and could have left if he really wanted. Years later, after beating myself up for my behavior, I realized he had his own mind and will to do what he wanted. I didn't make him stay. But left untreated, alcoholism causes nothing but pain toward the people around us as we try to steal their reality from them.

Each year, my revenue was increasing in my new career. Jesse babysat Jason so I could go out with clients at night. Drinking alcohol was no longer an issue for me, but living in sobriety was. At times, Jesse fronted me money to take clients to dinner and never asked for it back, even though I'd turn in the receipt and get reimbursed each month. He was good to both of us, and I believe he gave Jason a sense of security I wasn't able to give him since I was rarely home. Because I was busy with work, AA, and running from my own demons, Jesse played a key role in Jason's life during those fundamental years. At the time, I didn't realize the impact Jesse's influence had on Jason. I was too wrapped up in my own pain.

Jason and I still did a lot together. I'd take him to church on Sundays because it was important for me to teach Jason that God loved him. Even though I didn't always feel I was loved by God, I knew in my core he loved us, and I wanted Jason to know that too. For now, Jesse was my god in many ways, and that expectation would prove to be hurtful to all of us.

Jason and I spent the holidays and weekends with Jesse's family at their house in Hampton Falls, New Hampshire. It was a five-thousand-square-foot house set in an old apple orchard. It had an indoor swimming pool and a four-car garage. Jason would bring his toys and play with Jesse's nephew, Anthony. Jesse's dad teased Jason like he was his own. Jesse's mom, Neva, was a petite blonde woman who was a knockout in her younger years, a former majorette and dancer. I would sit in the kitchen and watch her cook while we talked about a range of personal topics. She taught me how to make chicken wings and chicken ziti with broccoli.

There's an expression I once learned: "The consequence of being a liar is you think everyone is lying to you." I felt so much tension while in New Hampshire with Jesse's family. I was constantly on edge, waiting for the dishonest life I was living to be discovered. I had constant fear that Jesse and his family were conspiring and hiding something from me, like I was hiding something from them. I may have been worried that Jesse had another girlfriend calling him. I didn't trust them because I didn't trust myself. Jesse and his family didn't deserve any of it.

At one point, Jesse found a journal I was writing in. While I was on an AA spiritual retreat that guided women to grow closer to God, he read about my episodes with Ken. Some truth was finally coming out. I was loaded with fear but also relieved. I probably would have never told him the truth about my escapades, being the coward I was. Jesse was watching Jason while I was away. He kept paging me on the retreat, and when I reached him, I believe he said he was leaving the house and leaving Jason alone because he couldn't stay there anymore. When I got home, we talked about what he read. He was very angry, but I recall him saying he was glad he now knew the truth. I'm sure I came up with some denial because I couldn't own up to my own nonsense.

By February of 1996, I had been sober and living on self-will for eight years, and I was tired. I couldn't look at myself in the mirror from the fraudulent life I was living. What does that mean to the alcoholic? Removing alcohol from my system was only the beginning of healing from the disease of selfishness, dishonesty, and fear. These were the underlying reasons I drank, and just because I took alcohol out of my system didn't mean I dealt with the causes and conditions of why I drank. Although I was going to a Catholic Church daily, I still felt like a fraud.

I was still "discontent," as the AA book says. I was still hurting myself and everyone around me. I needed to get to the root of my problem, which was self. This problem manifested itself in many forms but always resulted from trying to live by my own direction in reaction to fear. The kind of self-reliance I learned early in childhood, the drive to survive at any cost, was no longer serving me well.

Chapter 5

An AA friend told me about some new meetings in our area that he thought might be able to help me. The new meetings, called "Big Book Step Study," followed the twelve steps the way they were presented in the Alcoholics Anonymous book. I was as desperate again after eight years of sobriety as I was in 1988 when I first put down the drink. I had attended one of these Big Book Step Study meetings the year before, but because of my ego and because people weren't giving me the attention I felt I deserved, I didn't go back. This time, with the way I was living, I had nothing to say. I was ready to listen.

When I walked into the meeting, held in a Catholic Church basement in Revere, the atmosphere was peaceful. Rows of people sat in chairs with two people at the front table. One was chairing the meeting; the other was the speaker, sharing personal experiences on the step they were studying that night. At first, I wondered why the men didn't turn their heads when I walked in the room. That's where my thinking was—always looking for attention so I could feel good about myself.

These meetings were very different than the meetings I had been attending. At this meeting, no matter how long you were sober, if you hadn't done the steps as laid out in the Alcoholics Anonymous book, with the help of a sponsor who had also been through the process, you could not speak. In all my years of being in AA, I never learned a consistent way to follow the steps. People in the meetings I attended had different versions of how to do the steps, and that never made sense to me. Here, we would do the steps the way they were intended, not according to someone's opinion of how to do them.

I was attracted to the safety in these directions. Taking my friend's suggestion to go to these meetings was one of the best decisions I ever made. I had no idea what was in store for me.

My boyfriend Jesse was "punch drunk," as he later described himself to me, and I completely understood why. Every week we'd fight. I'd break up with him and then be crying for him to come back, and he would. His head was spinning after years of that. I didn't know what I wanted or what the heck I was doing. I was doing more damage sober than when I was actively drinking.

I told Jesse the importance of these meetings, and one night, he attended with me. For a short time, he was also going to Al-Anon. But when he told me he had made friends with a woman he met there, I was outraged. I suppose they were talking after the meetings about the difficulties of being in a relationship with an alcoholic. I was fearful that Jesse might realize he could be taking better care of himself and leave me. I suggested he attend twelve step meetings, and now I want to control who he talks to. It was always about me.

After we heard a speaker one night say, after doing the twelve steps and learning the truth about his relationship, he ended it because it was a lie. Jesse asked me, "Do you think that will happen to us?" I think for once I was honest with him. I said, "I don't know." I didn't want the relationship to end, but I had put so much dishonesty between us that I couldn't see how I or God could repair it.

While attending the Big Book Step Study meetings, I asked a woman named Sara to be my sponsor—in other words, to mentor me through the twelve steps. Sara was outgoing, direct, and dressed with great fashion. She had no problem being honest at the meetings about her past behavior, including her sexual conduct. I was floored at her honesty and ability to not worry about what people thought. She was free. I asked her to help me, and she said yes. She would be in my life for the next ten years.

Step four requires the alcoholic to "make a fearless and searching moral inventory of yourself." The first part is to list the resentments you hold toward other people. The second part is to see where you played a role in the resentment. I added many names from my past and present to the list. I realized I was playing the victim with people I was still angry at for events that happened long ago. When I wrote my resentments toward Jesse, there were about sixty of them. They ranged from "I don't like his friends," "He graduated from high school," "He doesn't give me enough attention," to "I don't like the candy he eats." Some of the resentments seem silly, but being an alcoholic, I believed everyone should like what I like.

I was going to church daily, asking God what to do because I was tired of hurting Jesse with my lies and Jason with my tongue due to the anger I was feeling. As soon as I saw that the relationship wasn't right for me, I wanted out. I didn't think to say, "Jesse, we need to take a break" or even prepare my son for the loss he'd now feel in his life.

* * *

Jason was a part of the ups and downs of the insanity of "untreated alcoholism" in our relationship. When we're not true to ourselves, we become resentful and blame everyone else for our misery. We also take it out on our children because they can't fight back. I know I did that with Jason. I bullied him at times. I'd yell at him when he was small and I was an adult. When I'd wake him up for school and he wouldn't get up, I'd scream at him all the way to school because he was going to be late. Then I'd feel bad after I dropped him off. When it was time to go to bed and he'd say, "I have homework, Mum," I'd start screaming at him about not getting it done earlier. If he had a project to do, he'd tell me at the last minute after I let him play his Nintendo. I was expecting him to be honest with me rather than asking if he had schoolwork to do. I didn't have a lot of structure in the house, and I expected him to parent himself.

When I behaved this way to Jason, he'd ask me, "Why do you hate on me so much?" I didn't understand that I was putting the anger toward myself and my father on him. I was bullying just as I was bullied growing up in my house. I felt powerless, and trying to control Jason made me feel I had power in my life. He belonged to me, or so I thought. My bullying wasn't twenty-four seven, but it came out enough to affect him. Like me, Jason told himself his own story about what took place in his childhood. He later told me he had a good childhood, and I'd always hold that close to my heart. It's easier to tell yourself a story than to admit the reality of the pain of feeling abused and unwanted. Praise God for the twelve steps because I'd later make amends for the bullying I inflicted on him.

I finally had the courage to end the relationship with Jesse in April 1996, right after attending Big Book Step Study. My last moment with him was in front of the glass company, where we met in his black Dodge pickup truck. He sat in his truck, resting his chin on one arm slung across his door and holding the pages of my fourth step in his hand.

He asked me, "Is it really over?"

I said, "Yes, Jesse, it is."

He gave me back the paper and said, "Okay," and I walked into the office feeling I had done the right thing by letting him go. I didn't know how much my heart would ache from this loss as time moved forward.

I didn't give one thought to how the breakup would affect Jason. I was tired of being in the lie, but I wasn't the only one in it. Jason was there too. I don't believe the breakup caused my son's future illness, but I do believe it was the catalyst that brought it on.

Jesse bought Jason many gifts over the years, including, just before I started writing my fourth step, a Dallas Cowboy's winter jacket. This jacket would play a significant role in future months. It's amazing how much an article of clothing can tell us about how a person feels inside.

For now, I felt scared about being alone but happy that Jason and I could start our life over. He was almost fourteen years old, and I was thirty-three. I continued going to meetings and finishing the steps, and every day, I got closer to God as he was beginning to heal my childhood wounds.

After seeing some truths in my life, I was starting to question whether I wanted to stay at the glass company in sales when another opportunity came my way. One of the company's owners, Tom R., wanted to hire a new manager for part of the sales team north of Boston. Through writing my fourth step, I saw that I was holding myself back, telling myself the lie that I wasn't good enough for the job. It didn't matter that I had already proved to be successful; my mind hadn't caught up with reality. I applied for the position, along with another sales rep. I was planning a trip out west with Susan and our kids, and I'd find out who Tom chose after I came home.

Susan has a son, Mathew, and a daughter, Stefanie. Mathew was fifteen and couldn't wait to get his license. He was a fun-loving kid and liked driving cross country. He kept an eye on the maps we had to follow in those days before GPS (global positioning system). Stefanie was thirteen and pretty much kept to herself during the trip. I had a little fear about returning home and doing my fifth step—reading my entire fourth step to my sponsor—even though she already looked at it every week. I would be feeling vulnerable for once, trusting someone else with my innermost secrets. I spent so much of my life trying to look good; now was the time to give it up.

While out west, we stopped in Phoenix. Our plan was to rent a GMC Jimmy and drive to Las Vegas and California. After picking up the truck, I noticed Jason wasn't feeling comfortable riding in it. He didn't want to sit in the back seat. The kids and I alternated sitting in the rear, which was tight, I have to admit. Looking back now, I can see how I people pleased Susan by renting such a small vehicle for five people to travel state to state. I wasn't feeling comfortable in the truck either. Jason was being real; I was the one not being authentic. Jason was quiet in the truck, and when anyone talked to him, he became irritated. I admit he was witnessing a mother who couldn't speak up and expected him to be okay with that. I knew our relationship wasn't healthy, and I needed to make some major changes.

I was just starting to learn who I was. I knew it would take time to mend our relationship and teach him that he couldn't always have his way and that his mother needed to grow a backbone. I treated Jason like he was special. When as a parent we don't discipline our children, they begin to feel entitled. While he was growing up, I told myself the lie that it was easier to give in to what he wanted so he'd be quiet. At the same time, I didn't stand up to him. I needed to become real with myself and with him. I needed to gain his trust.

I sensed there was more going on with Jason than just his behavior, but I wanted to believe the problem was his selfishness and being a teenager, acting as we all do at that age. On the trip, Jason asked me if I could see his eyes through his sunglasses. I said, "A little." That seemed like an odd question, but I didn't think much of it.

When we came back from our trip, I made an appointment to meet with my sponsor to read my entire fourth step inventory. I was ready to let another human being hear the whole story of the anger I was holding on to, the fears that were holding me back, and the unhealthy sexual conduct I was still participating in.

I met with Sara at her home in Brighton, a cute basement apartment in her mother's house. She sat on her loveseat while I sat on a recliner and read my fourth step inventory. I was "admitting to God and to another human being the exact nature of my wrongs." I was basically confessing my sins.

Each visit lasted between three and six hours, and the whole process took three weeks. As I read, Sara occasionally commented or gave validation and compassion to some of the material I was reading. At times, I'd feel a ball form in my throat after looking at what was on the page because it was too painful to say out loud. Some of the more painful resentments I had to read were toward my son. Becoming a mother at such a young age led me to be angry at feeling inept. It stemmed back to feeling like a failure from not being able to do more as a child in a home that was out of control. I wasn't prepared to become a teenage mother, just as I wasn't prepared to take care of myself and Jamie when my father left us those years before.

After each session, I'd leave Sara's house and drive home on the Massachusetts Turnpike, feeling a little bit freer from unloading the untreated alcoholism from my past. It took about three weeks to purge it all, and when I was done, I went on to take my sixth and seventh steps, letting God know I was willing to give up those behaviors I wrote in my fourth step to live a godlier life by being directed by him.

It didn't mean that I was going to be perfect, but at least now, I could see what was hurting me and holding me back from being the true person God wanted me to be. I felt like God was giving me a second chance at life. I couldn't change without God's help, and I couldn't change if I hadn't seen the truth of who I was and how and why I operated the way I did.

I went on to do steps eight and nine, to "make a list of the people I had harmed" and "make direct amends to them except when to do so would injure them or others." I needed a lot of guidance from my sponsor for these two steps. I thought I had to apologize to everyone. My sponsor helped by telling me not to go to the wife of a married man I had slept with and tell her I cheated with her husband. The amends were not about hurting someone else so you can feel better. I needed Sara's discernment, for sure.

During this time, I was still stopping by Jesse's office. Although he had already moved on with a new girlfriend, I couldn't let him go emotionally. I continued apologizing to him for my behaviors in hope that he'd come back to me. I was still hurting others with my selfishness. I couldn't change overnight the behaviors I had used for many years. I needed God's help.

One thing that was changing was my position at the glass company. After the trip, Tom R. offered me the position of sales manager. I met with him at a hotel in Harvard Square, Cambridge, to discuss my responsibilities and income. I was a little scared since most people at my company were intimidated by him. He's well educated—a Harvard Business School graduate—and hard to read. We had a nice talk about what his expectations were for the position. I appreciated his concerns, and to my surprise, I felt comfortable with him. I had the fear of failure and thoughts of not being good enough still swirled around my head, but I wanted to give it a shot. I had absolutely no idea what I was doing in life, but I knew how to sell our company, and I was confident I could encourage the sales team and help them reach their goals.

My career was the one thing I had that no one could take away from me. It provided me with a great income and the ability to have nice things and take good care of Jason. But my dependence on my job and the ups and downs of sales never gave me the security I craved. What I was beginning to understand is that God had been and always will be my source. I welcomed this new opportunity in hopes that God was ultimately guiding me. When we parted ways that day, I remember watching Tom walk away through Harvard Square and feeling this was a person who would have a significant role in my life. I felt like I had known him at another time in another place. I had never felt that feeling before. I was intrigued.

During the time I was going through the steps, I kept an open mind about who God was to me. I had been attending a Catholic Church in my town until one day I was invited by my AA friend Jerry to an evangelical church in Lexington, the historical town west of Boston. Jerry walked like a hockey player with skates on. He was a fast talker and was always joking around. But when it came to his relationship with God, he was quite serious. The conviction with which Jerry spoke and the knowledge he had of the Bible told me he knew Jesus in a way I didn't.

When I entered Grace Chapel, I saw a plain altar and a wooden cross on the back wall. Flags of many nations hung on either side of the sanctuary. I didn't see the statues I was used to seeing; the cross didn't have Jesus on it, and no one genuflected before sitting down or made the sign of the cross. I immediately felt disrespectful by not demonstrating these rituals. But I was beginning to understand that these rituals have nothing to do with knowing Jesus or with God's love for me. In fact, they are a form of idolatry. Idolatry is giving power to anything above God. I had given power to everyone and everything but God.

Some of the hymn lyrics at Grace Chapel made me uncomfortable; one of the songs was about Jesus's blood. For now, I thanked Jerry for inviting me but left it at that. I kept my new experience of an evangelical church in the back of my mind. I continued to attend the Catholic Church, but something was tugging at me. I kept an open mind and began reading New Age and Eastern philosophy books such as Emmet Fox's *Find and Use Your Inner Power* and Paramahansa Yogananda's *Man's Eternal Quest*. I was exploring new ideas that people had of who God was. I continued to seek him until I found him.

When I made verbal amends to Jason—which meant apologizing for the ways I had wronged him—I said I was sorry for being so angry toward him. I said it wasn't his fault; it was because I didn't know how to process my anger, and so I took it out on him. I apologized for all the crazy behavior with Jesse and said we were going to be okay. He didn't want to hear it, and he acted as if Jesse's leaving wasn't a big deal. I can't remember his exact reply, but he said, more or less, "Whatever." Jesse was in his life for seven years, and Jason was playing down the pain of him leaving.

I didn't realize it at the time, but I acted the same way when my father left us. I held the anger in until it came out in my drinking and looking for attention from men. "Living amends" would be required to heal this relationship. That meant I had to change my behavior with him moving forward. I couldn't keep getting upset when he didn't listen to me. I had to learn to communicate with him without taking things personally. It was finally time to let Jason in emotionally and not push him away because of my own fear of being hurt or rejected. Around this time, I wrote a poem about our relationship called "I Have Come to Know Him."

Since Jason and I were starting over, I thought we'd take a trip to one of my favorite places, Bermuda, before he started ninth grade. But this was another example of being selfish, choosing a place I wanted to go to. Still, I was trying to bring us together by going somewhere alone. We left for the trip the last weekend of August, just before school started. We spent a few days at the Hotel Sonesta, which is no longer there. The hotel was located at the bottom of a hill, spread across the rugged shoreline. It had three beaches and an indoor and an outdoor pool. While there, I could feel the tension between us. He gave me quick, short answers whenever I tried to talk with him. I knew things weren't going to change between us right away.

The last day of August 1997, the night Princess Diana died, Jason asked if he could go down to the recreation room in the hotel alone. I said, "Yes, just be careful." He came back ten minutes later, and I asked him, "Why did you come back so quickly?" I still had no idea why he wanted to go there. I sensed there was a girl he was interested in and thought he was afraid to talk with her. I told him I had fears about talking with boys at his age too. Or maybe he just saw a bunch of kids he could play with and wanted to approach them and then got scared. After our trip out west, with Jason asking if I could see his eyes through the sunglasses and his distant behavior, I wanted to believe there was nothing else going on with him. I wanted everything to be okay now that God was giving me a second chance. But deep down, I sensed something darker was going on with Jason. We flew out the next day, and I didn't think much about it.

Ninth grade started in September. Jason was now in high school. I was still on the road for the glass company, and a year and half had gone by since my breakup with Jesse. Imagine—I'm not with a man. I had found God and wanted to spend time with him and Jason. I'm not saying I wasn't feeling lonely at times, but the loneliness went away quickly.

Soon after school started, I learned Jason had missed fourteen days in the first two months. I was furious that he was being dishonest with me and that the school hadn't notified me. The school personnel said they left messages at our home. I didn't know for sure, but Jason may have deleted them. I told them they could have sent a letter or contacted my job if they really wanted to. To say the least, I wasn't happy with the way the school handled my son's absences.

I was told by the principal that Jason was wearing his Dallas Cowboy's jacket in class and refusing to take it off. At the time, I believed this was Jason's way of hanging onto Jesse. Neither Jason nor I realized how much he cared for Jesse. I understand now that we both felt a major loss at the same time in our lives. My father left us when I was around fourteen, and Jesse was gone from Jason's life when he was fourteen. My father never said goodbye to me and Jesse made a quick call to Jason that he wouldn't be around anymore. No wonder, Jason was angry and felt insecure. The good news is that Jason's story would be different from mine. He'd have someone "in his corner," as he'd put it, to help him.

Jason was becoming more and more preoccupied with his appearance. He was drinking SlimFast daily and was losing weight rapidly. His face was beginning to sink in, and one night while he was sleeping, I noticed the bones of his shoulder blades sticking out of his back. I grew increasingly concerned, but he kept telling me he was fine. He was isolating more and seeing less of his friends. He'd stay in his room, play Nintendo games, and listen to dark music like Marilyn Manson. I tried to discourage him from listening to that type of music, but he didn't listen. I wasn't strong enough at the time and was too fearful of his anger to set limits with him. I tried to get him to come to church with me, but he wouldn't go. This was the beginning of my neglecting what I was seeing. I needed to get him help, but instead, I continued to give him what he wanted, which was to be left alone.

I was leaving him alone in his room—never a good idea when someone is showing signs of depression. The first time I walked into his room and saw he had slept in his clothes on the floor, I didn't think much of it. As the weeks went on, he continued wearing the same clothes he slept in. These peculiar behaviors started to frighten me. I discovered he was smoking marijuana.

While cleaning under the couch one day, I found a pipe made from a plastic water bottle. I was afraid of what Jason would say or do if I threw it away. I knew deep down that this could not go on for long. I knew from my experience of being in recovery that I would have to deal with it, but I was devastated, and I couldn't believe this was happening to my child. I thought I had done everything I could to demonstrate to Jason how being sober and having God in your life was the key to good living. My dreams of a successful future for Jason, as I defined success in life, would take a major turn for the worse.

Part of the selfishness of alcoholism is the inability to put yourself in someone else's shoes. I was so wrapped up in my own pain from leaving Jesse I couldn't feel or even recognize Jason's pain. I was so busy obsessing about my job and men it kept me distracted from the reality I was living in. Jason was smoking a lot of marijuana and becoming agitated and paranoid. One day, I came home to find some items—a telephone, a radio, and some cash—missing from my house. I was sure he had traded them for drugs. When I confronted him, he started screaming to the point that I was frightened. I'd go to work, come home, eat supper, and run out the door the way I previously ran from reality. I did talk with Jason, letting him know we'd be okay, but saying that was like putting a Band-Aid on a wound that needed surgery. I didn't think to ask him how he was feeling. I didn't know how to ask myself that question, let alone someone else. I'd learn very soon there was more going on than defiance and teenage growing pains.

Jason was using marijuana and alcohol for about a year, which wasn't very long, but his using was intense. He was smoking marijuana all day, like sucking a pacifier. He had his first experience with the law one night while waiting for his drug dealer to come by the house in December of 1997. I was vacuuming the rugs when Jason came out of his room and asked me, "Who was at the door?" I said, "No one was there." He exploded in a rage and accused me of not answering the door. He thought I had blown off his dealer so he couldn't get his drugs. He told me he was going to kill me, and I was afraid I called the police. When the police officer came, he said I would have to press charges against Jason if I wanted him removed from the house. Of course, I didn't want to, but if I didn't, the officer couldn't take Jason into custody.

I said, "I guess I'll have to press charges because I don't feel safe with him here." I was devastated to have to do that, but I had no other choice. He needed help, and so did I.

For me as a mother, the change in Jason was painful and frightening to witness. I couldn't believe what was happening in our lives. I felt I was reaping what I had sown. I saw why I felt guilty all those years. I thought the guilt was due to Jason not having a father who contacted or supported him, but I now know I was dealing with my own guilt and my own unforgiveness. All the anger I had within myself when Jason was growing up I had put on him, which was unfair. I was angry with myself for the poor choices I made and the lies I lived that caused my own unhappiness. I was angry at God, my family, and myself because I felt robbed of so much. The dishonesty of bringing Jason home from the hospital and not admitting I wasn't ready to be a mom weighed heavily on me. I hated myself for that, and I projected that hatred onto my son.

God wanted Jason to be born to me, and he was in control. It would be some time before grasping that truth for Jason and me. For now, we were at a crossroads of taking care of his mental health.

After being held overnight, Jason had an appearance in court the next day. I was a wreck when I walked in, but I knew I needed help with him. Our lives were out of control. The district attorney was pregnant, and she was tough. She made it extremely clear to Jason that threatening someone's life is not okay. I started to worry that I had made a mistake having him taken from the house. I was afraid he would be sentenced and sent to the Department of Youth Services holding facility for minors in trouble with the law.

Instead, the court gave Jason a public attorney, and he was eventually put on probation, which consisted of reporting to a probation officer once a week at the East Boston courthouse. He was allowed to come home on the conditions that he go to school, not do drugs, and see his probation officer as scheduled. A psychiatric evaluation had not been done yet, but it would take place soon. I brought him to visit his probation officer weekly, and we discussed his self-medicating. We both agreed that he was depressed.

The using continued, and I was still in denial, assuring myself that he'd eventually pull it together or, even better, I'd fix him. That day never came. One day when I went out looking for him, I saw him walking up the street in my direction. He looked frightened and angry, and his frame was thin from not eating. I was scared when I saw his eyes. They were sad and dark, and I felt the emptiness in them. The look in his eyes was different than the one I knew. It was a glazed, staring look, almost in a catatonic state. I knew something was seriously wrong with my son. It was more than an addiction. It was the ugly beast of mental illness.

* * *

I'm in a crisis, and I haven't been able to own it. What am I going to do? When we were home together, he'd go in his room and blame me for what had happened with Jesse.

"You threw Jesse out," he would say angrily.

I told him, "I didn't throw him out. We fought too much, and it was time to part ways."

He was lost, and I was lost with him. I was nervous when he was home, so I did what I could to keep things calm in the house. I'd cook for him or get his favorite takeout, whatever it took to keep him from exploding. I was repeating living my life as a child with Todd and his explosive temper. Once again, I was beginning to feel controlled by the effects of mental illness. Because I was rarely home in the past, I didn't really know Jason emotionally. I was a good provider and did a lot of fun things with him and his friends, but I felt I had emotionally hid myself. Not intentionally, but I was too preoccupied with my own distractions. I was more like my mother than I thought.

Throughout Jason's life, he had to compete for his mother's love. Because I was busy between work and looking for "the one," Jason felt distant from me, as I had felt with my own mother. My trying to seek relief from my own pain, self-hatred, guilt—whatever you want to call it—Jason suffered from that too. The anxiety and fear he developed did not come from the sky; it came from being with a mother who had her own anxiety issues. I took on fear from my mother, and she took on fear from someone before her. It's all disease and generational curses, not the love and grace God wants us to experience with each other.

In addition to probation each week, Jason came to a few AA meetings with me. He had lost a lot of weight and was laughing to himself. I started noticing, when he was in the house with me, that he was talking to himself. I'd ask him what he was saying, and he'd shrug it off like I was imagining things.

I was more than happy to accept that all this wasn't happening. In June of 1998, I took a weekend trip to Bermuda alone. I stayed at the Sonesta again. Jason didn't want to go, so I lied to myself that my stepsister would come over and watch him. I had asked if she could, but she never really committed. I left for the weekend anyway. Jason was sixteen, and I had no business leaving him alone considering what we were going through. I had the denial of the alcoholic that tells me if I don't deal with it, maybe it will go away. Well, mental illness is the last thing you want to avoid and expect to go away. It won't.

I checked in with Jason while I was away, and he told me all was well, but in my gut, I knew I was fooling myself.

A few months prior to this, Jason asked if he could have a kitten from his friend's litter. I said, "Absolutely not," since I was afraid of cats because when I was young my mother told me a story about a cat attacking her dog. Fear steals from you what God can put in your life to bring you joy.

Despite my objections, Jason came running up the stairs with a kitten. She was a tabby with a mix of brown, black, and beige—no, white—and looked a couple of months old. I asked Jason what the specks on her nose were and that they looked funny. Like my mother, I was already having an issue with what the cat looked like. I also told Jason we needed to go to a pet store to buy food and a litter box. I had never had a cat before, so this was a first for the both of us. We left her alone and went to get what we needed to take care of her. Jason said the people he'd gotten the kitten from named her Gonzo. I suggested we name her Wednesday since that was the day he brought her home. Another relationship I didn't want, but God knew better.

When I arrived home from Bermuda, Wednesday was in the driveway. She never went out, so I knew something was wrong. I went into the house with my friend Kevin from AA, who picked me up from the airport, and my house looked like a bomb had gone off.

The phone rang, and a Winthrop police officer was on the line. He told me Jason had a party, and the neighbors called the police. When they arrived, they found marijuana in the house and arrested him. I couldn't believe it. What was I thinking, leaving him home alone? I was neglecting him because, once again, I didn't want to deal with reality. I wanted everything to be perfect now that I had left my boyfriend and was giving my life to God. The Department of Social Services was now involved. I was so embarrassed that I became angry at the caseworker when he questioned me about taking care of Jason. How dare he challenge me as a mother and say I was neglecting Jason and that he wasn't getting help! I still wanted to believe that Jason's illness wasn't that bad.

"Why did you think it was okay to leave Jason alone when you left for Bermuda, knowing he's a minor?" the caseworker asked.

"My stepsister was supposed to stay with him," I replied. I knew I was full of crap when I said that to him since she never committed to it.

"Do you know it's considered neglect if you leave a minor alone and don't seek treatment for Jason?"

"I realize that. I shouldn't have left him. I am getting him help."

He then looked in my refrigerator to see if there was food in the house. The fridge was full as it always was.

The caseworker was right. No Nintendo game I bought was going to make this go away. I was ashamed that I had brought a caseworker into our lives by being so selfish and remaining in denial. He'd only be in our lives for three months, but that was plenty of time for me to realize what was happening. He told me the truth. I had to step up and be the parent Jason needed me to be. In the years to come, I'd do just that to get Jason the services he needed.

Chapter 6

The first thing I had to do was get a lawyer. I asked Susan's sister, Jodi who worked at a federal agency in Boston, for help. Jodi gave me the names of three lawyers recommended to her by a judge. I called the first name on the list, Anthony Lochiatto, figuring the judge must have liked him the best. Anthony seemed focused and thorough. I explained my situation, and he said he wouldn't charge more than two thousand dollars for his services. I was good with that, so I hired him.

I went to visit Jason, who was being held at a cinderblock building with no windows in a tough section of Boston. When I pulled up to the building, I couldn't believe my son was there. I was horrified and frightened of what could happen to him. Jason's crime was a minor one, but in my gut, I knew there was more going on inside my son. Right now, it was substance abuse and behavioral issues.

All I recall was that Jason was angry and wanted to come home. I'm sure I brought him food or something because I usually used material things to make him feel better. I didn't know how to do anything else. It was now 1997, and Jason had been acting out for about a year. He was still expected to answer to the court for his actions. At the hearing, our lawyer suggested that Jason be sent to a substance abuse facility, and the judge agreed. That day, I found a facility in New Hampshire called Beech Hill. My good friend Kevin from AA took the ride with me to bring Jason some clothes.

About this time, I met a man named Brendan in AA. He was a friend of Jerry's and also attended Grace Chapel. God was definitely working through both of these men to get my attention. For a change, I was developing relationships with men who loved God. Rather than wanting to get in my pants, these men were teaching me that God came first.

Brendan was unmarried and had just given his life to Jesus. He had a calm sense of purpose when he spoke of who his God was. He told me he had grown up Catholic, didn't know the Bible, and was skeptical of the church's teachings. He didn't understand the idea of praying to statues and wanted a relationship with Jesus.

I told him I had similar questions and concerns. While attending the Catholic Church, I'd worry that if I didn't kneel during the service I was being disrespectful to God. I was told as a child that crossing my legs in church was wrong. I felt like I had to be perfect for God like I had to be perfect for my parents in order to be loved. I used to pray to the statue of Mary because I thought I needed someone to talk with Jesus for me. I'd pray to saints for help instead of praying to Jesus directly.

Brendan pointed out that Jesus wants a personal, intimate relationship with me, and I can talk with him whenever I wanted. Brendan bought me a Bible with my name on it and suggested I start reading the Gospel of John because that's a good place to start understanding who Jesus is, what his love for us means, and why he came. This Bible had a commentary to explain what each verse meant. It explained who wrote each book, when it was written, and to whom. All this was helpful since I had little experience reading the Bible.

Brendan suggested my next step should be to read the Gospels over and over. Reading them taught me that Jesus died for my sins and no one else has done that. Only he could save me from myself. I was a sinner in need of a Savior. That's what the expression "being saved" means.

I started attending Grace Chapel regularly, and within a few months, I gave my life to Christ as a believer in him and who he was, God in the flesh. I was confessing I believed in God the Father, Jesus his Son, and the Holy Spirit who was left behind after Jesus's resurrection to guide us into all truth. The Trinity, as they are called, are all one person, and that is a mystery of the ages.

Brendan suggested I also attend Grace Chapel's women's Bible study on Tuesday nights. I balked initially because I still had trouble trusting women after being scarred by my mother. But I went, and it turned out to be another good decision I made to let God help me.

While Jason was at Beech Hill, I met with two staff members to discuss his condition. Beech Hill sits on a hill in Dublin, New Hampshire, and looks like most hospitals. This would be one of many institutionalizations Jason would have in the next two years. I was ready to hear he was a drug addict who needed help, but unfortunately, there was more to it than that. When one of the staff members, a woman probably in her midtwenties, described my son's behavior as "bizarre," I felt offended. It sounded cruel.

She said Jason was lying on the floor in the shower, talking and laughing to himself. This was something I had seen him do at the house but not wanting to believe.

I felt like I was detached from my body as she described Jason's condition. As a mother, you don't want to believe your child is so far from reality. It's frightening to hear and see.

I asked her, "Why would he do that? What's wrong with him?"

She said, "He has inner stimulation going on inside of him."

I knew what she was talking about, but I didn't have those words to describe it. She explained this wasn't the right facility for him. He'd need psychiatric help. They didn't diagnose him yet, but they started giving him medication to help with his depression and anger.

When Jason eventually came home, I was on eggshells every day due to his unpredictable behavior. He struggled taking his meds; he didn't like the way they made him feel. We'd fight, mostly about me asking him to do something in the house or my going into his room to make sure he wasn't doing drugs again. He was self-medicating, as I suspected. It was a hard time for the both of us. He would get up in my face and swear at me if I questioned him about his using.

Jason would also get physically violent. He punched a hole in his closet door. One day, he came into my room and used his arm to sweep all the items off my dresser. I wasn't sure if we'd make it through this and be okay. One night, Jason was acting irritable, and I was getting nervous.

"Jason, come out of your room and have supper," I said.

"I don't want to, Mum. I'm fine."

"I'd rather you not stay in your room and listen to that dark Marilyn Manson music."

"Leave me alone, Mum! I'm not bothering you!" he yelled.

Later, he'd say, "I need some money, Mum. I want to buy a sub."

"Jason, I know what you want the money for, and I'm not giving it to you to buy pot," I said.

I tried to stay calm because I didn't want to upset him more. I asked my father, Jamie, and Bobby to come by and to talk with him, but that just made him angrier. They told him to calm down and stop swearing and being angry at me. They didn't know how to help either.

I realized that Jason wasn't going to listen to them. Jason knew Jamie and Bobby, but not my father. They had hardly spent any time together over the years. It infuriated Jason that anyone other than me would tell him what to do. He told me after they left the house that night, "Papa had no right to come here and yell at me." I told Jason, "I need help, and so do you with all the anger you have toward me."

I knew why he had that anger. The chickens had come home to roost.

Jason wasn't going to school, and I was still trying to work. The school was not being very helpful in providing direction for us. At one point, I went to speak with the liaison about his individualized education plan, an approach the school tailors to a child's specific needs. I was told she was on vacation and I needed to wait until she came back. I left and went home but then marched right back there, demanding someone to help me. I had no idea how I was going to keep Jason safe at home. I'm alone with an angry adolescent who needs help.

Not long after, Jason was in the back seat of my car, crying that his head hurt. While I drove through East Boston, he was holding his head and asking me, "Mum, if I don't trust you, who am I going to trust?" He told me he thought I was putting needles in his arms, and his mind was telling him I was trying to hurt him. He thought these symptoms had to do with the marijuana smoking. I was so scared for him I didn't know what to think anymore.

When I brought him home, he said he was okay. I knew he wasn't, but I left to visit clients in Everett. I drove there in a fog, exhausted from the stress and uncertainty. I wanted to run away. Talking with my client and friend Donna about Jason, I broke down and started to cry. She said, "You need to go home and take care of the two of you."

I called my friend Kevin, and we brought Jason to Winthrop Community Hospital, near our home. The doctor examined him, then looked at me, and said, "You have a long road ahead of you." I could tell by his tone and the look in his eyes that he felt bad for us. He didn't diagnose Jason, but I knew the situation was serious. He suggested I bring him to Massachusetts General Hospital in Boston. From there, Jason went to Westwood Lodge, a psychiatric hospital for children, about twenty miles south. Jason wasn't happy with me leaving him at the hospital, but I had to do what was best for him.

My father and I visited Jason the next day. I don't know why I brought my dad. I guess I still wanted to believe he could be there for Jason and me. Dad didn't say much during the visit. I told Jason the people at Westwood were going to help him feel better and that I was there to make sure he got the help he needed.

This was in December 1997, a few days before Christmas. A day or two later while at work, a doctor from Westwood called to tell me he believed Jason had schizoaffective disorder. This is when a person has symptoms of both schizophrenia (such as delusions and hallucinations) and mood disorder (such as depression or mania). According to the Mayo Clinic, they might also hear voices, become paranoid, and have problems with cleanliness and hygiene. Jason also had obsessive compulsive disorder, a form of anxiety. That part I understood, looking back to his behaviors of losing weight, obsessing about his appearance, and asking if I could see him through his sunglasses.

I was standing in my office when I took the call, and upon hearing the diagnosis, I froze and shut down. When I heard the *schizo*, I immediately blocked it out. It took a while before that diagnosis settled into my spirit. I didn't know Jason was hearing voices. He had never told me, but I learned that the times I had seen him talking to himself, he was trying to make the voices go away. Jason was fifteen and a half years old. The doctors put him on the antipsychotic Risperdal, along with Prozac for the anxiety, to see how he'd do. This was the beginning of a vicious cycle of trying to find the right meds.

I realized during this time that since Jason may not be able to take care of himself if I weren't here, I needed to have a will put in place. I had one drawn up listing my brother Jamie as the beneficiary to care for Jason in the event of my death. I felt better having it done. I thought at the time that I had all the contingencies figured out, but I would come to learn no one has anything all figured out in God's plan for our lives.

* * *

After coming home, Jason was still acting angry and using marijuana to self-medicate and not taking his prescription medication. We were having a lot of pointless arguments.

"Jason, you need to take your medication."

"I don't need any medication, Mum. Leave me alone!" he'd yell.

"Please pick up the empty can of cat food you left near Wednesday's bowl after you fed her."

"Mum, it's no f——ing big deal. I left it there on purpose." He'd pick it up and storm out of the room. I knew it was odd that he'd feed the cat then leave the empty can next to her bowl instead of throwing it away, but I couldn't talk to him about his behavior.

Next, Jason was brought to Bournewood Hospital in Brookline. I'm not sure what I did at the time to have him put there. I might have taken him to the hospital again, trying to keep him safe. I was so stressed that I'd bring him to various hospitals, hoping they'd keep him. I was afraid that if he ended up in jail he wouldn't receive treatment.

After a few days at Bournewood, he escaped. The police later found him at a train station, trying to come home. He had no shoelaces in his sneakers. The hospitals remove them so you won't hurt yourself. The police returned him to the hospital, and I believe he stayed a few more days before coming home with new medication. This was the cycle we were in. The health insurance I got from work only covered so much a year for inpatient psychiatric help, and we were rapidly nearing the limit.

By the middle of 1998, I had Jason in the well-known McLean Hospital in Belmont for treatment. He was furious with me, but I was doing everything I could to keep him safe. I was running out of insurance benefits, so I took a loan from my 401k to keep him at McLean. I eventually ran out of money, so Jason came home again, still not stable. What else could I do? Fortunately, I got the money back somehow from the health insurance company. God was always there helping us.

Around this time, we started to receive help from the Massachusetts Department of Mental Health, a state agency that provides funding and resources for the mentally ill. This agency was a great help for us moving forward, with benefits and suggestions of placement. One of those placements was the Lighthouse School in Brighton, a school that was also a residential treatment center for children with psychiatric issues. Jason hated it because of the rules. During one visit, he got so angry he put a hole in the wall. I was afraid for him and what was going to happen if I didn't get control of things soon. Every day, he complained and talked about getting out. I'd do my best to redirect him by being positive and bringing him food.

One night, he decided he had enough. The school called to tell me he took off. I didn't leave the house. If he made it home, I wanted to be there for him. Eventually, I got a call from the state police barracks in Cambridge informing me that Jason had been picked up at the Hatch Shell on the Charles River in Boston, where the Boston Pops perform for the Fourth of July fireworks. Apparently, Jason was on a pay phone calling me when a man approached him and asked if he wanted a cigarette. As mentally unstable as Jason was, he told me later he had a bad feeling about the man. Thank God, a state trooper was patrolling the grounds and picked up my son since the man was someone the police suspected of being a pedophile. The grace of God protected Jason that night.

I went to the barracks with a friend. When we arrived, the police had Jason handcuffed to a railing outside so he could smoke. The trooper asked what I wanted to do. I still had a court-ordered custody in place in case Jason decided to leave a facility, which was now becoming a pattern. I told him we'd bring Jason to the Department of Youth Services detention center in Roslindale. It killed me to take him there, but I had to keep him safe, and bringing him home was not an option. It was one of the hardest decisions I have ever made. My friend and I followed the officer to the facility. We arrived late at night, which made it scarier for me to leave him there.

During his stay, there were a couple of guards who looked out for Jason, realizing that he wasn't a criminal but was mentally ill. I wanted the staff to take care of Jason, so I'd make brownies for them. I still felt I had to do something more for people to get what I wanted or needed. I was being a protective mom.

When I'd visit Jason and we were seated facing each other, he'd look down and repeatedly dig the dandruff off his head and watch it fall onto the table. I'd ask why he was doing that and asked him to stop, but he wouldn't answer me. His behaviors were becoming more and more frightening. Doctors treated Jason with medications while the correct facility was found for him. One day, Jason and I were playing cards when all of a sudden he started shaking all over and squirming out of his seat. Terrified, I screamed for the staff to help him. He was having a seizure in reaction to the medication. I thought I was going to lose him that day.

* * *

When you have a child with mental illness, you're on a road you'd rather not be on, a road that's very dark and uncertain. You want to believe people can provide the support and direction you need, but as I'd learn, only God can do that. Professionals can be helpful, but when you're lying in bed at night in the fetal position, crippled with fear over what can happen to your child, only God can comfort you.

By now I had developed a great relationship with Tom R., one of the company's owners, who had promoted me to sales manager. Tom supported me during the first few years of Jason's illness. He allowed me to go to medical appointments that took up a few hours of my day. At one point, I had to drive to New Hampshire a couple of times a week, and Tom never questioned whether I was getting my job done. He knew I was doing my best. I also sometimes talked with Tom about God and all the insights I learned on my fourth step. I felt compelled to share with him what God had done for me in helping me get sober and the positive changes taking place in my life. God was healing me in so many ways, and Tom was a man I had come to trust, which was astonishing for an adult child like me.

After going through the steps in AA, the way the first one hundred alcoholics did it out of the Big Book, my life was changing. According to the ninth step, I needed to make amends to Tom. I had taken money from the office in 1986 when I was actively using drugs. Now I needed to return it. I was in management now, but I didn't feel deserving of the job so long as I had this dishonesty within me. This wasn't just a company but a family I had taken from, and I needed to make it right.

Mind you, the company would have never known since it happened so long ago, but God and I knew, and that was all that mattered. How could I look Tom in the eyes, knowing I had this dishonesty between us? How could I tell Tom about how great God is and what he had done for Jason and me while being such a hypocrite?

I spoke to my sponsor Sara about it, and she said I needed to make an appointment and tell Tom what I was doing. So I called him and asked if I could meet to discuss something I needed him to know. We decided to meet at the Boston Harbor Hotel. It was a snowy and slushy winter day. I was shaking like a leaf, worried that he would fire me. His opinion of me was also an issue. It's not easy to admit your deceptive behavior to someone whom you have grown to respect.

Making amends is about correcting a wrong, immediately if possible. I already had a plan to pay Tom back right away so the situation wouldn't drag on any longer. We met in a quiet area in the lounge, and I told him what I had done. I explained while working as a customer service representative in the company's Chelsea location I stole about two thousand two hundred dollars from a cash job invoice I never processed. I'd been working for Tom's family for fourteen years at this time, and I was sober for nine of them. It was humbling to sit with a Harvard Business School graduate and tell him I stole money from his company. The Big Book states that we are willing to go to "any lengths" to stay sober, and this was an example of that. If he had fired me, God would have provided another job, and I believe I would have been okay. We all have a destiny, and if mine was to not go on with his company, I'd have to accept it.

Tom looked into my eyes for a moment, looking concerned. He said, "Karen, if I didn't know you for who you are today, I would have to dismiss you." I was so relieved he had the compassion and grace to let it go and not judge me for it. I can't tell you how powerful it is when you have that kind of honesty with another human being. That was something my own father didn't extend to me. If I had let my fear get in the way of making that amend, Tom and I both would have missed out on seeing the power of God and what he can do to heal relationships.

During the late nineties, God was doing a lot of healing in my life. He was also preparing me to deal with Jason's illness. Early on, I was naïve, thinking that doctors could just give Jason some medication and he'd be okay. Mental illness is not as simple as that. Doctors select meds by trial and error with each patient, attempting to find the right combination that will work with that person. By late 1999, Jason had been evaluated many times, in many places, and placed on many meds. It took some time before the doctors found the combination of medications that worked for him.

Unfortunately, when you're a teenager and going through puberty, feeling like you're "losing your mind," as my son would say, is exceptionally difficult. Jason always felt his marijuana use brought on his mental illness. Jason had insight like no other person I ever met. He'd describe how each medication made him feel and why some worked and others didn't. Some of the meds could cause you to lose your sex drive, as Jason described, and make you feel flat, like you have no feelings. As a mother of a child with mental illness, I had to make some very hard decisions, which sometimes led to locking Jason up to protect him and others. Sometimes he was strapped down in the hospitals. Jason never hurt anyone, but his mind was sick and needed to be medicated.

There have been stories in the news these last few years about children with mental illness committing murder. I feel for the mothers of these children, the victims, their families—and also the perpetrator. If a child has cancer or some other visible physical illness, people have compassion for them. With mental illness, the brain is sick, and the effects are not visible; therefore, the parent may be coping with their own ignorance. As a child, Jason could be challenging, no doubt, but I never dreamed he'd develop schizophrenia. At first, I refused to accept the illness Jason had and what his limitations were. Because of my selfishness, I refused to believe he couldn't change who he was. I needed to accept the disease he had and not try to change him just so I could look and feel good. I had to accept him for who he was instead of who I wanted him to be.

After an extensive interview with a forensic psychologist at the Carney Hospital in Dorchester in June of 2000, Jason was to be placed in an IRTP (intensive residential treatment program). In this case, Centerpoint, which was a locked facility for adolescent boys on the Tewksbury State Hospital grounds. When the Department of Youth Services caseworker first suggested a locked facility, I was scared, but in my heart, I knew it was time for Jason and me to separate. At this point, he was eighteen years old, and I had legal guardianship, which he did not contest. If I hadn't taken this step with the lawyer who wrote up my will before he turned eighteen to prove Jason's incompetence, Jason would have had the authority to sign himself out of any facility.

During Jason's stay at Carney, Karen Richardson, one of the salespeople I was managing, and I became close. She's a married mother of three girls, a great listener, and a blessed writer. She provided encouragement by telling me I was doing a good job taking care of Jason and doing my best. We'd spend time seeing clients near the hospital and then drop food off for Jason. I was also grateful once more that my company gave me the flexibility to attend appointments at the hospital. It's hard for a working mother to produce business and train salespeople, all while trying to figure out how to help her son. I'd think of how tough it could be for parents who had nine-to-five jobs with no flexibility to make their appointments. My way of life was draining, to say the least, but at this point, I was getting it all done.

By this time in my recovery, I had taken a hard look at myself as a mother, daughter, sibling, employee, and friend. I was finally making good decisions for my son that didn't involve giving him what he wanted but what he needed to get better. I had to admit I had been part of the problem. We enable our children by lying to ourselves that we're helping them when we're not. We can also be participating in their not getting well. At this point on our journey, we both needed to not be involved with each other on a daily basis. I was everything to him, and he listened to and believed everything I said. Well, his mom wasn't right all the time, and with schizophrenia, I had no idea what I was dealing with. I may not have been the most emotionally connected parent in the past, but I was now in a different place.

I was attending Grace Chapel and had given my life to Christ. I was developing a personal relationship with Jesus. Does that mean I became perfect? Absolutely not. When I told my father I no longer practiced Catholicism, he wasn't too happy to hear it. Honestly, I said it to him because I knew he'd disapprove. He didn't say anything but just shook his head from side to side as if to say, "No. What are you thinking?" I explained that I had become a born-again Christian and given my life to Christ as an adult. I explained, "Dad, born-again Christians believe what Catholics do. We just don't believe in the man-made traditions." I explained being "born again" was accepting Jesus into your life as a believer. You want to live for him, not when you're a baby but when you're mature enough to know what that means. I said, "Dad, there is only one God, and he is Jesus Christ."

Until I knew God, I wasn't capable of giving or receiving love. I couldn't truly believe Jason loved me because inside me a voice constantly whispered, "If he only knew the truth." This is what Satan does. He whispers lingering thoughts and false beliefs in an attempt to keep a person in bondage. Due to the lack of self-forgiveness, I was still in bondage, and that is why I couldn't get close to Jason. The truths were that I wanted to abort him and that I was a young mother who was angry from her past who didn't have help to raise her child. I hadn't wanted to be a mother. That was the truth that Jason needed to hear that would set us both free.

* * *

I was learning about love through Jason's illness. Love is doing the right thing, even when your son is telling you he hates you and claiming that you don't want him. Love is putting your son in a facility because he needs more safety and structure than you can provide. I was still not disciplined enough to have any structure at my house, and I would have fed into his demands.

During this time, God brought a few women into my life I could sponsor through the twelve steps. God knew I needed to get out of myself and be helpful to others. One of the women lived in Manchester, New Hampshire. Before visiting Jason on Saturdays at three o'clock in the afternoon, I'd meet her in my car and review her fourth step. By the time I visited Jason, I was no longer wrapped up in worrying about how the visit would go. Jason still wanted to come home, of course. I'd always bring food, and sometimes Jamie came, along with Jason's cousin Jay. Jason loved it when he had visitors, but when he started obsessing about going home, the visit could turn ugly. Sometimes I felt a little unsafe with him, which is hard to admit about my son.

By this time, I could see his OCD (obsessive-compulsive disorder) escalating with the insistent questions of when he could come home. He'd describe his bad thoughts and then get stuck in them. The thoughts were usually fears that someone was going to take something from him or hurt him in some way. I'd do my best to comfort him and let him know he was safe and in a safe place. Once he talked about his obsessive thoughts, he felt better. At times, he said he liked where he was, which contradicted his desire to leave. I think that deep down he knew he needed to be in the facility.

I was only allowed to visit him an hour a week, which turned out to be good for the both of us. He didn't see it as a good thing at the time, but it was. I was what is called an "enmeshed mother," very controlling. I was starting to admit I was powerless over his illness, but it didn't save me from the denial of wanting to change him.

I believe Jason was starting to realize his mom loved him after all despite her shortcomings. I was advocating for him in ways I never dreamed I could. In many ways, I couldn't advocate for myself in my own life, but when it came to Jason, my claws came out. I was a protective mother and would do anything to help him.

I have to give Jason credit because while he was at Centerpoint he was dealing with a significant lack of freedom. Jason was there for one year. He did very well and was ready to be released since he had aged out of the juvenile program in late 2001. He was now nineteen years old.

One of the caseworkers from Centerpoint called and gave me a few suggestions about where Jason could be placed next. Coming home was not an option since he still needed professional care. Jason had such good insight that he could be honest with himself that his illness was more serious than he had thought. His main desire in all the facilities he was in was to come home. Now he had matured enough to realize that living with me again would probably not happen. I was sad for him, but he needed his space now as he was growing into a young man.

I was also dealing with some anxiety of my own. In the winter of 2000, I was driving home on the highway, having left a work party around midnight. The temperature was in the teens, which created black ice on the roads. I was driving in the far-left lane doing about fifty miles an hour when my car hit the ice and went spinning around. I was trying to get the car under control by stomping on the brake and fighting with the steering wheel. An instant later, I remembered being told that if you lose control of your car on ice, you should let go of the steering wheel and brake and let it stop on its own. I did that, although I was petrified that if I let go I might die. I didn't know what the car was going to do.

This was a vulnerable time for me but also for the country. The day after the September 11 World Trade Center attacks, I drove to Western Massachusetts to visit one of the treatment programs Jason's caseworker had suggested. I felt uneasy driving on the Mass Pike toward New York, thinking the terrorists would get me. This self-centered fear almost gave me a panic attack. I interviewed the staff there and knew it wasn't a place I wanted Jason to be. The setting was rural, with only a few one-story buildings spread across the property. Pretty—but far from home—and I didn't want Jason that far away from me.

I had one other alternative, a program in Cambridge called the Castle School. I made an appointment for an interview and was praying they'd accept Jason. The school had never had a student with schizophrenia before; Jason would be the first. Thank God, they accepted him. Jason was transferred from Centerpoint and lived there for the next two and a half years.

Castle School was in an old green Victorian building on the corner of Harvard Street, just outside of Central Square, that held twelve to fifteen students. The students could graduate solely from Castle School or in conjunction with a nearby public school. The school had a principal, teachers, a nurse, and staff running the school twenty-four seven. It also had a dog and a cook and was coeducational. I loved that Jason was there, and I was grateful to have him close by.

I'm sorry to say that getting good care for your child is all about the money. The cost for Castle School at the time was $105,000 a year. I didn't pay a cent for Jason to be there. The Department of Mental Health was involved with Jason since the beginning of his illness. I was told that without their involvement, I wouldn't get the services Jason needed. Three resources were paying for Jason's stay at Castle: the Department of Mental Health, the Department of Education, and the town of Winthrop, where we lived. I was told at the time it was very unusual to have three resources pay. I didn't care who was involved; they were responsible to educate my child until he was twenty-two. I wasn't aware at the time that this is the law in Massachusetts.

Mental health services are available, contrary to what agencies and others may tell you. Although there may be fewer facilities to help these children now, parents and guardians should fight for everything they can to get help for their children. Never give up helping your child if he or she is mentally ill. Ask the tough questions and don't let people throw an answer at you, hoping you'll go away. I wasn't going anywhere. The educational and mental health systems were going to help my son. Some days I had no idea what I was doing as I tried to find my way around the bureaucracy, but I knew Jason needed to be in a safe place. My lawyer was even able to have Jason's juvenile criminal record wiped clean. He only had the one charge for possession of marijuana, but I was glad his record was clean.

When I went to parent meetings at Castle, I felt lost because Jason was not complying and no one else there had a child with schizophrenia. Most of the kids were depressed, and some were cutters or bipolar. Jason had difficulty following the rules, but he hung in there. I also noticed the lack of inner-city children. Other parents like myself were from more affluent communities. This led me to believe that a little education and a sense of how the schools and the mental health system work would be helpful to parents trying to assist their children. In the beginning, we had an advocate assigned to us, but she was not moving fast enough for me, and I knew time was money. I spoke with Jason's social worker quite a bit, and together, along with a few kind caseworkers at the hospitals, I was able to successfully navigate the system.

Jason had to earn visitation privileges, which of course he didn't like, so our visiting was limited. By now, Jason was significantly heavier due to the meds he was taking, but his face still looked very young. It saddened me to see him with so much weight, but he was stable, and at this point, that was more important.

These were difficult years for Jason and me, but we were getting closer, and I'd always talk to him about God. When he was at the Carney Hospital, he once told me that during a psychotic episode, he saw crosses hanging from the ceiling. Although I knew he was delusional, I believed God was letting me know he was with him.

Jason called a few times a day asking to come home. "Mum, I want to get out of here," he'd beg me.

"Jason, you have to do what they're asking of you, and then you can come home," I'd tell him.

"Mum, I don't feel safe here. They're trying to put stuff in my food."

"Jason, honey, no one's trying to put something in your food. You need to take your medication."

"My mind is telling me if I take the medication, they won't let me leave."

"Jason, listen to Mommy. If you take the medication, you will be able to come home."

This went on every day while I was in my car trying to train salespeople. Those times were awful; many times, I wanted to go get him, but I knew coming home was not safe for him. He'd eventually do what was asked of him and come home.

I directed Jason to talk with the staff to help him do what he needed to be released. I was learning how not to try and fix him myself but to direct him back to the people who could help him. I had to do the opposite of what I did in the past, which was to feed into him. I still had a job to do and felt very loyal to Tom, as now I felt I was bringing business in for a friend. I went on the road daily to talk with clients and get business for the glass company, but I was dying with fear inside. For a time, I looked for relief in a few men, but I got back on track pretty quickly. I'm an alcoholic, and that's what alcoholics do—look for relief. I knew God was the only relief for me, but we can still lie to ourselves and fall into bad habits.

* * *

Jason was doing much better on his medication, praise God. The doctors prescribed Clozaril, which turned out to be the golden drug for Jason, along with many other people with schizophrenia. Because the drug can cause a decrease in white blood cells, he'd need to have his blood tested every week. By this time, Jason and I were telling each other, "I love you." It was a far cry from where we had been for the last few years.

I also learned more about Jason's fears and his thought processes. Jason blamed me for throwing Jesse out. He didn't understand why we had broken up, and he thought I just wanted to be alone. Because of this, he felt like I was getting rid of him like I got rid of Jesse. He said as much to the caseworkers and doctors. I don't think it helped that Jason never had contact with Jesse again. I also understood why Jesse stayed away from us. Why would he want to be near someone who hurt him so deeply? Of course, it wasn't true that I threw Jason out, but I completely understood why he felt that way.

Castle School did many positive things with their students. Jason went skiing, camping, and white-water rafting, which were a great way for him to get away and experience life. I was happy for him. I felt my son was finally getting what he needed to enjoy being a teenager. He had already been through so much with his illness.

During Jason's stay at Castle, the staff connected their students to a counseling center outside of Harvard Square. The first therapist they connected him to in December of 2001 was a female. I'd occasionally go with him to meet with her, and I could see it wasn't working out. Jason needed a male influence, and that's exactly what Jason got.

By June of 2002, Jason was a client of Daniel Sprintzen. Daniel and Jason connected in a way I never could have connected with him. Daniel had dark hair and glasses, was in his early thirties, and had an easy way about him. I'd meet with them occasionally when Jason wanted me to. We were both a work in progress. We still had moments when we didn't agree with each other, and Jason could be explosive at times. Learning to trust me was a slow process for Jason because he was waiting for the angry mother to come out, which she still did on occasion. I was doing my best to become a "safe person."

I was praying that Daniel wouldn't leave the counseling center. While going through the system, Jason had lost far too many people he really liked, including the cook at Castle, who passed away after Jason started there. Castle's dog, Rea, was put down during Jason's time there, and a few of Jason's counselors changed jobs. It can be difficult for a child with trust issues to keep having people leave. I tried to explain to Jason that it wasn't his fault and that these people were just changing positions and weren't leaving him. This is the way things are; we have no control over it.

Daniel and Jason met on Thursdays and then eventually on Tuesdays. Daniel worked with Jason to get him slowly acclimated into the community. They'd walk to the coffee shop or maybe get a sandwich at the local pizza place. Jason described to Daniel, with his great insight, the ins and outs of his schizoaffective disorder and his obsessive-compulsive disorder and how the paranoia plays a part in his everyday life. Though the medication helped tremendously, Jason told me it can only do so much, and the rest was on him. Daniel continued to see Jason during the rest of his stay at Castle. This would be the start of an eleven-year relationship.

I started dating someone in AA around the time Jason began working with Daniel. Many people date in AA because they find common ground. I let Jason meet him when we went to dinner one night. The relationship lasted only a few months. The night I broke up with him, as I drove home I promised God I was done looking for men. For the first time, I felt like I had given up that area of my life for God to take care of. I usually picked the men I dated. I thought I knew better than God when it came to relationships with men, but I'd always end up unhappy and bewildered. When you step before God, you don't get what you need. Now I wanted God, not self-will, to bring someone to me.

Chapter 7

In February of 2003, I was scripturally baptized by immersion as an adult. The ceremony took place in the indoor pool at the Sea Crest Hotel in Falmouth on Cape Cod during a weekend Christian women's retreat. I have a picture of that occasion, with my pastor's wife and the woman who was the head of women's ministries at Grace Chapel.

I continued visiting Jason, going to the parent meetings, and hoping for the best for my son. I also tried to be a good daughter to my mother. The old car Chris bought my mother broke down for the last time, so I donated it to a local high school for the kids in automotive mechanics to work on. I bought my mother a decent, cheap car to replace the old one, but she kept complaining about missing her first car. At her apartment one night, Todd started giving me a hard time.

"There was nothing wrong with that car, Karen. You should have had it fixed."

I replied, "The mechanic said the cost wasn't worth it."

He continued to badger and bully me about it. "You shouldn't have gotten rid of Ma's car!"

Sometimes he'd point his finger at me or get too close while he was badgering, which made me feel uneasy. The car really was no good, but my mother said she missed it because she knew that would upset my brother. Once again, I was the bad guy. She loved to throw me under the bus.

One day, I was out seeing customers and walked into an office I had been visiting for ten years. The agency was located in East Boston and established in 1994 by two partners, Ralph and Greg. In all this time, I had been the first salesperson to visit them. That year, I sent them a Christmas card, and Greg didn't recognize my name. Ralph said, "I think it's the girl from the glass company." By now, when I visited once a month to ask for referrals, Greg and I would have long talks. He was going through his second divorce and having a difficult time, so I'd sit and listen. At the time, Greg had salt-and-pepper hair that was greased and combed back. He was a little overweight and somewhat sad. He told me he liked to play cards and bet the horses—not realizing that he reminded me of someone else I knew. In fact, he and Ralph named their agency after a famous horse track in New York.

For a while, I gave up this agency, but my coworker and friend Karen wanted to give it back to me. "They're always asking for you," she said. "I think you should go back in."

Little did she know where her suggestion would lead. Because we talked so often and were both unattached, Ralph kept suggesting that Greg and I should date.

I told Ralph, "I'm all set. I have my own problems." Greg was still married, after all, and he told me he was drinking nights to get through this difficult time. Lo and behold, when I walked into the agency one day in June of 2003, Greg stepped out of his office and asked me to dinner. I declined. He said, "Just as friends?" Yeah, right. I gave him my business card and said he could e-mail me.

A few days later, he sent me a beautifully written e-mail, once again asking me to dinner. It said something like "I like the talks we have in the office. I'd like to take you to dinner sometime." I swear, when I read it, I thought the people in the office must have helped him write it. A couple of weeks passed before we went out since we were both busy with plans we already had. I felt that the fact we both kept our commitments before getting together was a good sign.

Our first date was on a Thursday night in June 2003. Greg picked me up in his white Cadillac. He arrived at my house a little early, which I liked a lot. He made reservations at Gavins Steak House in Middleton. So far, he was a man with a plan, which was a breath of fresh air. We had dinner and talked about our families, and I remember feeling very comfortable eating with him. After dinner, he took me home, and we walked around my neighborhood, talking some more while he smoked a cigar. He called again a few days later. We went out again and have been together ever since.

Falling in love and caring about someone again was scary for me. In October, I was driving on the highway to see a new account in Marlboro, a city west of Boston, thinking about how my relationship with Greg was going. I was in the far-left lane, going down a hill when suddenly I felt a paralyzing, crippling fear, and I couldn't move the steering wheel. I didn't know what was happening, but as I pulled over to the right lane to feel more secure, my hands were sweaty.

"What the hell was that about?" I thought. I couldn't wait to get to the exit. When I arrived at my clients' office, I told them what I had just experienced. I also told them about hitting black ice a few years before and that the incident must have created a fear of driving on the highway. I had one more sales call to make, so my clients suggested a back road to take to avoid the highway.

My body was telling me I needed to deal with something, but I wasn't listening. I continued to drive on the highway despite that crippling fear because it was part of my job. It would be years before I'd ask for help. As always, I tried to figure things out or fix them myself. Unfortunately, when you ignore fear or trauma, it gets worse. I'd call Karen at work, and she did her best to get me through the most defeating times. The fear brought an awful feeling of powerlessness, something I knew well.

My mother also got nervous at every passing car when I drove her places on the highway. She went to the same bars every day or to the beach when we were small. She was afraid to travel or eat out or be with people in general. When I planned a trip, she'd say, "Why are you going so far away? Are you crazy?" I'd say, "Ma, it's fine. Nothing's wrong. It's okay to travel." I'm afraid to travel far from home, but I go anyway because I don't want to live the way my mother did. I believe now that my mother was agoraphobic. Medication would have helped her, along with a relationship with God. The alcohol was her medicine all those years.

* * *

Because of my obligation to Jason, I wanted to make sure whoever I dated understood my relationship with my son and how he needed me. Greg was the perfect guy for that. They met for the first time on Thanksgiving Day 2003 after we had been dating for five months. We had lunch in Boston at Grill 23, a steak restaurant in the Back Bay with a sunken dining room and high ceilings. It felt so good having a nice, stable man to meet my son. Greg was someone Jason felt safe with, as he eventually expressed to me. He said, "Mom, Greg takes charge of things." He liked that about him, as did I.

Jason was still struggling with his surroundings at Castle, but he didn't run away. He was now stable and staying on his meds. He was growing up and getting a better understanding of his illness and what he needed to do to take care of himself. Since we had been through so much during this ordeal, Jason and I now have a much closer bond than ever. He trusted me; I trusted him, and we both knew we needed to continue to move forward in our lives, along with Greg.

By February 2004, I wanted to go on a weekend Christian women's retreat on Cape Cod with my church. Greg offered to see Jason over the weekend. I can't tell you what it meant to me, knowing someone else was in Jason's life, a man I trusted to spend time with my son. It had been many years since I shared my son with anyone other than my family and the people in the programs he was in.

However, I was still protective of my relationship with Jason. Deep down, I feared he would leave me. I know it's natural for most parents to not want their kids to grow up, but my fear was more about emotional abandonment. I knew the fear was irrational since he needed me, but I was concerned about losing his love. My feelings had a lot to do with how I felt about myself. I didn't feel worthy of Jason's love. I was always trying to prove myself to him. That lack of self-love was transferred onto Greg once we started dating.

When you're a child growing up with parents like mine, you do everything you can to be perfect because you're afraid that if you fail your parents will leave you. That is a frightening mindset to have with the two people who are supposed to protect and care for you the most. I transferred those reactions onto the people I loved out of fear I'd be alone. With all the recovery work I'd done, I was still using twelve-year-old behaviors to prevent my boyfriend and son from leaving me.

When I first started dating Greg, we learned that we had different views on sex before marriage. He expressed that he probably couldn't be in a relationship without sex; I wanted to wait until I was married. Unfortunately, I heard that discussion as "If I don't do what Greg wants, he'll leave me."

My fear led me to do things I wasn't ready to do, which caused anxiety. I was also being dishonest with myself and with Greg. I blamed him for not honoring my wishes, but I was also giving mixed signals. I told myself that having sexual relations would connect me to him emotionally. I didn't have to stay and give up my beliefs. If I didn't like what I heard from him when we had a discussion, I needed to let him know. I was still being controlled by my past. I was abandoning myself again.

Sex clouds everything in a relationship. That's why God said to wait until you're married. We no longer see the differences and work on them when we are caught up in the flesh. Too often, we make decisions on the basis of fear—fear we may not get what we want, fear of losing what we have, fear of people's opinions, and so on. If we are true to ourselves and trust God in everything we do, we can avoid being led into trouble. One of my favorite scriptures, Proverbs 3:5, says, "Trust in the Lord with all your heart and lean not on your own understanding; in all your ways submit to Him, and He will make your paths straight."

* * *

Jason was now allowed to leave Castle and move into a group home in Somerville with about a dozen adult men and women. Castle had a farewell party to wish Jason the best. I still have the books they created and the pictures and messages they wrote to him. He was at Castle for two and half years, and although he wasn't graduating, he had done very well. He was thrilled to be getting out of there. The staff was great with him, but Jason was sick of programs, and I couldn't blame him. He was twenty – two years old. It was time to move on.

I was proud of Jason, but I was also petrified. Greg and I went to see the new place, and I was not happy. Perkins, as it was called, was a three-decker house on the Somerville-Charlestown line. It had large private rooms with a shared kitchen and living room. Some older men lived there, and I was worried Jason would be in danger. At twenty-two, he was still very vulnerable. Greg assured me the people looked docile. Using his pet name for me, he said, "Sweetie, he'll be okay. We're here for him." That sounded good, but I still wasn't convinced. We got Jason a cell phone and set up his room with a bedroom set, television, and of course his video game console.

His room was on the second floor, and his window overlooked the street. Lindsay, the young woman who ran the house during the day, was very dedicated. She looked about twenty-two years old and seemed a little shy. Many employees in the mental health field are young and right out of college. They really mean well and are truly trying to make a difference, but I was concerned for her. With grown men living in the house, taking medication, and possibly drinking, she could be at risk.

A few years before, a young woman was assaulted and killed by a resident in a group home that did not have enough staff support. I never wanted people to be afraid of my son. He was on the correct mix of meds and wouldn't hurt a fly. At the same time, I had some fear of others who were mentally ill. I guess I thought my son was special, and I wanted him to be treated that way.

Thank God, Jason went to a day program in Jamaica Plain, a few miles away, which enabled him to spend time out of the house. I was so proud of him for taking the train from Somerville and becoming independent. He told me one woman had a male visitor who was bringing in alcohol. I told Lindsay because that was definitely against house rules. I was advocating for Jason and letting people know I was paying attention. The truth was I wanted to run the house. If the residents threw cigarette butts on the ground, I would go crazy. I kept thinking about how selfish the other residents were.

Schizophrenia affects people's motivation and their perception of things. Trust is an issue, as is paranoia, and they sometimes have trouble with personal hygiene. But the thing I couldn't get past was the selfishness. To me, it's Satan taking over their thought process because they think everything is about them. I'd have conversations with Jason about it because I knew it well. AA helped me learn about my own self-centeredness, so I was able to see it in others.

While staying at Perkins, one resident asked Jason to take a taxi with him to the bank and split the fare. When they arrived at the bank, the resident got out and left Jason to pay the entire bill. Is that mental illness or just selfishness? My son wouldn't do that to anyone. When he told me what happened, I wanted to kill the guy.

Some of the tenants panhandled at the end of the street, and Jason asked if he would have to do that. I told him, "If you handle your money well, you won't have to." He was now getting a check every month from Social Security and learning how to budget. Perkins would help him with that too.

This was the beginning of Jason being in the real world. I had to stop protecting him from everything and begin letting him go. I knew I couldn't be with him twenty-four seven, so I'd do my best to teach him how to take care of himself. He deserved to keep his dignity and his freedom, which he so desperately wanted. He was doing a great job so far.

One of the character traits I admired about my son was his ability to adapt to change. Growing up, before he got sick, Jason had so many friends. They hadn't been in touch with him for years, and most of them had moved on. It's tough to witness your child losing friends because of something beyond his control. He was in so many different facilities, but he always found a way to adjust to his environment. I really don't think I could have done what he did without self-destructing.

Jason had been so brave going through what he did, especially when he didn't know what was happening to him. He knew by now he had a mental illness, and he said, "Mum, the medications can only do so much. The rest is on me."

He was right. The OCD was something he could work on, and the paranoia was something he'd learn to share with me and his therapist to help him get past the lies in his head. At the end of the day, what Jason heard in his head were lies. He was able to express himself more as time went on, and he found that very helpful. Jason was becoming a great young man.

* * *

In 2004, I was still dating Greg, and we were attending Grace Chapel in Lexington. On my own, I purchased a two-bedroom condo in Winthrop. The condo was on the top floor of a large three-story house, beige with brick-red trim. The living room had beautiful light hardwood floors and skylights, and straight across was a brand-new galley kitchen with granite counters and a porcelain floor. The bedrooms were off to each side, and the round glass solarium straight ahead was heated for the winters with a wraparound deck. The deck overlooked Winthrop Bay coming in from Boston Harbor. It felt good to invest in something. I had never owned my own home, so it felt freeing, but I was a little stressed by the responsibility of paying a mortgage.

Jason was growing up and moving on. Greg and I were getting closer, and life was getting better for all of us. The three of us still spent time together. Jason loved his rock music: Metallica, Pearl Jam, the eighties hair bands, Pink Floyd, AC/DC, and George Michael. In October, Greg and I took Jason to see Metallica in Boston. We had the best seats Greg and I ever had at a concert. Jason was thrilled Godsmack backed them up.

I was still working at the glass company as sales team leader when my boss Tom decided to move in a different direction and hire a manager for the entire sales group. I felt it was only a matter of time until I would no longer be working with the few salespeople I had left. The new manager would replace both me and another team leader, so I couldn't take the reorganization personally.

That being said, I doubted my performance as a team leader. I wondered if I had done enough or if I was just a fraud, pretending to be someone I'm not. Tom and I were no longer meeting regularly, and I once again felt like the little girl whose dad was not there emotionally for her and realized he never was to begin with. Having Tom to talk to during the early stages of Jason's illness had given me a false sense of security. The pain of my childhood scars came rushing back to me in the present.

My mother was still living in Chelsea with her boyfriend Chris, and I'd visit her a few times a month. Although my father went to see Jason several times, my mother only visited Jason once, very early on. My father's health started deteriorating from congestive heart failure, and it looked like he'd soon leave us. Greg and I went to see him at the rehab, and my father and I would talk about God. I told him he could give his life to Christ before he died. He said he believed what I was saying.

In one of our talks, he mentioned that my mother was envious of me. I hadn't seen it at the time because I was too busy trying to please her, which was impossible.

I was saddened to see him so frail, knowing he was dying. I felt for him, although I never told him how much pain he caused me as a child and how frightened I had been from his anger and drinking every day I lived in his house. I felt I had forgiven him. Every abusive man I looked to for love but didn't care about me and who I didn't care about was the consequence of my father not protecting and loving me as his daughter.

I knew at this point that I was the daughter of the Most High King Jesus, but I think it might have helped me to tell Dad before he got sick how his untreated alcoholism affected me. We all have to take responsibility for our actions in life. They affect other people, especially those we love.

One Sunday, I brought him a Bible to read and suggested he read the Psalms for comfort. He didn't complain. God bless him, but I felt he was afraid to die. I too was afraid to die until I understood the love of God and where I'd be when I died, which was with Jesus. It's a hard world to live in at times, and being in heaven with Jesus is something to look forward to.

I went to work on Monday, January 3, and one of the salespeople I worked with told me she was retiring. Her area was on the North Shore of Boston, mostly the Cape Ann area. She had about ninety accounts, and I needed to transfer them to other reps or hire another salesperson. I went home that day, thought about what I should do, and asked for a meeting with Tom.

The following morning, my stepbrother Bobby called about eight thirty. Dad was now in a hospital in Everett. "I think you better get over to the hospital. They took your father there early this morning. It doesn't look good."

"Thank you, Bobby. I'll head over there now." A ball of fear formed in the pit of my stomach as I wondered what I'd see when I arrived. I was pondering whether I'd have the courage to be with my father when he passed.

When I arrived at the hospital, I was the only one there. I looked at him with the life support tube coming from his mouth and the machines beeping. To see my father, who was not a big guy, so frail and aware there was nothing he could do to save himself was humbling.

"Dad, Karen's here," I said. "You're not alone. God loves you. I love you, and I'm here. You're not by yourself."

Dottie, Dad's wife, had been a patient in the rehab with my father. Now she was en route to the hospital.

"I'm here alone," I told Dad, "but everyone's coming, including Dottie, Ma, and Wayne." Wayne lived the farthest away in Lowell where he worked for a cabinet company. He, my mother, Greg, and I, along with a relative of Dottie, were present when my father was taken off life support. Dottie arrived shortly after Dad died. When I looked at him after he passed, it seemed like twenty-five years was taken from his face. All the stress of trying to stay alive had left him.

It was January 4, 2005, and it was time to say goodbye to my father. We all stood there in silence. After a moment, Wayne looked at me and said, "I don't remember anything good." That was painful to hear, but years later, when I finally allowed myself to mourn the love of a father who abandoned me, I understood my brother's feelings. I was still holding a torch for my dad. I spent my life trying to measure up to earn his love, not processing in my heart what he actually did over and over—leave me. I felt I had forgiven him, but I later realized I had forgiven him so quickly I never honored my own feelings and pain. Isn't it funny how we can be so concerned about how others feel about us that we don't even notice how we're feeling ourselves? The Holy Spirit has shown me a lot, as did the people God brought in my life to help me along the way.

We had Dad's service at St. Rose in Chelsea, where we went to church and took CCD classes as children. We met with the priest at a local funeral home. It was a small place with a fireplace in the sitting area. My father had picked the funeral home, along with his urn. My family agreed I'd do the eulogy and read a passage from scripture because no one else in the family wanted to do it.

I chose to read John 3:1–21, about the Pharisee Nicodemus, who believed in Jesus but didn't want anyone to know, so he visited him at night. As I was speaking, the priest was looking at me.

I said to him, "Oh, wait a minute. I can't read the Gospel in the Catholic Church, can I?"

He said, "No, you can't." Only the priests can read from the Gospel. He gave me a copy of a passage from a book in the Catholic Bible that I was not aware of and asked me to read that. Greg was baffled. He never realized all the years he went to Catholic schools and a Catholic Church that laypeople couldn't read the Gospels at the altar, especially during a funeral for a family member.

I was being stubborn, so at the service, I read from Psalms instead and then talked about Nicodemus. I couldn't help myself; I had to do what I believed. I went up to receive Communion, which I knew wasn't a good idea because I don't believe in Catholicism—but I do believe in Jesus. When I approached the priest, he refused to give me Communion. Instead, he crossed my forehead. I, a believer in Jesus, was not given Communion, but many others who don't go to the church or talk about Jesus received Communion that day simply because they were Catholic. Many people died to give us the good news, so who is anyone to deny a person that? I knew Jesus wouldn't.

Four and a half months later, my stepmother Dottie died. Her health had already been poor, and she was heartbroken. Most likely, she no longer wanted to be here without Dad. I guess God felt the same way because he let her go. There we were, at the same funeral home, now having a service for Dottie. I have to give credit to my stepfamily, my five stepbrothers and one stepsister. Although some of them have very little, in times of need, they stick together.

Shortly before Dad and Dottie died, Jamie moved in with them. He was struggling being on his own, still unable to get his life together, and was slowly drinking himself to death. This gifted guy—who never realized how much he was loved by me, my son, and many others—was unable to bring himself to go to our dad's funeral service. I found it sad and hard to believe that my youngest brother was in such despair he couldn't attend his own father's funeral.

Afterward, Jamie had to leave my father's apartment and stay with one of our stepbrothers for a short time. He met a woman in the suburbs he moved in with. I'd occasionally hear from him, usually when I wasn't home during the day. I think he called during that time because he had so much shame about his life. It was painful to hear him on my voice mail because I could tell by his voice he had been drinking. I loved him no matter what, and I still do today.

Todd and me about 1969 Congress Ave.

Ma and me at Watts St. about 1974

Castle School Cambridge Ma.

Jamie and Jason (age 19) at CenterPoint – 2001

Jason and me at Castle School – 2003

Jamie and Jason at Grandma's house Krakow Wisconsin.1994

Greg and Jason at my condo 2005 – Jason is 23 years old.

Jason graduating Kangaroo Pouch - 1988

Jason about eleven years old.

Jason at the Hoover Dam – 1997

Jason a year old with Dad.

Jason with Peter about eight years old – 1990

Jason and me on his sixth birthday 1988.
Nine days before I got sober.

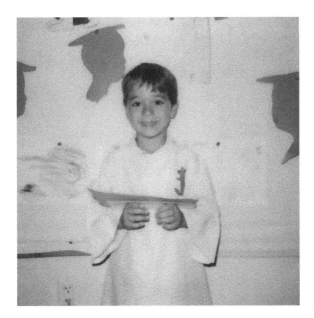

Jason on graduation day Kangaroo Pouch. 1988

Ma in her green leisure suit. 1974

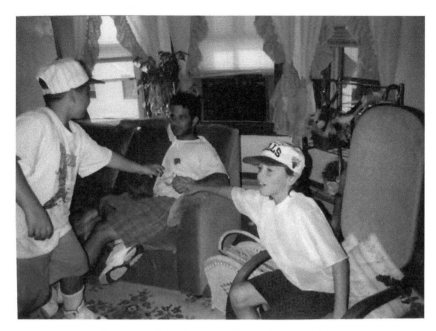

Jason on left, Jesse and Jay. About 1991

Jason in Wisconsin – 1994

Pictures of Ma and Dad in Wisconsin. The child is Wayne.

Ma and Dad on their
wedding day. 1954

My paternal grandparents, great
grandparents, Dad, his two
sisters and my brother Wayne.

Wayne

Bobby and me on my wedding day – 2006

Jason and me on my wedding day – 2006

Wayne and me in Wisconsin for Grandma's funeral – 1995

Wednesday our cat.

Chapter 8

In the summer of 2005, about seven months after my dad passed, Greg asked me to marry him. We set the date for June 11, 2006. Greg moved into my condo shortly thereafter, which was a big step for me. I had been living alone for eight years and loving it. Not only that, I was a Christian woman living with a man and not married.

Greg and I were still attending Grace Chapel, which offered classes for newly engaged couples. As a born-again woman marrying a man who wasn't, I thought it would be helpful to go. The few classes we took discussed handling finances, communicating with your spouse, and sharing feelings with each other. After each class, Greg said he didn't think we needed to go back. He said, "I don't want to attend these classes. We get along well. I don't feel we need them." I was a little surprised to hear that since he had been married twice before. I didn't tell him that was how I felt, but I was thinking it. In addition to being a licensed insurance agent, Greg is a certified public accountant, so I guess he felt he had mastered the financial aspect. The class wasn't something he wanted to do, so we stopped attending.

Looking back, I'm sorry we didn't stay because there are always things you can learn in life. I was still grappling with my discomfort over Greg saying he couldn't be in a relationship without sex. He told me he was being honest, but at the same time, he wasn't honoring my wishes as a Christian and a woman. Greg and I had different belief systems, which was fine, but I wasn't being true to myself or standing by what I believed. I still didn't want to believe I could trust God with the consequences if I was true to him. I was the one being dishonest with myself, and I would make amends later to Greg for that.

I don't recall when I told Jason we were getting married, but telling him was hard for me. Jason and I had been on our own for seven years after I broke up with Jesse and before I met Greg. Now he was saying, "Whatever you think, Mum. I'm happy for you, Mum." Jason was so good and kind. A child's love is like no other. It's unconditional.

Jason spent a year at Perkins before getting another placement. This time, he would be living with three other men in a single-family house in a quiet neighborhood near the center of Hyde Park, a neighborhood of Boston. When Greg and I went to see the place, a man answered the door, and I got an uneasy feeling from him right away. He started mumbling angrily about Jason, saying, "I'm living here now." I could sense he was very controlling, and it wasn't long before he was removed from the house after running out in the street naked. I have to be honest: I was glad he was gone.

Each resident had his own room and bathroom, which was nice. The kitchen and living room were in a common area on the first floor. I was concerned, of course, but Jason had proved to be responsible while living at Perkins for a year, and this was the next step toward living independently. Jason was taking his medicine regularly and started working at Fenway Park for Aramark, a food vendor. I was proud of him but also concerned about him taking the late train and bus home after night games. I give him a lot of credit for the effort he put into the job. Jason's meds made him sleepy, and he couldn't take them after a late-night game and then get up early to be at the park for a day game the next morning. It became too much for him, so Aramark let him go.

Between jobs, Jason volunteered at an animal shelter. The mental health organization that found him an apartment also found him a job working at a kiosk in Downtown Crossing in Boston, selling pretzels and sodas on the corner across from Macy's. Linda, who owned the business, had a store in Faneuil Hall and kiosks around Boston. The job was flexible, which was good for Jason, and Linda was kind to him. Life was moving forward for Jason and me. He was living somewhat independently, and I found a wonderful man to spend the rest of my life with.

Greg was good at helping me with Jason. Sometimes while Jason was living in Hyde Park, he'd run out of money, usually from ordering takeout food too often, and I had to run over to his apartment with some cash. Greg helped me not to continue that behavior since it prevented Jason from learning how to handle money.

One night, Jason had no food. His caseworker was coming the next day, so I suggested he go to a food pantry. It killed me not to go over, but I didn't. As I grew spiritually, I realized I was not helping my son learn how to be responsible. We were both on a learning curve.

I wasn't taught how to handle money as a young person, and like Jason, I was terrible with it. I always had money coming in from work, but I was deep in debt with credit cards and never seemed to be able to save. When I wanted relief, I shopped instead of going to God. As soon as I'd get money, I'd find a way to spend it. I bought clothes mostly and items to decorate the house. I'd put three hundred dollars a week on my credit card at Ann Taylor at the Cambridge Galleria mall. The salesperson's name was Sonya. She loved the patchouli oil I wore, which I bought at Whole Foods, so with my characteristic overgenerosity, I'd bring her in a bottle. Meanwhile, my credit was being jacked up every week in a vicious cycle. Before I got married, I'd use my tax refund, which was a substantial amount, to pay off my credit cards each year and then start all over again. I was trying to teach Jason to do things differently. Jason knew I was making the right decisions for him. Sometimes he'd laugh when he recognized his own selfishness. He was becoming a responsible young man.

Just before Greg and I got married, Jason had an incident at his house. He was friends with David, one of the other tenants. The staff learned that Jason and David were drinking and notified me. This was one of my biggest fears—that Jason would start drinking and drugging again. I attended a meeting at the house with Greg, the staff, Jason, and David. I made it clear to David that I wasn't going down that road again with my son. I let Jason know he'd be on his own if he chose to start drinking because that would only complicate his condition, and he knew it. Jason complained that

David harassed him to share his food and cigarettes. Jason was feeling trapped because he really liked David. I see now I feared Jason being trapped in a relationship the way I was trapped in my house with my brother. I didn't want to be controlled, and I didn't want Jason to feel that way.

On June 11, 2006, Greg and I were married. Before the wedding, he took Jason to New York for the Belmont Stakes and then to Foxwoods so I could spend time with my friend Susan and prepare for our wedding day. Greg and I decided to write our own vows, and of course, I waited until the night before to write mine. The wedding was on a beautiful sunny Sunday afternoon, and I was so grateful because we had had rain every day leading up to it. My gown was simple, forties style, long, sleeveless, fitted with lace and pearls, with a collared neckline.

It would have been nice to be married at Grace Chapel, but Ruth, the head of women's ministries, said she wouldn't marry us.

"I baptized you, Karen," she said. "How can I marry you now that you're living together?" She laid out my options. "Greg can move out. He can sleep in another room and refrain from sex, or you can have someone else marry you," she said. I wasn't surprised. Instead, we were married in the Veronique Ballroom at Longwood Towers in Brookline by a justice of the peace. Here I was, early on, giving up my beliefs because the man I was with didn't agree. I wasn't living in God's truth that being born again means you live by what the Bible says or at least you try to. I guess I still didn't think I was worthy of his promises.

Still, it was a beautiful ceremony. With all Jason and I had been through, I was so proud when he walked his mom down the aisle that day and brought me to my husband. Jason cried a lot that day, but he said it was only because he was happy for me. I felt inside he might have been afraid he'd lose me, but I knew that would never happen. I'd always be there for him, and he was getting a loving stepdad, someone he knew he could depend on.

The venue had an Old Europe architectural style with high ceilings and long draperies. It felt like a castle. Greg and I did our best to make sure everyone enjoyed themselves. When I was young it would have been all about me, now I wanted it to be about our guests. I was forty-three; Greg was forty-four, and we were now growing together on our journey through life.

During the reception, Jason and I danced to the song "I Hope You Dance" by Lee Ann Womack. The lyrics tell of wanting someone you love to keep their sense of wonder and live their life to the fullest. It says, do things that make you uncomfortable, don't miss opportunities, and, most of all, give faith a fighting chance. I felt trapped a lot in my own life, but I so wanted Jason to live a life of freedom. Greg and I went to California for our honeymoon and drove up and down the coast. It was a magical time for me, but hidden fears and conflicts continued to trouble me.

For a recovered alcoholic who is the adult child of two alcoholic parents, getting married was a big step. Although I was still going to meetings, talking with my sponsor, and going to church, marriage was scary. During our honeymoon, I had obsessive thoughts about a woman my husband just hired, whom I had not yet met. I worried that she might be pretty and Greg would like her more than he liked me. Because of my traumatic childhood, any type of change in my security can cripple me in fear.

On our honeymoon, I was able to express my fear about Greg's new employee. Thank God, Greg understood me for who I was because I felt fine after that. Any relationship relies on communication and not being afraid of who you are. It's hard to be authentic sometimes, but my relationship with God is what keeps me honest.

I believe that after the wedding, submitting to Greg as my husband brought up my old traumas about sexual abuse. Greg's gray hair triggered my experience of the older guy who raped me when my brother left me in the apartment. Although I wasn't having sex against my will, having been born again a few months before I met Greg, I was going along with it against my better judgment. I couldn't stand by my beliefs when it came to men. Even in my forties, I was still seeking my earthly father's approval instead of the approval of my heavenly Father.

* * *

When we came back from our honeymoon, we decided to sell the condo. I was sorry to see it go, but the other owners were very difficult to deal with. I loved my condo, but it was not the same as having a home together on our own piece of land, which Greg and I could now afford. I considered Swampscott and Marblehead, both a little north of Boston, but I preferred to stay in Winthrop. It's close to Boston and where Jason lived in Hyde Park. I also loved the town since visiting there as a child.

I hired the wife of one of my clients, a real estate agent in Swampscott. Carol Beatrice is a wonderful woman with a kind disposition. She exhibited patience with us as we looked for our new home. Greg, Jason, and I probably viewed over twenty homes within a few months.

We put an offer on a house in Winthrop that I was sure we would buy, but we lost the offer by a couple of hours. I was sad about it. I remember saying to God, "Wow, I was wrong on that one." Sometimes things take a little longer than we think they should.

We were running out of time once the condo had sold, so we settled on a house that was more desirable to Greg than to me. It was in Swampscott, a colonial on a tree-lined street overlooking Harold King Forest, a piece of conservation land. The benefit of this location was that no one could build behind us. The house needed some work, but it was near the most desirable elementary school in town, which would be a plus if we ever needed to sell. The ceilings were very low, which we didn't realize until after we moved in. The kitchen was small, but we decided to tear down the wall to create an open floor plan. The house also had a finished attic and a basement that could be used as a recreation room. It was the first house for both of us. We had both owned condos or town houses but never a house.

When we moved to Swampscott, my cooking, which I had always enjoyed, became compulsive. I was looking at recipes every day and cooking a couple of dinners at a time, along with desserts, for Greg to bring to the office. Greg took food into work because during tax season the accountants couldn't get out. Shrimp scampi, veal marsala or piccata, coconut cupcakes, madeleines, and chocolate chip cookies, whatever was someone's favorite. Ina Garten, the

Barefoot Contessa, is my favorite recipe writer. When we lived in Swampscott, my holiday dinners were five-course meals: appetizers, soup, pasta, meat and sides, and dessert. Cooking gets me out of myself like writing does. Cooking was my way of coping with getting married and leaving my own home.

We moved into the house in early November 2006 and had our Thanksgiving dinner there. Jason came for the holidays, along with Greg's family. I had inherited hosting Thanksgiving and Christmas since dating Greg. Each year on Easter Sunday, Jason and I went to Bobby's or to my sister-in-law's since it was usually tax season and Greg was busy working.

I was struggling living in our new home since I was no longer looking at water. Both of the homes I lived at in Winthrop were on the ocean. Now, after thirteen years of looking at the ocean, I was seeing conservation land instead of water. I felt a stillness and a deadness. I was not feeling alive. I'd mention to Greg now and then how much I missed the ocean view, and he'd gently say, "Sweetie, if you're not happy here, we can put the house back on the market after tax season." I felt bad that I was reacting that way, but something inside of me was not right.

During this time, I was listening to a fourth step at the Cambridge home of someone I was helping in AA. I'd drive over there a few times a week so she could read to me. This activity was helpful because it got me out of myself during the stressful early days of marriage. God gives you what you need at just the right moment. I didn't realize it at the time, but my perfectionism (a character defect I learned in my fourth step) was starting to take off into a new dimension.

When Greg and I got married, I feared that if I wasn't perfect I could lose him. I had to be the perfect wife in every way. Cooking the perfect meal. Keeping the house perfect. Giving him sex since I took the lead by feeding into my fear about it. I gave up nights at the gym so I could be home more. Looking back now, that's how I felt when Jason was born. I didn't think I was good enough to be a mother or that I was a good mother at all. Fear is the great stealer of life. The abandonment was slowly creeping in again. I was being that little girl, trying to be perfect so my father wouldn't leave us. I believed that if I was perfect, I wouldn't have to deal with loss, pain, or criticism. But life is filled with loss and pain, and we all have to deal with it at one time or another. How we deal with it, if we choose to deal with it at all, determines if we become stronger.

My people-pleasing issues flared up over communication in the marriage. Greg thought the best policy was to keep the peace instead of bringing issues up. He said, "I won't criticize you, and you don't criticize me." If I said something simple like "Please shut the door when you're going to the bathroom," I'd get the silent treatment just because I asked him to change a behavior. If I asked him to close his mouth when he was chewing, I'd get the silent treatment. I spoke up at times but still felt like I was doing something wrong until I realized he was emotionally immature too. Finally, we had a long talk. I told him I couldn't be in a relationship if I couldn't express my dislike for something he was doing. I also stated that if I can't ask for my boundaries to be respected, I feel like I'm living with Todd.

Being a Christian, I wanted to work on the marriage. I wanted more emotional intimacy. I said, "Greg, if I can't be myself in this relationship, either we get therapy or we admit that this isn't a healthy way to live." We started therapy and have been doing much better. We brought out our feelings about aspects of the relationship we didn't like or felt uncomfortable about. Greg enjoys church and has been more open to talking to people there. My pastor loves him.

I was a newlywed. This should have been a joyous time for me. Instead, I was feeling scared, and I wasn't sure why. I was living in a new home in a new town and wondering if I had done the right thing in giving up my freedom. I was starting to feel like I was being put in a box again, this time by my own doing.

It was hard to let someone love me since I had spent my life trying to get love from people who didn't love me. Before Greg, I always guarded my heart and my finances. I didn't want anyone telling me what to do with my money or with my life. Unfortunately, I hadn't always handled that freedom very well. I was forty thousand dollars in debt when I married Greg. Over the next two years, I paid it all off on my own, with the help of a couple of noninterest credit card loans

Greg got for me. Now I have just one credit card. I pay it off every month and have not paid one penny of interest.

I told Greg again how much I missed living on the ocean. For several nights, I awoke in the middle of the night and felt like God was trying to get my attention. While lying in bed one evening, I asked God not to let me burden my husband with how I was feeling. I thanked God for our new home, and I asked God that if we didn't belong there, please reveal that to us. Two weeks later, my husband called to tell me the house we loved in Winthrop was back on the market.

"That was what God was trying to tell me," I explained to Greg. "We're going to buy that house after all."

I was so excited that I ran to the address in Winthrop to see the "For Sale" sign, but there was none. At a donut shop, I ran into the neighbor who lived next door. I felt this was another affirmation we'd buy the house. He explained that the new owner couldn't sell her other property and was upside down with her mortgages. It was early April. We had just bought our house in November, and we still had boxes in the basement, but God was working everything out.

As soon as Greg and I walked in to see it again, we put in our offer and listed our house in Swampscott for sale. We sold the house in one day. We were on our way back where God knew we belonged.

When God has a plan, it doesn't matter what things look like; he'll bring you where he wants you in his time.

I was so happy to be moving back to Winthrop and live on the water. The house is located on the bay as you come into Winthrop through the East Boston side. It's a three-bedroom colonial built in 1920 with leaded glass on each side of the front door. The rear of the house looks out to our deck and the ocean. You can see one of the runways from Logan International Airport directly behind our home. We have a great view of the planes coming and going each time they use that runway. You can jump into the bay right from our yard, and when it's low tide, you might see people fishing. Living on the water gives me a feeling of freedom. The idea that the ocean is always moving, with its tides coming and going, makes me feel like it's alive, which is how I want to feel inside—alive, not dead, spiritually.

Greg and I unpacked everything and got all the painting and repairs done. After all the years of working hard, it was rewarding for us to have a home on the water to call our own. We felt blessed.

Chapter 9

The first year of marriage flew by, and it was now 2007. Jason was still in Hyde Park waiting for his Massachusetts Housing Assistance (Section 8) Certificate so he could get his own apartment. He came by to have dinner with us on the weekends he wasn't working. I'd visit him in Hyde Park to make sure his room and bathroom were clean because he always needed help with that. I have to be honest: at times, I'd go to his house and struggle to accept how he kept it. He'd tell me I didn't have to come and clean, and he was right, but I did it anyway. Just as when he was little, Jason had a difficult time organizing his responsibilities.

But he went to work and stood on that corner selling pretzels in any weather from summer up until December. I'd walk by and talk with him once a month, when I visited my Boston agents. When it was freezing outside, Jason would have on just a light jacket. I'd stop by and bring him something to eat and ask, "Jason, aren't you cold in that?" He'd say, "I'm all right, Mum." His boss Linda told me she was concerned too. He had six jackets in his closet, but he'd always wear the same one. That was Jason. He didn't want to listen to anyone—he preferred the beat of his own drum.

Finally, around May of 2008, Jason received his Section 8 housing certificate. He was excited, and so was I. A client of mine gave me the name of a realtor she knew, but as soon as I told her Jason was on Section 8, her tone changed. I felt the discrimination right away.

We got help through a regional mental health organization that connected us to an East Boston property manager who had an available apartment. When a caseworker brought Jason and me to see the apartment, we knew it was perfect for him. The street ran parallel to the bus line, which would bring Jason to a train into Boston.

We were thrilled. Jason would be like his mom and many other people in society, living in his own place. He would be living close to us while working and paying his own bills. He was still seeing Daniel once a week in Cambridge and visiting the Lindemann Mental Health Center in Boston to pick up his Clozaril, have his blood checked, and enjoy camaraderie with other patients on the same med.

By age twenty-six, Jason had been through hell and back, but he was persevering. He may have been lazy at times, as we all can be, but when he wanted to, he had his mother's tenacity.

Yet I knew inside I was still trying to manage Jason's mental illness. With him living on his own, I had a fear that something bad might happen to him, and Greg and I wouldn't know. My fear stemmed from the fact Jason was overweight and took his meds before bed. The meds made him very tired, and he fell into a deep sleep within a half an hour of taking them. I was concerned that he might choke or stop breathing. A mother's instinct maybe. What I mean is I hadn't really given this situation to God. I felt like we were beating the odds, but only because I was controlling Jason's life.

By this time, I had gotten away from church completely, and not being connected to other believers was definitely wearing on me. We changed churches because Greg wasn't attending Grace Chapel with me anymore, and I didn't want to go alone. I was moving away from my beliefs and succumbing to Greg's. I usually tithe, giving 10 percent of my gross income, but I talked myself into thinking I didn't need to go to church or tithe. When we moved to Swampscott, we attended a congregational church near our home, but the preacher was all over the map each week, and I couldn't follow him. When we moved back to Winthrop, I started looking online for a non-denominational church close by. We started attending a church in downtown Boston, but that wasn't moving my spirit either. I missed Grace Chapel, but at least, I was hearing God's Word. We stuck with the church in Boston for about a year while I prayed for God to help us find a new church.

Jason's apartment was on the third floor, a one-bedroom with a cute little balcony off the living room that overlooked the parking lot. I was thinking the back was better since the front of the building could be noisy. Jason couldn't care less—he was going to be on his own. He had saved some money and was able to buy his own kitchen set. He brought his own TV and the bedroom set he used when we lived together, and we pitched in for the sofa. Of course, he had his PlayStation. He was all set.

There were some challenges, of course. Jason was a huge boxing fan, and he'd order the matches whenever he could, which increased his cable bill. I'd give him a hard time about becoming a slave to the cable company. He also started shopping at the nearby supermarket, which was too costly for him. We decided to shop together at another supermarket on the weekend.

Each Saturday morning, he'd call and ask what time I was picking him up. It was usually between eight o'clock and eight thirty. I have to hand it to Jason; he'd take his meds by eight thirty in the evening and be up by six thirty in the morning with no issues. Motivation is hard for people with mental illness, so I was grateful he had this ambition. The only days he didn't get up early were when he felt down or overwhelmed about something; then he'd sleep in most of the day. On those days, I'd encourage him to walk to the nearby gas station to get an iced coffee or something. I'd explain that it's good to get out of your head by getting up and doing something—anything. He'd say, "I know, Mum." Of course, he wouldn't do it, but I tried.

Jason's OCD caused him to experience denial of truth. Before walking out the door, he would check everything in his house multiple times. Once he closed the door, his OCD had him counting, staring, and pulling his door to make sure it was locked. He'd have the key in his hand and ask me if he was holding the key.

I'd say, "Yes, Jason. Can't you see the key in your hand?" He'd stand there and stare at the key. He didn't trust his own mind. I had little patience and started walking away while he was going through his routine. It was hard to witness, and of course, his anxious mother was always in a hurry to go somewhere.

A minute later, I'd be at the elevator, looking down the hall at him, amazed that he was still in such bondage. It was sad to watch him.

I'd yell, "I'm getting on the elevator!"

Jason would yell back, "Mum, I'm coming—wait!"

He'd start laughing because he realized how crazy the behavior was, but he couldn't help himself. Some days I'd pick him up and he'd say, "I did really good with the door today, Mum. It only took a few minutes." I'd reply, "Good for you, Jason. I'm proud of you."

First, we'd stop at the Starbucks in a nearby Target and get our coffees. Sometimes we'd run into my brother-in-law John, and after Jason sucked down his iced coffee, he'd talk with John a hundred miles a minute. A tall, easygoing guy, John is married to Greg's sister Roseanne, and they live near us in Winthrop. He'd laugh and tease Jason, saying, "Who wound you up this morning?" Jason was a chatterbox, just like his mom.

Then we'd go to the Market Basket in Middleton, which was about twenty-five minutes from where we lived. People asked me why I drove all the way to Middleton when there was another Market Basket close by. I'd tell them it was the time my son and I could get caught up with each other. We talked all the way there, and I loved every minute of it.

One of the effects of schizophrenia is poor hygiene. For the most part, Jason did a good job taking care of himself, but at times, he would get in my car and his glasses would be dirty or his shirt might have stains on it. Although he showered regularly, he sometimes had a bad odor about him. Sometimes it was the cigarette smoke on his clothes. When you're in close quarters, an odor is more apparent. As his mother, I could let this drive me crazy, so I had to keep remembering he wasn't doing it on purpose. It wasn't about me.

It's a funny thing. When Jason was younger, I thought other people could take better care of him, and now I was realizing what a good job I had done, even with all the ups and downs. Jason was doing a great job living his own life and taking care of his illness. We were together in a car having conversations every week about his obsessions, his job, and a customer who might have bothered him that week at his pretzel kiosk.

Once we were in the car, it was hard for Jason to not obsess about someone breaking into his apartment. Along with his therapist Daniel, Greg and I told Jason that everything in the apartment could be replaced. He also had paranoid thoughts of someone taking something from him or trying to put one over on him. Clearly, he believed that people could not be trusted.

I completely understood that from my own upbringing and Jason's relationship with me during his earlier years. I believe mental illness stems from people stealing your reality from you. When you see and experience one thing but your experience is denied by someone you trust—like your parents—you become confused. I knew Todd molested me, but my mother claimed he protected me. As a baby, Jason sensed my distance from him, and that was not his imagination. What he felt was real: it was the same distance I felt from my mother.

One day when Jason was working at Downtown Crossing, a young man was shot in the middle of the afternoon not too far from the kiosk. I thought for sure Jason wouldn't go back because it might be dangerous, but he did. I told him I was proud of him for not letting fear get the best of him.

My birthday was in late March 2008. Greg took me to dinner and gave me a DVD of the movie *Ratatouille* and a card with a travel itinerary inside. Greg knew I wanted to go to Paris, so the trip was my gift. I was excited but a little nervous since I wasn't thrilled about flying overseas. Although I had been to Italy with Susan in 2005, I didn't like to fly. Flying requires a person to give up control to someone else who must make good decisions to keep their passengers safe. Coming from a home with a father who drove drunk with us in the car, I didn't feel comfortable trusting someone with my life. It never occurred to me that the people flying or driving also value their own lives.

Greg and I went to Paris in late August and had a wonderful time. We stayed at a hotel in the Madeleine area, across the street from the American Embassy. We visited Versailles and the Louvre.

We also visited Montmartre with its outdoor art galleries and little cafés. We stopped by the tunnel where Princess Diana had her fatal car crash. I was loving Paris, as I thought I would. Greg didn't think he'd enjoy it, but he was pleasantly surprised and did a great job learning the Métro.

Jason was doing well. Greg and I were traveling again after the huge expense of the house and wedding. This was a blessed time for all of us.

* * *

An old flame had reentered my mother's life: Andrew Petersen, or Andy, whom Ma had met in the fifties and dated before marrying my father. Ma had moved out of the apartment she shared with her current boyfriend Chris because he was suffering with dementia. Ma didn't want to help Chris, so she decided to move out. She asked the manager of her building to let her know if another apartment became available. Ma had been with Chris since I was sixteen, but my mother was done using him, and she wanted out. Even though he had supported her for twenty-eight years, she wasn't going to stick around when things got tough and he needed her for a change.

But God wasn't going to let her off that easy because the apartment that became available was just across the hall from Chris. Once Ma moved in, Todd got in touch with Andy, and he came up from Virginia to see her. Andy was still married, but he began leaving Virginia every month or two to stay for two weeks with my mother in Chelsea. Chris's family shortly thereafter put him in a retirement facility called the Soldier's Home in Chelsea. My mother visited him a few times a week. I guess she felt some responsibility to him even though she had already moved on.

In June of 2008, Chris passed away. My mother went to the wake with Todd where she told Chris's ex-wife that she had a new "friend" in her life. My mother, who betrayed my father and Chris's wife all those years before, is now telling Chris's ex-wife she has someone new as glibly as if she was talking about the weather. I was embarrassed when I heard her, and I felt ashamed, wondering what people thought of me because of my mother's actions. Greg and I took time off from work the next day to be at the funeral. My mother and Todd, whom Chris gave so much to, were nowhere to be found. Unfortunately, Chris had made the mistake of falling in love with someone who was incapable of loving him back.

After Chris died, my mother's seventeen-year-old dog Susie, a light-brown Pekingese, had to be put down. Todd, who was now living with a woman in New Hampshire near the Canadian border, had a hard time with my mother being sad, so he bought her a gray-and-white shih tzu named Candy. My mother was a survivor. She moved forward with her new dog and her new man.

My brother Jamie called my cell phone one night, concerned about who Andy was and what my mother was doing with him. The deep, low tone of his voice scared me. It sounded like something was seriously wrong with Jamie. In a couple of weeks, I'd learn my fears were justified.

On a Saturday afternoon in October of 2008, Greg and I took customers to the circus in Boston. After the show, we stopped by my mother's in Chelsea. Ma said she was worried about Jamie. She said, "There's something wrong with him. His head is so swollen." I told her, "Ma, he's an alcoholic. It's the booze doing that to him." She said, "I don't know why he's drinking so much." She was still in denial about the pain he had been in since childhood.

At five thirty the next morning, Greg and I were awakened by a phone call from my mother telling us Jamie was on life support. I quickly threw my clothes on, and we picked up my mother. It was still dark outside as we took the forty-five-minute ride to Lowell. I had been concerned over the years that my brother would commit suicide, and drinking yourself to death is a slow manner of suicide. I thought, "My brother will be in a vegetative state if he survives this. He'd rather be dead than live like that."

Upon arriving at the hospital, the woman Jamie had been with the last couple of years greeted us. She had a trailer in the suburbs, and Jamie was living with her. I asked her what had happened, and she said, "He went to the doctor recently, and the doctor told him he had to stop drinking."

She told us she had been getting ready to walk her dog and wanted to call the ambulance because Jamie wasn't feeling well. He said not to call, and when she came back, he looked like he had passed out. She thought he was teasing her. I believe his body organs were shutting down slowly, and he just didn't care anymore. She called the ambulance, and they brought him to the local hospital.

I saw my mother crying, not knowing what to do. I was distraught thinking of what Jamie and I had lived through together, knowing that he could have had a much better life. Like most alcoholics, it seemed he was always trying to start his life over. He left our company after problems arose with his drinking. He went to another glass company for a couple of years before going to work at a body shop and couldn't always get to work. Many times, he didn't call in, and his boss, someone I went to school with, would call and ask me to check in on Jamie. I'd go bang on his door, and he wouldn't answer. All of us would be concerned that he was dead. He'd go back to work, feeling shameful the way I did when I drank and didn't call in.

Then Jamie was in the Salvation Army in Saugus for a while, trying to get help. He came out and stayed sober for a while, then started not showing up for work again. His boss gave him a lot of breaks but finally had to let him go. After this job, he never quite got back on his feet again. He lived with a sequence of girlfriends and was "irritable, restless, and discontent" as the Big Book of Alcoholics Anonymous describes. He needed healing from God desperately, but he couldn't let go of the lie that alcohol was his solution.

"I'm not angry at God," I told my husband while I paced the halls waiting for another doctor to come in. I knew my brother had plenty of opportunities to get help, but he continually refused to accept that help. We alcoholics think we're so unique, and our pride gets in the way. We think we're not like "those people" who drink in alleyways. My heart was broken for Jamie. To be honest, I knew he was gone, and I just wanted it to end. That may sound selfish, but the thought of him lying there any longer, knowing he wouldn't make it was excruciating.

As far as I knew, my brother had no religious beliefs, but my mother considered herself Catholic, so I felt it would be helpful to have a member of the clergy come in to pray over him. In reality, I could have done it myself. We all can pray to our heavenly Father; we don't need someone else to do that for us. Peter said we are a "royal priesthood" (1 Peter 2:9). Jesus died so we can all have a relationship with our Father. But this wasn't about me and my beliefs. I wanted to help my mother feel comfortable.

The hospital contacted a priest. When he arrived, he read from the New Testament. We said the Lord's Prayer; then the priest stood awkwardly beside me, not saying a word. Distraught, I thought, "Is he looking for me to pay him?" Then he handed me the Bible he had read from, which had only the New Testament in it. I said, "Oh, you want me to have it?" He did nothing else to comfort the family. He didn't even ask about Jamie or who he was. Still, I think my mother felt better someone had come in.

A young nurse was taking care of Jamie. I can't say enough for the tenderness I felt from her as she continued to look after him. She wrapped his feet—I guess they were getting cold as his body began shutting down.

We waited with Jamie for seven hours. The doctor finally came to talk with us, and she had a terrible bedside manner. She said bluntly that Jamie was dying of "septic shock" from an infection in his bloodstream. She made it clear there was nothing they could do, so it was time to take the life support away. I kept telling Jamie that he wasn't alone, that we were all there and how much we loved him, and how gifted he was. I told him, "God loves you. God is with you, Jamie. You'll never be alone."

Jamie had just turned forty a few months before, and it was already time to say goodbye. The nurse took the life support from him, and I asked her to cut off a small piece of his hair. I thanked her for her kindness toward my brother. Her eyes teared up with compassion, which told me she was being genuine. After a few short minutes while we were standing in the doorway talking, she said, "He just left us."

Jamie was an intelligent human being with a quick sense of humor. He was handsome, smart, funny, and talented but also sad and angry inside. He was a wounded soul, trying to live as an adult but still feeling inside like a scared and unloved child until the end.

As I looked at my mother, I couldn't help but blame her. She was never there for him, and she'd show more of that in the days to come. We drove back to Boston. It was early Sunday afternoon, and we needed to make the necessary calls. We had already called my oldest brother Wayne, who was now living in North Carolina. After graduating from a trade school, Wayne worked for a company that built cabinets. He had been employed there for about thirty-seven years, thirty-five in Boston and two in North Carolina. When the company offered him a position at their new location, he accepted, then packed up his family, and made the move.

Before Greg and I returned home, we asked if my mother wanted to come to our house. She said no, so we dropped her off to deal alone with the pain of losing her son. I don't know how she did it, sitting there by herself. Greg and I went home, and I was devastated. I couldn't believe my brother was gone. He had no life insurance, so we all came together to pay for his service and make the funeral arrangements.

Greg and I were attending the Congregational church in Boston at the time, and Greg suggested I call them. I was able to have a member of the church come and speak at the service, which would be at a funeral home in Chelsea, close to where we grew up. There wouldn't be a church service, just a wake and a memorial service in the funeral home.

I prayed about what to do about Jamie's service. My mother had the final say since she was his next of kin. She had no issues with him being cremated, and she didn't want an autopsy. Honestly, I later regretted that because of a conversation I had with Jamie's girlfriend the night we were at the hospital. She said she was married before and her husband had also died from septic shock. I know my brother was drinking excessively, but who knows what happened with him that last night of his life or how he developed an infection in his bloodstream?

I don't think Jamie would have wanted a wake. He was very private and wouldn't have wanted his body being laid out for everyone to look at. But my mother and I wanted one for him. I felt his friends would want to say their goodbyes. They had not seen him in quite some time, and they felt sad about his passing. His good friend TJ was very saddened over Jamie's death. Their friendship had lasted for years before Jamie started to isolate.

When you grow up feeling unloved, it leaves you distrusting of everyone. Jamie struggled to have relationships, as most adult children of alcoholics do. But he was very well-liked—he didn't know how much. Many of his friends came to the service. I displayed a lot of pictures of him. He had done some fun things with Jason—taking him fishing and to drag racing shows—and I had pictures of the two of them at an air show. Like me, Jamie had a fear of flying, but he was fascinated with airplanes.

After leaving the wake, my mother and Todd stepped into the bar down the street from the funeral home. I couldn't believe it. My mother just saw her son dead lying in a casket, and she thought it was a good idea to walk to the local gin mill. Wayne came out to ask where she had gone, so I told him. He was still playing the "hero," one of the roles in an alcoholic family. He was still acting like the fifteen-year-old in our house, who tried to stop my father from beating her. So off my brother went to try to save her again. He would try to make sure she was okay, and he might have coaxed her to come home. Wayne's eyes would soon be opened.

Greg and I went home, and I wrote the eulogy. I wanted to tell the story of our trip to Krakow, Wisconsin, with Jason in 1995 to visit my father's family. Jamie sat in the front of the car with me, and Jason sat in the back with his wrestling figures and his Game Boy. Jamie used his fake Boston accent all the way to Wisconsin while Jason and I cracked up laughing.

My son was devastated to lose his uncle Jamie. Although they hadn't been together in years, Jason was happy that the last time he spoke with Jamie he told him he loved him. Jason said, "I'm so glad, Mum. That's the last memory I have of him." I said, "I am too." I believe that's also the last thing Jamie and I said to each other the night of our last phone call. It's so important to tell those we love that we love them, every day.

Jason and I had been through so much, and now we'd get through Jamie's death together. Greg was there too, but unfortunately, he had only met Jamie a few times. What a tragedy—they would have liked each other.

I told my mother I'd buy the clothes for Jamie's service. Jamie wasn't a suit wearer, so I wanted to clothe him in an attire he enjoyed wearing. I went to Marshalls and walked around in a fog before buying a white T-shirt, a pair of jeans, and sneakers. Jamie also wore a motorcycle jacket with the American flag on the back.

I gave the eulogy for my brother, and I made sure it reflected who my brother truly was. I expressed his gratitude for TJ and his family and how much he appreciated their friendship and love. My stepbrother Bobby was crying; he was about eight when Jamie first came to live with his mom and my dad. I spoke about our trip to Wisconsin and the fun Jason and I had with Jamie. About all the gifts God gave him and how much he was loved by those who tried to love him. We all said our goodbyes that day, and Jamie was taken quickly to be cremated.

I picked up the ashes a few weeks after Jamie's service. We chose a blue urn with white seagulls flying free in the air, a place I hoped Jamie was now. My brother came home to our house and is now resting there, where it's peaceful and quiet. When God calls me home, Jamie will be placed in my casket with me. I hope I see him in heaven. The Bible is clear in John 3:16: "For God so loved the world that he gave his one and only Son, that whoever believes in him shall not perish but have eternal life." I don't know what Jamie believed, but I pray he is with God, no longer suffering, and feeling love from him he couldn't feel here on earth.

I have a letter Jamie wrote me in December of 2005, three years before he died. He talked about being my shadow when we were kids. He also talked about how sometimes all a person has is hope. It's so painful to read it now. He apologized for not calling me more and said how it's hard to talk about family but that he was reading books that said it's better to talk about it. He told me to keep the faith. He sent me a bunch of pictures he wanted me to keep. Most pictures were of an ex-girlfriend whom he had loved very much. I think he was really heartbroken about their breakup.

Although I was Jamie's big sister and he once called me his shadow, I looked up to him. When you lose a sibling, it's a much different feeling than losing a parent. It's losing a friend who you grew up with. When I received Jamie's ashes, my mother never visited them or asked what the urn looked like. I realized my mother didn't deal with feelings that caused her to be uncomfortable. Who was I to judge? I didn't always deal with my feelings, nor had I lost a son.

But I wanted to encourage her to talk about him, so I'd stop by the house to share funny stories about Jamie, and my mother would chime in. Like the time when he was about four and he took the trim comb and cut down to his scalp on the top of his head. I used a Band-Aid to cover the bald spot. We talked about Jamie being a great gift wrapper. My mother got a kick out of how he spent more money on his wrapping paper than he did on his gifts.

That year, my mother had three losses in a five-month period: her longtime boyfriend, her dog, and her youngest child. But she was fine going home and spending time with her married boyfriend. Andy continued to travel from Virginia every couple of months, leaving his wife to stay with my mother. It was the only way she knew how to cope. We all sin and fall short every day, but we can repent and do better in life. I want to believe my mother knew what she was doing was wrong, but I really don't know if she did. She had to deny so much in her life to survive. We as alcoholics need to stop being selfish and justifying our behaviors. We're so caught up in ourselves we don't realize the hurt we cause to our family and the families of others. Not to mention God.

I see more clearly now than I did growing up in my house with my family. I can now identify the web of lies and deceit that occurred. I believe every family has generational curses, but I also believe God can heal them. With my family, it's just complete denial of truth. No wonder, I questioned and doubted myself and my own experiences. If I spoke the truth in my house, it was not welcomed. If you called my family members on their behavior, you got the silent treatment from my mother or yelled at by Todd. People can steal your reality when you're a child, and you don't even know what hit you. You no longer trust what you see. That's something I was experiencing more and more driving on the highway. My anxiety was getting worse. The road could be clear, but I was questioning whether I was safe and protected. What the heck was going on with me?

Chapter 10

As 2008 came to a close, we got through the holidays. Although it had been years since I spent Thanksgiving or Christmas with my father or brother, I was keenly aware that I had now lost two of my family members. Little did I know 2009 would bring still more sadness.

Before I dated Greg, his niece Adrianna had a bout with cancer. She was a beautiful young lady with a Sophia Loren look. When Adrianna was in her teens, she developed cancer on her ankle. The doctors were able to treat it, and she was in remission. In November 2006, she gave birth to her daughter, Gianna, and shortly thereafter, she found a lump on her side. In a short time, she was given a grim diagnosis. In the months to come, her parents—Greg's sister Roseanne and brother-in-law John—fought tirelessly to get her the care she needed. John took her to Mexico to seek treatments that are not approved in the US.

It was heartbreaking to watch John taking care of his little girl, feeling so helpless and unsure of what was to come, and to see such a beautiful, vibrant young woman slowly succumb to this terrible disease. Every time I saw Adrianna, she never complained. She was a sweetheart, with an honest and innocent approach to life. In July of 2009, Adrianna finally lost her battle. Adrianna was only twenty-eight years old and mother to a toddler who was now being raised by her paternal grandparents. I couldn't imagine what Roseanne and John were going through. They decided not to have a funeral service, and who was anyone to question them? None of us could imagine the pain they were in. I only had one child, and I couldn't imagine what I would have done if I lost Jason.

My son felt bad because Adrianna was so young. I told Jason we don't know why God allows these things to happen, but we must trust him. He decides the day we are born and the day he takes us home. We belong to him, and he has control, not us.

* * *

My longtime friend Susan was still living in Georgia and making a home for herself there. After moving there, she got involved with some things that could have taken her life. Now she was calling from Atlanta, telling me about her experiences with God and how she had been saved. She was going to church regularly and sharing what God had done for her with anyone who would listen.

When I first got saved in the late nineties, I was on fire for God. Susan said she now understood what I was doing years before when I constantly told her about God and his love. I was truly happy for her, but I also resented her for feeling that way because I had lost my fervor for my Savior. I knew that I had to get back on track. God was letting me know through Susan what was missing from my life. I prayed that God would guide me to a church Greg and I could attend regularly.

God answered my prayers. My friend Karen from work told me she and her daughter had been visiting a church in North Reading, and she thought I'd like it there. I trusted her, so I took her suggestion and walked into Trinity Evangelical, where I heard the Holy Spirit through Pastor Ray that morning. I heard truth in his message, which meant he knew the Word of God. I immediately made an appointment to talk to him about the anxiety I was experiencing.

Pastor Ray grew up in South Carolina and then attended seminary in Massachusetts. He's an army veteran and lawyer, but his calling was to pastor a church. He's been at Trinity for over thirty years.

We met in his corner office, which had a large model sailboat in the window. I told him a little about myself and what I was experiencing with my anxiety. I immediately felt comfortable in his presence.

He couldn't have been nicer with his Southern charm. He told me his first assignment while in seminary school back in the early eighties was to fill in for a pastor at a congregational church in Chelsea. I knew right then and there I was in the right place. He also told me he knew Ruth, the woman who had baptized me.

Pastor Ray loaned me a book by Beth Moore, *Praying God's Word: Breaking Free of Spiritual Strongholds.* I don't like lending books to people because I rarely get them back without having to ask, but I read the chapter he recommended and returned the book to him on Sunday morning. I started attending church each week and got involved in the women's Bible study on Wednesday nights. I knew God was answering my prayers and helping me to get close to his Son again.

Jason was doing his best selling his pretzels, but his daily sales were down. Downtown Crossing in Boston was becoming more of a ghost town after one of the major retail stores closed. At times, Linda had him work on another side of town, and I'd drive by and beep the horn to say hello. I was so proud to see him out there working at a job that gave him confidence. Late in 2010, Jason left the pretzel company. He told me he was tired of being outside during the cold months not selling anything, so he just stopped showing up. I explained to Jason that I didn't think he handled it well. He needed to go back and tell Linda he quit. I don't think he did, but he did his best for a long time, and I don't fault him for that.

While Jason was working for Linda, I called his hours into the Supplemental Security Income (SSI) office each week so they could adjust his benefit check. That was a constant headache because the hours changed each week. Jason and I would go to the SSI office in Chelsea to straighten out his paperwork. I'd leave the information with them, but they'd later tell me they didn't receive it. The poor kid was only making about one hundred twenty dollars a week, and they're cutting his eight-hundred-dollars-a-month benefit check. Because of the nonsense I had to deal with, at times I'd be livid. Jason spoke up to them when he had to, but without a parent, Jason—or anyone with mental illness—wouldn't have been able to advocate for themselves.

Initially, I encouraged Jason to find another job. But as time went on, he didn't seem that interested in finding work, so I let it go. I told him that if he became bored, it wasn't my job to entertain him; I didn't want to see him sitting in the house gaining weight and falling apart. He was still seeing his therapist weekly, which occupied an entire day. By now, he had been seeing Daniel for eight years. Jason enjoyed his time with him, and in a sense, they had become friends.

Next, Jason decided to leave the state outreach program. The program sent a nurse to his house once a week, but he was having a hard time with the last one who visited. Although Jason was my son, I realized he could be difficult and become paranoid regarding people he didn't know. Sometimes the outreach workers didn't show up or call Jason, which irritated him greatly, and I'm sure Jason wasn't always showing up for them either, but accountability is important to me. Occasionally, I'd stop by their office to complain to the director. Whenever he saw me walk through the door, he'd run and hide in his office because he didn't want to deal with me. When I'd inquire where his staff was during certain hours, I wouldn't get an answer. I asked him, "You're being paid by the state, and you have no record of where your staff is during the day?" I reminded him that my tax dollars were paying for him to have a job.

Jason had been taking his meds regularly for years, and there had never been any issues. Jason had the support he needed from Greg and me. As Jason frequently said, "I know you and Greg have my back, Mum," which made me feel good because I didn't feel that way about my own parents. I was a little nervous that Jason wasn't connected to another source, but he had other supports in place. He wanted to be free and on his own, as he was an adult now.

Looking back, I can see how much I still struggled with control. I was trying to allow Jason to be the adult he was while I lived with the fear something bad would happen to him. I looked at him in the car one day and thought to myself, "I need to step aside and let him be the young man God wants him to be." I had so much anxiety that he wouldn't be okay. I didn't want anyone to take advantage of him, like they did with me. Our relationship had become more trusting, and we were able to come to a place my mother and I would never reach. I felt distant from my mother because of her lies, but Jason knew I wouldn't lie to him. He was beginning to trust me again. That trust came by my showing up for him during his darkest days.

As Jason enjoyed his newfound freedom in his cute little apartment, I was still on the road for the glass company. The years had passed by so quickly. I started with the company when Jason was fourteen months old. As of 2010, I had been working there for twenty-seven years. The last few years at the glass company had been difficult following some personnel changes. I wasn't doing well practicing my tenth step, which is "continue to take personal inventory and when we are wrong promptly admit it." I was getting caught up in a lot of nonsense I really had no control over, and my anxiety while driving on the highway was not getting better. I was getting more and more irritable with those around me. I felt like I was carrying a burden, but I didn't know what it was. Was it something from childhood that I needed to deal with? I continued to pray daily and ask God to show me truth and what the root of the anxiety was.

Around this time, I started attending Al-Anon again to deal with my adult child issues. I needed to talk about some of the fears I had about being married and about Jason living on his own. It was time to admit I wasn't always so "put together." I needed to be vulnerable again, and going through the twelve steps was only a part of my healing. I had more work to do.

I heard years ago in AA, "What you bury inside of you, you bury alive." God will stir up that piece inside of you that needs attention and healing. Because God loves us so much, he wants us to get to that truth of what's causing our anxiety. God wants to heal what's keeping us from our destiny.

I was reading a book by a local psychiatrist that was moving my spirit. The doctor grew up in a town not too far from Chelsea. After reading his book, I contacted him. I met with him a few times, and he gave me some insight on what could be going on with me: childhood stuff was playing out in the present. The times I didn't speak up for myself mirrored the times I had felt trapped as a child.

On Easter Sunday 2012, Jason and I were at church when the pastor asked anyone in the congregation who would like to give their life to Jesus Christ that day to please come up. The church had a little bridge set up at the altar for people to walk across, demonstrating leaving the old sinful life for a new one with Jesus. Jason never wanted to go up for prayer during Sunday services, so I didn't think he'd go on this day, but I took a shot and asked him anyway. To my surprise, he said yes. I was so happy for him and so proud to walk over that bridge with him so he could give his life to Christ. Giving his life to Christ meant he was acknowledging he needed a Savior and his soul after death would be secure. He received a little booklet the church gave to all new believers to help them on their way. It was a great day for both of us.

While driving home, I called Susan and told her what Jason had done. She was thrilled and congratulated him. I wanted him to be encouraged by another believer and to hear that what he did was the best decision he could ever make.

Jason's thirtieth birthday was coming up on June 1, 2012. The last party I had thrown for him with guests from outside the family was his twenty-fifth. He was at the age where I thought attending a party every year would be asking too much of people outside the family, but thirty was a milestone, so I had a few people over to celebrate his accomplishments. One of the gifts God has given me is the gift of encouragement. I didn't receive much of it growing up, but it comes naturally to me. I was proud of Jason and told him that as often as I could. Jason and I had become friends, and we were continually growing together.

We continued our ritual of Saturday morning food shopping. After doing most of our shopping at the supermarket, we'd stop at a local meat market. Jason enjoyed talking to Jim, one of the employees about his video games. He'd also chat with Helen, the owner, while he waited at the register for me. I'd step in at times to make sure he wasn't talking too much and distracting them from their work. Jason loved to chat with people, just like his mom. He would have made a great salesperson.

Sometimes when we were out shopping, Jason would admire some of the girls he saw. They were often much younger, like fifteen, and I'd tell him, "She's very young, Jason." In his mind, he probably felt fifteen even at thirty because he lost a lot of years in institutions.

One Saturday, we stopped at another store in Revere to pick up our sausages. While looking at the lettuce, I noticed Rob Dolan, Jason's biological father, standing at the counter near the register where Jason was. I felt this terrible fear in my stomach, and I didn't know what to do. I walked over to them, and as Rob noticed me, he asked if the person standing next to me was Jason. Rob had met Jason only a couple of times when he was a toddler and he was paying child support for a very short period.

I looked at Jason and said, "This is your father, Rob."

The two of them said hello; then Rob said to Jason, "I'd like to call you sometime." I kept quiet and got in the car with Jason, wondering what Jason would say about him. He was quiet too, so I asked him if he was okay, and he said he was.

Then he said, "Mum, how is he going to call me when he didn't ask for my phone number?"

I replied, "Jason, unfortunately he said that to make himself feel better, not you. I'm sorry you had that experience with him."

I didn't want to pretend that Rob cared about him because he didn't. If he really wanted to talk with Jason, he could have offered his phone number. He would have disappointed Jason over and over, like he did with his other children and my father did to me. I waited a couple of minutes and again asked if he was okay.

Jason replied, "Mum, I don't even know him. You took good care of me."

I said, "Well, I told you in the past he's a sick guy and lives a selfish life. You were better off without him. In fact, you probably have more going on in your life than he has."

I believed that 100 percent because Jason had people who loved him and were there for him because of who he was. Rob, on the other hand, had not changed his behavior. He didn't take care of Jason and only lived life for himself.

At this point, my son was an adult and could make his own decisions. Jason knew he had half-siblings, but he never asked to meet with them. He was very cautious around strangers. I guess he felt he had a family that loved him, and that was enough. We went about our day, and he never mentioned Rob again. It's sad that a man in his seventies was so wrapped up in himself that he would make a statement like that to a young man with a mental illness—a statement he never intended to support.

* * *

In the fall of that year, my brother Wayne decided to take a plane to Boston from his home in North Carolina. When he arrived, he walked from the airport to my mother's house in the middle of the night without letting her know. Chelsea is about a ten-minute car ride, so walking probably took him about half an hour. What the heck was he doing back in Massachusetts without notice?

It turns out he was taking what we call in AA "a geographical cure." A geographical cure is when you move to another place in hopes your problem will get better or go away. Unfortunately, you also bring yourself, which is the real problem. Apparently, Wayne's alcoholism was getting the best of his marriage, and he had some court issues going on. He was struggling to put himself together. As he expressed it, "I wanted to come home."

I learned that after two years in North Carolina, the cabinet company where Wayne worked for decades made the decision to lay him off. My brother was devastated and felt abandoned, as I'm sure most adult children would. It seemed he made his job and his accomplishments his source of security and peace, just like me. To do so is wrong because God, not my job or people, is my true source of income and security. People come and go, and so do jobs, money, houses—anything can change in life, but not God's love. God created me, and therefore, he is my source and knows my destiny. As Jeremiah 29:11 states, "'For I know the plans I have for you,' declares the Lord, 'plans to prosper you and not to harm you, plans to give you hope and a future.'"

Wayne's wife and daughter were both in North Carolina. In his alcoholic mind, coming home, I believe, meant getting comfort from our mother. Wayne had been distant from our family due to his own drinking and the hurt he felt from his dad's treatment as a child. I kept thinking about Wayne saying, when my father died, "I can't remember anything good." He was still feeling that hurt deep in his soul, and drinking was the escape he used to avoid it. My pain was still there, but I was covering it with people pleasing and caretaking.

Wayne and I weren't very close, due in part to the eight-year difference between us. I was twelve when he left the house and married his first wife. I remember thinking back then, "Who will stop my father from beating on my mother when Wayne leaves?" It certainly wasn't Wayne's responsibility. Todd had been there for a while until he started coming in and out of jail. None of us could really stop the chaos, so through the years, my brother found solace in alcohol. He has since experienced some sobriety.

Growing up, all three of my brothers defended my mother. I didn't realize or admit she treated them differently than she treated me. My father said she had been in competition with me. My brothers saw my mother as a victim, but I didn't. This time around, Wayne would have an eye-opening experience with our mother.

Ma was angry that Wayne came to see her without notice. She called and told me how angry she was and that she was in subsidized housing and couldn't have him there for long. In her mind, when her married boyfriend came from Virginia and stayed in her apartment for two weeks, that was perfectly fine, but not her son. She said Wayne was working a temporary job and wasn't drinking. The drinking part I didn't buy since I know the behavior of an alcoholic.

When I called Wayne, he asked me to visit him at his job. Shortly after arriving, he found a temporary job at Bed Bath & Beyond in Somerville. I'll never forget walking into the store to see him one day. My oldest brother—who worked hard for thirty-seven years as a cabinetmaker at a job he loved, with people he trusted and to whom he was committed—was relegated to putting merchandise in a cardboard box.

As he told me how much he liked his coworkers and how much they appreciated him, I looked at his face and couldn't help but see a little boy still searching for validation and approval. It was sad that he was getting his self-esteem from people he hardly knew, who saw something special in him. Wayne was like me, an adult child of two alcoholic parents, desperately trying to be loved. As children, we were not nurtured or valued as people who had gifts to share with the world. As adult children, we didn't know or appreciate our own value. We were too busy trying to seek approval from people who don't have the power to give us the self-esteem and love we so desperately crave.

I felt sorry for him that day. Although I too look for validation from people at times, I am now aware of when I am doing it. Although I still struggle with disbelief at times, I know my self-worth does not come from people or what I do for them. It comes from God.

I was heartbroken to see my oldest brother so lost. But I have to say, it felt good to have him nearby and be able to introduce someone as my brother, who I was related to by blood. I invited him to an AA meeting I attended on Thursday nights, but he evaded the suggestion. While giving him a ride one night, I could smell the alcohol on his breath. I didn't say anything until Greg and I had him over for dinner and we talked outside in my yard.

"Wayne, I know you're drinking, so let's be honest with each other." I told him his life could be much more fulfilling if he could get off his self-pity and get some help. He had some times of sobriety in the past, but he got away from meetings. He could have also used help with adult child issues.

I said, "Wayne, what are you waiting for? Dad is long gone, and you're still giving him power over your life. Aren't you tired? You're going to be fifty-seven years old this year." He didn't say much, but I could tell he still wasn't ready.

After eating dinner together, my husband drove him back to where he was staying. I felt terrible for him and wondered what his next move would be since he wasn't getting much temporary work. He talked to me about how mean my mother was being to him. He couldn't believe how she was treating him when he had come to her for help. He was shocked and said that when Ma died, he would probably not attend her funeral.

I told him, "Our mother has always been like that. You're just finally seeing it."

He said, "No, you don't understand—Ma is evil, Karen. She's evil."

I said, "Wayne, I've felt that way my whole life. She's always been mean to me."

I told him how Todd molested me when I was young and how I remembered a man coming into my room when I was a baby in my crib. Wayne brought up Ronnie, Todd's father, being in the house when Wayne was about eight or nine and our father was out working. Our mother hid Ronnie in the bathroom so Wayne wouldn't see him, but Wayne said he knew there was a guy in the house.

I said, "Yeah, Wayne, he was probably the man who scared me when I was in my crib."

Wayne was horrified. He hadn't realized I may have been affected by this man coming into our home. Wayne probably also felt conflicted, knowing my father didn't know. I think his drinking through the years is partly due to the betrayal he witnessed. During the visit, we shared a lot from the past, like we usually did on the rare times we got together.

Wayne said one more poignant thing to me. He said, "I don't know how to love." I told him, "God is love, and when we have a relationship with God, we will feel loved and in turn know how to love ourselves and others."

He started crying, and I could see he still had a lot of pain that needed healing. I was grateful for staying sober because I was able to have a relationship with my son and enjoy life, but I felt sad for Wayne. During his stay, I felt I had escaped from much of the past, but my brother was still living in it. When you spend time with people who have been hiding in alcohol, you see how much they haven't moved forward. It's painful to witness, especially when you know there is something they can do to help themselves.

Wayne told me he hadn't wanted to be like our father and that he didn't feel like he was because he had kept the same job for thirty-seven years, but he was now starting to realize that he had become the very thing he dreaded. He thought he could come home and be comforted but now was realizing home was not with our mother. Home is where love is, and there still wasn't any of that back here in Boston. She wanted nothing to do with him or his problems, which was not news to me. He was finally feeling like I felt: unwanted.

When parents have an opportunity to help heal their children due to the role they have played, they should try to make things better. Now there wasn't going to be any conversation about my mother's role in raising Wayne or the men she brought into the house. Wayne and my father would not have a conversation about how he beat up Wayne and locked him in a closet.

That's why the steps in AA are so important. The ninth step gives us an opportunity to make direct amends to those we have harmed. We all could have felt some healing if our father and mother would have admitted their wrongs to us. For me, with Jason, they were living amends, and I was trying to demonstrate them one day at a time.

Wayne decided to call his wife, and she said it was okay to come home. Greg offered to pay for his ticket and booked him a flight home to be with his family. His wife texted to thank us, and I told her not to worry about paying us back. My husband is a good-natured man, and he didn't care about the money. Wayne has only called once since that day.

Chapter 11

During Wayne's visit, my mother developed a hoarse throat. As Wayne returned to North Carolina, Todd called to tell me the doctor said Ma may have throat cancer. She was going for additional testing and receiving rides to Boston Medical Center from a local social services organization. I felt sorry for her and pondered what this would mean for her future. I was happy she had help getting her needs met.

The holidays were approaching, and I wanted to have a real tree for Christmas. Before meeting Greg, I'd buy a tree in Winthrop and have it delivered to my house. I loved coming home and finding the tree on my front porch. When Jason was in and out of institutions and schools, I didn't get a tree because he wasn't there to share it with me. Eventually, I bought a fiberoptic tree that I displayed along with my beautiful ceramic Nativity.

This year, Greg and I went down to the local lot and bought ourselves a real tree. I bought all-new decorations, and I enjoyed every moment of decorating my fresh tree. The cat Wednesday was being Miss Busybody, getting into everything. She was Jason's cat, not mine, but I took care of her when he was receiving help. During the years he was away at school, I was grateful to have her company. Still, Jason was the only one allowed to pick her up and rest her on his shoulder. He called her Furball.

We got through the holidays, but the doctors seemed to be taking their time coming up with a treatment for my mother's cancer. In early 2013, I started to help Ma with her appointments. I had mixed feelings about this since I never felt emotionally safe around her, but I felt I had to help since I was the only child nearby. I also knew it was what God wanted me to do. It's hard to love people who don't show love to you, but Jesus said to love and forgive your enemies.

Ma stopped drinking after she was diagnosed, and I was feeling good about helping her until she started making negative comments toward me, like she always did. She asked me, "Jeez, how many pocketbooks do you have?" which really meant "I'm envious that you have so many pocketbooks." She'd say she liked the haircut I had twenty years ago, which meant she didn't like my current haircut. Sometimes she'd even ask, "Did you gain weight?" That was a classic with her. In public, she told people what a great job I had, but alone with me, she'd say I worked too hard and they didn't pay me enough.

Coincidentally, while waiting for her at her medical appointments, I read the book *You're Not Crazy—It's Your Mother: Understanding and Healing for Daughters of Narcissistic Mothers* by Danu Morrigan. The doctor who treated me for anxiety, recommended I read the book *Narcissism* by Alexander Loren. As I read and did more research, I began to realize that the book's definition of narcissism was a perfect portrait of my mother. Narcissists are vain, selfish, and overly self-involved. They struggle to integrate their needs and desires with those of their children. Narcissists don't have the capacity to love anyone; they're too busy making sure others are feeding them with praise. They view their children as mere objects or burdens. They compliment their children in public to make themselves look good, but in private, they make them feel not good enough. In public, they look great to everyone, except the child who experiences their evil.

One day, when we were sitting in the hospital waiting for the doctor, Ma said, "I wish you had married a doctor." I couldn't believe what I was hearing. Greg is one of the most loyal and caring people you'll ever meet, but she never bothered to get to know my husband because he didn't give her much attention. From what I told him of my childhood, he knew who she really was, so although Greg never said a bad word about her, he kept to himself around Ma. I was at the hospital for God, but when I look back, I can see I was allowing myself to be victimized by her again.

While taking Ma back and forth to her appointments and encouraging her to stay positive, I finally realized that my mother did not know how to love. I was coming to the understanding that no matter what I did for her, it would never be good enough. I thought it was my father who I relentlessly tried to please, but it was both of them. If you weren't praising Ma and living in her lies, you were the enemy. Needless to say, I was the enemy most of the time.

The 1981 film *Mommie Dearest*, about actress Joan Crawford, is an excellent depiction of a narcissistic mother. If you're a woman who has a mother who acts like that toward you, you are not alone.

My mother lacked empathy. If it wasn't about her and what she liked—usually drinking and men—she wasn't interested. I think back and realize my mother didn't have one girlfriend in her life. You can't have girlfriends when you're in competition with other women, including your own daughter. It's sad when I think of all she could have had and what God would have wanted for her. After all those years, I was finally starting to grieve the loss of not having a mother who loved me.

My mother never wanted anyone to call her out on her behavior. While at her appointments, I cringed when the nurses and doctors told me what a wonderful lady my mother is. They had no idea about the life she led and how selfish she was. How, at the age of seventy-four, my mother thought it was okay to take up with a married man. They had no idea she abandoned her children and spent her days with men in barrooms. I had to bite my tongue and smile a lot, which was killing me inside. Sometimes I made negative comments about her to the nurses, but I had to stop because I knew God didn't want me to do that. I thought I had forgiven her, but I had to forgive her every time we were together because she continued to insult me. One day, I finally told her that if she continued to talk to me and insult me the way she did, I was going to stop taking her to her appointments. I had the right to speak up or, better yet, walk away.

No matter what I did, I couldn't win. Before I picked her up, I had to pray I wouldn't get sucked into the insanity. At times, I believed I was helping her, and she told the doctors she appreciated it. I had moments when I'd think maybe she wasn't that bad. Then one day, I dropped her off at the front door of the hospital, and she took off on me. I ran around the hospital looking for her since I didn't know where her appointment was. When I found her, I said, "Ma, have some consideration for me instead of making me go looking for you." But she was all set; she had her ride, and she really didn't care that I didn't know how to find her. I told her that if she was going to be that selfish, I wouldn't take her anymore.

After the doctors saw where the cancer was, they created a treatment plan and started chemotherapy. Ma's voice came back right away, which was a good sign. During those few months, my mother let me walk Candy, the dog Todd bought her the year Jamie died. Ma had no other choice because Candy had a lot of energy. Candy and I got to be good friends, and she was a great distraction from the pain I had to endure.

* * *

"Has anyone not been anointed with the Holy Spirit?" Pastor Gus asked during a small-group meeting one evening at church.

Gus is Greek, a father of two sons, and a very passionate speaker. I raised my hand. He suggested I come after Sunday service so he could pray over me. I knew God was speaking to me that night. I had been feeling a prompting in my spirit for a while to be vocal during prayer and meditation each morning.

The Bible speaks of the gift of tongues: "For anyone who speaks in a tongue does not speak to men but to God" (1 Corinthians 14:2). The apostles spoke in tongues in the Book of Acts after Jesus ascended to heaven. They did this in order to communicate with the different nations and lead them to Christ.

I thought such people were delusional until my own spirit was moved to speak aloud. I sought Gus after Sunday's service. He prayed over me, and since then, my walk with God has become much deeper, as I pray in tongues every day. When I meditate in the mornings, I let sounds come out of me, and I don't know what I'm saying. I let the Holy Spirit guide me to speak, which allows me to worship God at a deeper level. It makes me feel freer to communicate with God. I now had the power of the Holy Spirit, which I needed to carry out his will.

I would be turning fifty in March of 2013, and I wanted to have a little party at our house. Greg was unable to plan it since it fell in the middle of tax season, so I took care of it. I decided to have the party catered. Greg put my invitations together. On the card was a picture of me with my brother Jamie when I was seven and he was about two. I wanted him to be there in memory because I missed him so much. He looked so cute in the picture, dressed in a tie with his round face and round eyes. He looked so much like Jason at that age.

I wanted to make sure my good friend Lisa, whom I grew up with in Chelsea, and her husband Frank were at the party. Of course, I invited Susan's family along with Greg's family. Bobby would be there with his wife, Danielle, and of course my son Jason. My mother declined the invitation, which was no surprise. My brothers Wayne and Todd were not invited.

A few weeks before my party while driving on Route 114 to Market Basket, Jason and I talked about his past and his accomplishments. He liked to emphasize the negative while I tried hard to remind him of the positives that took place during those years. I told him that I was grateful I had him as my son and I was sorry for being angry toward him while growing up.

"I didn't want to be a young mother, Jason," I said. "I was resentful and frustrated because I didn't have anyone from my family to help me. It wasn't your fault, and it wasn't you that I was angry with. I was angry with myself and the decisions I made."

Jason replied, "I never asked for much when I was young, Mum."

I told him kiddingly, "No, you didn't, but the few things you asked for weren't cheap." I was referring to all the Nintendo games I bought him when he was a kid. They were fifty dollars apiece, which was a lot in those days. I'd buy several at a time, along with other stuff. He had very good Christmases.

I didn't directly say I hadn't wanted Jason because that would have hurt him. Instead, I wanted him to understand that the pregnancy was not wanted. He must have thought about this conversation during the next few weeks because he brought it up again on my birthday. That day, Greg picked up Jason at his apartment. I have to be honest here because I want to help out other parents who may have a child with a mental illness: I was concerned what people would think of Jason if his hygiene wasn't good or he looked disheveled when he arrived. I thought about that while running around the house trying to get things ready. I never knew how Jason would be dressed, so I was going to look him up and down when he got to the house.

When he arrived, I noticed he had his dress pants on. I also noticed they had a broken zipper, which Jason held together with a binder clip. Even after all the years had passed, I couldn't comprehend how Jason could come to our house with a clip on his pants. I became upset and asked him how he could possibly think this was okay. He snapped at me, shouting, "You never wanted me!" and then sat in my home office, crying his eyes out. I yelled for Greg to come upstairs because Jason hadn't cried like that in quite some time.

I went into the bathroom and kept quiet while Jason sobbed to Greg that I never wanted him. "He's right," I thought. "I didn't want him when he was a baby." I felt good that he was expressing that out loud with no one, including me, telling him he was wrong. Greg talked with him and calmed him down, then told him we'd find him something to wear.

I felt like a complete jerk. I stood in the bathroom, thinking, "It's all about you, Karen, isn't it?" I walked out into the hall and apologized to Jason, and he apologized to me.

Then something happened that I will never forget. He hugged me in a way he had never done before. He wrapped his arms all the way around me and held on to me for about a minute. People with schizophrenia are not physical people; they're usually very distrusting. I stood there thinking to myself, "Wow, he's really hugging me."

Then Jason said to me, "Mum it felt good to get that out." He didn't mean the hug. He meant yelling, "You never wanted me," and no one was saying it wasn't true.

I said, "Jason, you know I love you. Look at all we've been through together." I told him I was glad he felt better by getting out what he had to say and that he had nothing to be sorry about. As he was going through the early days of his illness, he'd sometimes say I didn't love him but now he realized I did love him. The hug told me that.

When I was pregnant with Jason and God didn't allow the abortion, I had a lot of guilt over wanting to end the pregnancy. I never wanted Jason to know I had considered having an abortion. Taking him home from the hospital, not knowing how to be a mother, was the second dishonesty I lived with.

We fool ourselves, not realizing what we hide in our heart comes out through our actions. I wasn't really hiding my feelings from Jason. In fact, the thing I feared I brought to pass. I was afraid he'd know I didn't want a baby, and that's what he felt from me growing up. His sense of being unwanted always needed to be validated.

Next, Jason asked me a question I never thought he'd ask. After he settled down and we got him something to wear, he asked me why I didn't give him up for adoption. As I was running around the kitchen, trying to get prepared for the party, I was stopped dead in my tracks.

I stood in front of Jason and looked directly into his face and said, "Because you were meant to be my son, and I was meant to be your mom." I couldn't have answered it any other way. I told him I wasn't going to give my son to anyone. I was his mother. I didn't ask him why he asked me that question. I guess because we both knew.

I'm sorry now that we didn't talk more after that day, but I felt he understood what happened to us. At the time, I was also sharing more about the neglect I suffered during my childhood. I didn't tell him about the rape or sexual abuse. I felt that with his mental illness, it would be too much for him to process.

I now understand that when Jason was born and my mother stated that she wouldn't help me, I told myself the lie I couldn't be a good mother. I also told myself the lie I was doing something wrong keeping him which I wasn't. I was angry at my parents and took it out on Jason. I also believe having a child triggered the trauma of worrying about Jamie when my parents stopped parenting us and were out drinking instead.

I believe that my parents' abandonment was Satan's entry point into my life. I started to believe God didn't care and began worshipping other things like alcohol, men, and money. I was thirteen when I was trying to discipline Jamie and keep our house together with no heat or food and no one to turn to. Self-reliance was a way to survive, and my mind gave me many solutions to fill the hole in my soul, none of which was from God. When you're still living with that trauma and trying to distract yourself from it, you're not fooling anyone. The truth comes out in the tongue and sometimes in just a look. When a child doesn't get needed attention from a parent, the child feels worthless. When everything else comes before the child—such as alcohol, men, drugs, gambling, work, whatever—they feel like they don't exist.

I've realized that I had narcissistic ways, just like my mother. During his younger years, I did to Jason what my mother did to me: ignored him. I know I affected Jason by being overly concerned about how he looked instead of how he felt. That eventually changed in our relationship. Because of the twelve steps and my relationship with God, I was able to ask him how he was feeling. My mother was never in touch with her own feelings, never mind ours. Since I have some empathy for people, I know I don't have the same limitations my mother had. I believe she had her own hole in her soul, where she felt her own emptiness that she had to fill. Perhaps her impeccably dressed father was the narcissist in her family.

Thank you, Jesus, for the love and healing you've given to Jason and me.

* * *

Greg and I planned a trip to southern California in the spring. We had been there a few times before and enjoyed it immensely. This time, we'd be staying in Santa Monica, right down the street from the pier.

We left the first week in May. Although Greg hates the Hollywood scene, we enjoyed LA. We visited the Warner Bros. lot and were amazed at how uninspiring the sets appeared in cinder block buildings. God bless the TV actors going in there to film each season; it was just depressing to me. While Greg and I were driving on the freeway one day, I almost had a panic attack. My anxiety on open highways was still there, regardless of whether I was driving or Greg was. I was frustrated that the anxiety was still with me. I knew it stemmed from a wrongful belief I was holding on to, and I wanted it to go away so I could be free again. When Greg drove up Mulholland Drive, I freaked out and made him drive back down. I couldn't believe that people drive up there at night with no barriers on the side of the roads.

Jason took care of himself while we traveled, and I checked in with him regularly. The Friday night before we got home, he said he was thinking of ordering the boxing matches. He struggled to pay off his cable bill, so I told him it might be a better idea to wait until next week and see it for free rather than to pay the high cost for HBO. He called and told me that when he was about to order the fight, my stepbrother Bobby invited him to a relative's house to watch it instead. I was happy for Jason and thanked Bobby for inviting him.

There weren't many people Jason often spent time with. He had lost many of his friends, but he made new ones over the years, and they were the people he could trust. They included Greg and Daniel and Gail from the counseling center Jason loved. Jason was very wary of new people. He liked going with Greg to the cigar store. He felt safe because of Greg's presence. He also liked going to the gym at the Erich Lindemann Center in Boston, where he would talk with the staff.

Jason loved watching boxing matches with my stepbrother Bobby and the rest of his family. During the fights, they teased Jason because he commented a lot and wouldn't stop talking. It was all in good fun, and Jason would laugh and appreciate the attention. He knew boxing better than anyone, and just like with basketball, he could tell you the history of the games and how many rounds a boxer had gone in a previous fight. He was unbelievably knowledgeable about the sports he loved. He was a man's man for sure.

Years back, I took Jason to see a Chicago Bulls game in Boston, and he forgot his eyeglasses. We're both nearsighted. I was mad at him, but I gave him my glasses so he could see better. Jason had loyalty to a player, not a team. He loved to watch Michael Jordan, when he stopped playing with the Bulls and signed with the Washington Wizards, he rooted for them. When Lebron James came on the scene, Jason followed him like he did Michael Jordan. I took him to a Cleveland game in Boston about five years ago, and I told Jason to keep it down because he was rooting for Cleveland instead of the Celtics. I was just teasing him; I didn't really care. He laughed when I said that. My husband and Jason's friends told him that in boxing he liked the thugs. He loved Mike Tyson and Floyd Mayweather. Jason was disappointed when Mayweather hit his wife and went to jail. He was thrilled though when Floyd got out and tried to make a comeback. Jason also loved to watch the Bulls Classics on television. He remembered all the games and scores.

Greg and I returned from California the day before Mother's Day, 2013. The next day, I picked him up for church. He had spent most of his money while we were away, and I was disappointed he had done that.

I asked him, "What came over you to buy so much takeout food?"

He said, "I don't know, Mum. I messed up."

He had about forty dollars left to get through the rest of the month, along with his food stamp money, which was about a hundred dollars. While driving through the McDonald's drive-through to get our coffees, he handed me my Mother's Day card. He wanted to let me know that although he went crazy with his money, he made sure he bought me a card and a gift. I opened the card and found a McDonald's gift card for ten dollars.

I said, "Thank you, Jason. And of course, I will be spending it on you anyway since we're going through the drive-through now." He started laughing. I told him how grateful I was to have him as my son and how I was grateful that we were friends as adults.

I still have almost every card Jason gave me. He always wrote a note and added a smiley face. When I asked him why he added the smiley face to his signature, he shrugged and said, "I don't know." I guess it was his way of telling others to be happy. Some things come naturally to people. Jason's spirit led him to sign with this symbol.

One of the things Greg helped Jason with is reminding him to buy me a card on special occasions. In those cards, Jason apologized many times for not getting me cards in the past. He told me once he thought I didn't care if I got a card because I never said anything about it. It was true. I'd be hurt, but I also felt undeserving of his love. I didn't want anything from him but his love, which I thought I had to earn, due to my guilt. Jason just wanted his mom. He didn't care about anything else either.

Jason understood more now about the relationship I had with my own parents, the neglect we endured growing up in Chelsea, and why I acted like I did toward him. Right before we left for California while helping him clean his house, I explained all the responsibilities I had growing up. I took Jason to an Al-Anon meeting in Melrose and an adult child meeting in Arlington. I wanted him to hear from people who grew up with untreated alcoholism and how they were taking care of themselves. Jason was one of those people, just like me.

There was a time when I'd do anything to prevent Jason from making me look bad. It was more important now to live in the truth and see Jason heal from the wounds I played a part in creating. Jason never got into going to Al-Anon, but we talked as much as we could about our feelings and behaviors. I felt at times like I was a sponsor to Jason, and I was fine with that. He had Daniel, his therapist, to vent things he felt regarding me. I wasn't afraid for him to talk with people and tell them how crazy his mother could be. I knew God was with us.

Chapter 12

The weekend before Memorial Day, we had dinner at the home of Carol and Peter Beatrice. Carol was the real estate agent we had used a few times, and her husband Pete is a client of mine. She knew Jason from when we were looking for homes to buy in Swampscott. She was always gracious with him, and I appreciated that from her and her family. When you're a mother who has a child with a mental illness, it means the world to be around people who accept him for who he is, a human being.

I was still periodically taking my mother to the hospital in Boston. She was getting better, and I felt I had done the right thing by assisting her with her appointments. I was learning a lot more about myself being around her, especially in how I interacted with Jason. God was mirroring my behavior back to me through my mother's behavior.

My mother was still all about how we looked. She worried about what other people thought of her and was preoccupied with keeping up a good appearance, but it was all smoke and mirrors. I realized the way I eyeballed Jason up and down, as I had done at my party that day, was exactly what my mother did to me. As long as he showered and was clean, I needed to keep my mouth shut.

On the Friday morning of Memorial Day weekend, 2013, Jason called to see if he could ride along with me on my business calls. Occasionally, if he had nothing to do for the day, he'd keep me company in the car. If I had to go to places farther away, like Andover, I didn't bring him. I didn't want him to see me freeze with my driving anxiety. However, he knew I was experiencing it, and that was bringing us closer together.

I picked Jason up, and we headed out to Lynn so I could see my customers. I told him we'd work, and then I would participate in a conference call at two o'clock. After my call, we'd have lunch at Dube's, a seafood place in Salem, a couple of towns over. Then we'd go food shopping in Salem at Market Basket. He didn't care what I had to do; he just wanted to spend the day with me.

When we discussed plans for his birthday coming up on June 1, Jason asked if Greg and I could take him to the sushi restaurant on Route 1 in Saugus. I said, "Jason, wherever you want to go." I figured I'd get him a gift card at Market Basket, along with dinner.

I saw my customers in Lynn, then headed over to Salem so I could park and make my conference call. It was pouring while we sat in the car and I listened to my sales director. The sales team had no idea what the call was going to be about, and at first, I really wasn't worried about it.

The manager said there was a complaint from an unknown source about a sales rep. I guess they made a negative comment out in the field regarding something in the industry. Our manager said to call her right away if any of us thought we may have been the subject of the complaint.

I panicked right away that I may have done something wrong. I was very upset as I walked into the restaurant with Jason. I was obsessed with the fact I might have done something that made my company look bad and hurt my boss Tom. My being caught up in fear was weighing heavy on Jason. My self-centeredness was getting the best of me.

Poor Jason had to listen to me for the next two hours. He didn't even understand what I was talking about. I couldn't enjoy my time with him because I was feeding into my fear. We finished our lunch, and off to Market Basket we went. I called Karen, my coworker, about the incident, and we talked the entire time I was shopping. While I paid for our groceries at the register, I was still on the phone. The tenth step in AA teaches us that when fear comes up, we are not to entertain it but to ask God to "remove it" right away. Of course,

I didn't do that. I was actually magnifying the fear by talking about it incessantly.

After shopping, I finally got off the phone and drove Jason home. I'm sure he was glad to get away from me that day. I went to my six o'clock in the evening class at the gym. Working out has a way of getting you out of yourself, and I certainly needed it that night. The next day was Saturday, and since Jason and I had already done our food shopping, I took it easy in the morning and then went to my Al-Anon meeting in Revere. I felt nurtured there, which I truly needed.

On Sunday morning, I got a call from Jason saying he wanted to come to church. My response was "Jason, you should come to church because you want to, not because you have nothing else to do." At the time, I thought he was using me because he had no money left and couldn't do much outside of his house. I so regret saying that to him now. In fact, Greg sometimes planned other things to do on Sunday mornings, and Jason said he felt bad that I was going alone and that he liked going with me. I said, "I know you do. I'll pick you up at ten." Although it would've been nice if Greg came with us more often, I enjoyed my time alone with Jason.

Memorial Day came, and I had plans to walk with my friend Harlene, an elementary school teacher I had met a few years back at the gym. It was a sunny, bright, puffy-cloud day; and we took a long walk on Revere Beach. I was still caught up in the issue at work, and I asked for her advice. After we parted ways, I thought I'd go home and run my treadmill. We had walked about three miles, so I decided to run another three and make it an even six. Exercise has been a constant in my life since I stopped smoking in 1993.

Jason also started to work out more at the Lindemann Center in Boston. He'd take the train and walk the treadmill in their gym. I used to give him a hard time about wearing jeans on the treadmill because they'd give him a rash. Of course, I'd get an "I'm okay, Mum." I just wanted him to be more comfortable, but he was his own person. I was happy he was working out and taking care of himself, God bless him. I'd recently noticed he lost a little weight, and I told him what a great job he was doing.

About nine thirty that evening, before going to bed, I asked my husband if he had heard from Jason. He said he hadn't, so I said, "I'm going to give him a call." Jason's phone rang and rang, with no answer. I thought it was kind of odd because Jason usually takes his meds around eight thirty, and then if I called, he'd answer the phone in a tired voice. If he didn't answer, I'd get nervous, and Greg would tell me, "He's fine." This night, I said, "God, I'm giving Jason to you. I'm not going to be afraid," and I went to bed.

A few minutes later, I felt an odd pain in my chest. It was noticeable enough to mention to Greg, and he asked if I wanted to go to the hospital. It was a dead pain—quick, heavy, and sharp. I've never felt it before or since. I'd frequently think of this moment after the events of the next day unfolded.

* * *

When I woke the next morning, it was a bright, sunny Tuesday, and I did my morning routine: coffee, Bible reading, and meditation. Still no call from Jason, but I was letting it go. I took a shower, drove to a popular donut place in Saugus, and picked up some goodies for the clients I was visiting that day. I was in a really good mood that morning. I felt like some bondage had been taken from my spirit and God was truly taking care of things. It was about ten o'clock in the morning when I arrived at my client's place of business. He mentioned how nicely I was dressed, and I said, "I feel good today." We talked for some time, and as I left, I told him I'd stop across the street to visit another one of their offices.

As I was leaving, I saw that it was almost eleven thirty in the morning. I thought, "That's not like Jason to not call me this morning." I wasn't panicking, but I called him again. No answer. Sometimes he'd sleep all day, and I thought maybe that's what he was doing. Maybe he felt bad that he had no money. I didn't want him to be stuck in the house, so I stopped at an ATM to withdraw forty dollars—twenty dollars for me and twenty for Jason to go out and enjoy the day. I had forgotten he had therapy on Tuesdays with Daniel.

As I rang Jason's bell, I noticed the maintenance man standing in the hallway near the door. I asked if he knew Jason. The man said he did, but he hadn't seen him today. I told him I was going up to his apartment because I was worried about him. The janitor replied, "If you can't get in, let me know."

I went up to the third floor to Jason's apartment and knocked on the door. I was yelling his name. I could hear the air conditioner, which told me he was there. He'd never leave the air conditioner on when he was out, due to his OCD. I headed back into the elevator to get the maintenance man to let me in. I was growing more concerned. The maintenance man opened the door, and I said to him, "I really don't want to walk in here right now."

I looked straight ahead and saw Jason's sneakers. I proceeded into his bedroom, which was to the left, and saw him on the floor on the right side of the bed. He was lying between the bed and the wall with his head at the foot of the bed, wearing only his boxers. I ran around him to look at his face, screaming his name, hoping he was okay. He was on his back, with his arms straight out, and I could see dried blood coming from his mouth and his nose. I touched his left arm, and I knew he was gone. I noticed the bit of gauze taped on his arm from getting his blood drawn that week. I was only there with him for five seconds when I ran out of the room into the hallway, screaming for the maintenance man to call 911.

For some reason, I hadn't brought my phone with me, which I don't think I could have dialed anyway. I was on the floor in the hallway, on my hands and knees like a dog, circling around, screaming to God, "Why didn't you take me instead?" I had been so selfish my whole life. I knew in my heart while I was screaming that I couldn't tell God what to do. In my mind, I was saying, "It's over between Jason and me." I couldn't help but think while scrambling around on my hands and knees of what the Bible says, "Therefore we are always confident and know that as long as we are at home in the body we are away from the Lord" (2 Corinthians 5:6–7). I knew Jason was not in that room; he was with God. I continued screaming at the maintenance man because it seemed like it took forever for the ambulance to get there.

Three women standing at the end of the hallway tried to comfort me from a distance, and one asked if there was someone else I wanted to call. I had her dial Greg's office, and she told him it was an emergency. Greg's office was ten minutes away from Jason's house, so he was there rather quickly. By the time he got there, the police and paramedics had arrived, and he walked in to see Jason. I was thinking, "Why don't I have any tears coming from my eyes? Do I not care?" No, I was in shock and didn't realize it.

When the paramedics went in, I had a small piece of hope that maybe Jason was still alive, but I already knew from touching his arm that he was gone. The police came mostly to make sure there was no foul play, which there wasn't. The one moment I'll never forget was the callous way one of the paramedics came out to tell me Jason was no longer with us. I was on the floor in the hallway when he grabbed my shoulder, looked straight into my face, and said, "He's gone," with a very stern look and tone of voice. I know I was distraught, but that was an awful way to tell a mother her son was dead. He could have approached me and said, "Are you his mother? I'm sorry, but your son has passed away." I wanted to call the ambulance service and complain about how cold the paramedic was to me, but I never did. I told myself, "What's the use? My son is gone, and that complaint won't bring him back."

When Greg and I got in the elevator to drive home, I was hysterical. Right before entering Winthrop, I asked him to stop at Constitution Beach in East Boston because I couldn't go home. I just found my son dead, and what, I go home now like nothing had happened? I really didn't know what to do with myself. Greg pulled over at the beach, and I told him to call my boss at the glass company. Greg told Tom about Jason, and that was the beginning of a huge series of calls Greg made to notify everyone of Jason's death. I couldn't think straight. I wanted to jump out of my skin. It was a hot day, with the temperature in the mid-eighties. The humidity, along with the anguish I was feeling, made me want to scream.

Greg got us home, and when we arrived, our contractor, Buzzy, was working on our kitchen, which he started while we were in California. The first floor was blown out, so we were living on the second floor where the bedrooms are and in the finished basement, which had a full kitchen and bath that we could use during the construction. When I walked in crying hysterically, Buzzy didn't know what was going on until Greg told him what had happened. His boss called to tell him to leave the house.

I went upstairs to our bedroom and sat on a little bench we have, just wailing with sadness. I had just recently been asking God to heal Jason's mind. I had also been asking God to help me have more patience with Jason's illness and to love him more. Since I had been attending church again for the last few years and going to Bible study every week, God had been showing me more changes I needed to make. And now Jason was dead? Jason was my family. He was all I had since my brother Jamie passed. They were the only two people in my family I felt truly loved me, and now they were both gone. I loved my brother, but losing a son and the love from a child is like no other loss.

That night, after Greg made more phone calls, we finally went to bed, or I should say we went into bed. How do you go to bed after you just found your son dead? You don't turn on the television. You lie there and talk to your husband through the tears and heartache that neither he nor God can take away. I said to Greg, "Even God can't bring Jason back to me here on earth." It was a sobering thought. I wasn't yelling why because I knew I had no right to ask that question. Some readers may think, "What are you talking about? You're not wondering how your thirty-year-old son died?" Of course, I wanted to know how he died, but I knew I may never get that answer. I thought of my sister-in-law Roseanne after she lost her daughter Adrianna, asking God why and demanding he tell her when she came before him one day. I couldn't go down that road. I felt for her, and now it was my turn to feel the heartache she and her husband felt since their daughter's death.

The weeks to come would be grueling with pain, but we had the love of my husband's family and our friends. We sat in the yard since we had no first floor during the remodeling, but God was good and gave us good weather. I still couldn't believe Jason was gone. The day after I found him, I was sitting in the yard looking out at the water when a thought came to my mind, "Aren't you glad I'm gone, Mum? You didn't want me anyway." I cried out loud to God that I loved Jason, and that wasn't true. I knew the thought was from Satan, trying to condemn me for my sins of the past, but I had learned enough in my walk with God that I wasn't going to condemn myself. I knew God and Jason had forgiven me. It was my unwillingness to forgive myself that was still lingering.

I couldn't imagine my life without Jason. All the guilt of being impatient with his illness came rushing into my head. The thought I always had—that I could lose him—had come true. Greg reminded me that I always worried something bad would happen to him in that apartment. He said, "You never thought he'd be mugged or hit by a bus." He too was surprised that my fear had come true. I was sad that Jason had passed away alone in his home, but as time went on, I realized he wasn't alone. God was with him. I would have done anything to have saved him that night, but I couldn't. I thought of the odd feeling in my chest the night before I found him. I believe that my heart broke the moment he died. I believe that at that moment, Jason was gone from here and was with the Lord. That pain was the ache of a loss I didn't know had taken place. My husband isn't one to believe in these things, but he too felt that conviction.

I was ever so grateful that Jason and I spent two days together that weekend, thanks to him calling and asking me. The last day we were together, we went to church and then stopped by my mother's in Chelsea. Candy kept jumping on Jason and pulling at his belt. Jason loved animals but wasn't comfortable with them when they were out of control. I didn't blame him.

I'll never forget my last moment with him. What we said to each other was so important. I dropped him off at his house, and as he walked away from my car, I was looking down at my phone. I glanced quickly at him as I saw him walking toward his building, and we said, "I love you" to each other. Usually, day or night, I waited to make sure he was secure in his building before I drove away. That day, I didn't watch him walk in because I was so obsessed with that nonsense at work. Little did I know that would be the last time I'd see him alive. As I write this and relive those moments, I have to type through the tears of wanting to redo that moment again. I'd have so many more memories rushing back in the days to come, both good and bad. I was only in the beginning of my grief for losing my son's love here on earth. I knew I'd always have him in my heart, but that doesn't take away the pain.

* * *

Greg was my rock during this time. We had to find a funeral home for Jason's service. I never dreamed I'd someday have to arrange funeral services for my only child. As I said, I had a trust in place for Jason. It has been said, children are supposed to bury their parents, not the other way around. If events had followed the natural order and I died before him, there would have been funds for him and someone trustworthy to manage them. If I died before Greg, he'd have taken care of Jason, and I felt completely comfortable with that. There was no one in my immediate family whom I could trust or who had a relationship with my son. My stepbrother Bobby would be the beneficiary when Greg and I were gone. I discussed these arrangements with Jason, but he didn't want to talk about death. It didn't matter anyway because Jason had now gone home to be with Jesus, before Greg and me. I said to Greg, "We do not own our children. They are loaned to us from God." I encountered that idea years ago in Khalil Gibran's book *The Prophet.*

Greg and I went to the same funeral home in Chelsea that we used for Jamie's services. The date of the funeral was important to me. My son died on Tuesday, May 28, and his birthday was the coming Saturday, June 1. He would have been thirty-one years old. I couldn't have his service on his birthday, so we needed to have it on Sunday night, with the funeral on Monday, June 3. Unfortunately, after telling Greg on the phone that the days we requested were available, when we got to the funeral home, the owners changed their tune. I was livid to say the least. I needed this nonsense like I needed a hole in the head. The young man tried to sell us their other venue down the street, so Greg and I went to look at it. I walked in and immediately said, "Forget it." It was very dated, and I didn't like the way the owners tried to manipulate the dates in order to salvage our business. Now the owner was suggesting we skip a day after the viewing and have the funeral two days later. It was ridiculous what he was doing to get business. I was disgusted.

Greg suggested a place in Winthrop that my brother-in-law had some business connection to. As soon as I walked in, I knew this also was not the place for my son. The interior was dated. I wanted a place with more brightness since Jason was so young. After thanking the funeral director for meeting us, I walked out so quickly I forgot my pocketbook.

My husband then suggested Vazza Beechwood Funeral Home, a place in Revere I had been to in the past and I thought was nice. The furnishings and design weren't as dated, and the bathrooms were remodeled. The room where wakes are held has an entire wall with engraved scripture from the Bible and a beautiful outline of Mary and Jesus. Greg knew the owner, and upon meeting him, I felt connected to him right away. Louie was an Italian man, about eighty years old, with a tan and "I'll take good care of you" attitude. He told me he too had only one son, whom he was very close with. That statement alone made me feel this was where we belonged.

We selected a casket, and Louie was kind and practical about everything. We decided to have my pastor from Trinity Evangelical officiate in the funeral home. Greg, my friend Susan, Jason's therapist Daniel, and I would speak that day. I had to be there for my son and make sure he had a beautiful service. The truth of our relationship would be spoken that day. Jason deserved that.

* * *

I think the hardest part for me was to buy Jason's clothes to be buried in. Greg came with me, and we were lost walking around the store. I had shopped for Jamie's burial clothes alone, but I couldn't do this for my son without Greg by my side. He stayed with me through everything while feeling his own pain from losing Jason. I tried my best to remember to comfort him too. Although Greg wasn't Jason's biological father, I knew Greg loved Jason.

We bought Jason a green short-sleeved collared shirt and a pair of black dress pants, along with a pair of shoes. We didn't want to dress him in a suit because that's not who he was. In the same way, I had dressed my brother Jamie in a motorcycle jacket because that's what he loved. Jason's appearance had always been about me and what I liked, but not now. Jason's life would be honored and remembered in such a way that if you didn't know him before, you would after the funeral.

Greg and I went to find a plot for Jason at the cemetery. I wanted him buried, not cremated, so I could visit him. We went to Woodlawn Cemetery in Everett, just down the street from where I lived when Jason was born. The salesman directed us to an area of the cemetery in the back where new graves were available. In one section, the graves have three plots, for couples like us who have only one child and may need to bury their child with them. We chose the first grave on the end, near the road, under a small tree on Richardson's Way.

In the days that followed, many people came to our house to be with us. We got all kinds of plants and flowers from friends, family, coworkers, and clients. My good friend Stacey, who became my sponsor in AA in 2012, dropped everything and ran over to my house, as did my good friend and massage therapist Ketna. A beautiful Haitian woman with a smile that can light up a room, Ketna knew all my history with Jason. She had listened intently over the years, giving me love and biblical guidance.

I was surprised I was okay with people coming over because, in the past, I wouldn't have wanted anyone near me while I was in such pain. Being an adult child, you really don't know how to accept love because you're used to working for it. But I had grown enough in my walk with God to know I needed people with me who were safe. I felt truly loved by their immediate response to want to be near me. Some people act strange when a person loses a child. They don't know what to do. After going through this loss, I can assure you that doing nothing is not the answer.

The following night was Wednesday, Bible study night. Of course, I wasn't going, but my pastor asked if he could bring my study group by the house to pray with us. I said, "Of course. I'd really appreciate it."

I can't tell you how grateful I was to be connected to a church and a group of people who would do something so kind. I was pleased that Greg's family was at the house when the church group arrived because I wanted my husband's family to see how the group conducted themselves as Christians. They arrived with all kinds of food and comforted us with their love. I felt loved and cared for, and I know that's what they wanted to achieve because that's what Jesus would have done. By being there, they also reminded me that I was a Christian, as was Jason, and that this life on earth was not the end. I was also grateful they didn't downplay my pain because even Christians sometimes do that. They say, "Well, he's in a better place"—which I believe is true, but it doesn't take away the grief of losing your child.

People who were not believers also made that statement to me. They don't know what or where the better place is; it just sounds good to say to the bereaved. I'd rather hear "I'm sorry for your loss, and I can't imagine what you're going through," which sounds more genuine. I'd hear many hurtful and inconsiderate statements in the months to come. I have to believe people don't know any better, and I have to forgive them. I've had my own ignorance to work on.

Along with my stepbrother Bobby, Greg's family continued to visit every day. My friend Susan came from Atlanta on Thursday, before the services, and prayed with me. Her sister, Jodi, was also there. My friends checked in every day to make sure I was okay, and Stacey was frequently by my side. The talking helped, although no one except for my in-laws, Roseanne and John, had any idea what I was going through. My biological family, specifically my mother and my two brothers, were not there. They were showing me who they really were again, people who were unable to be there for me.

God demonstrated to me early and often that he had my son. The first time was when I was on the first floor of my house and the doorbell rang. When I opened the door, I saw a florist's delivery man walking toward the front door carrying an arrangement.

I said, "Excuse me, sir. I'm right here." Then I looked at him again and said, "I know you from somewhere."

He looked puzzled. Then I noticed his shirt was imprinted with the logo Trinity Evangelical.

I said, "We go to the same church. I see you walking up for prayer sometimes." The man's name was Craig. He lived in Revere, and we both drive to a church twenty-five minutes away to be fed spiritually. After I told Craig about Jason, I hugged him and said, "You were supposed to come here today so God could assure me my son was safe with him." I gave my testimony about Craig with every-one who came to the house. I was grateful God had used someone from my church to comfort me.

Another way God comforted me was by showing me smiley faces, like the ones Jason made when he signed a card. Greg and I decided to order our flowers from a place in Chelsea, not too far from the glass company. I knew Valerie, the owner, and her husband, and I felt comfortable going to them with such a tender loss. One of their children was there, all grown up, and from his appearance, it seemed he was transgender. On the counter was a cup with a smiley face asking for donations for his operation. I glanced at it but didn't notice the smiley face until my husband pointed it out. Damian was gentle and loving while helping us order the flowers, and he showed us more of his loving spirit when the flowers arrived at the funeral home.

* * *

I was in another world, and all I could think about was Jason and the insightful conversations we'd have. All I could see were shad-ows of my son shopping with me and sitting in my car talking. All I could do was cry when I thought of him. I knew crying was healing. I knew I needed to get the grief out of me.

The grief process, as I've read, involves denial, then anger, then acceptance. My mind knew Jason was dead, but I frequently shook my head back and forth as if I were saying no to God. Emotionally, I was trying to deny the truth. What anchored me in reality was finding Jason lying on the floor that day. I believe I was the only one Jason would've wanted to have found him. Apparently, God did too. The image of Jason on the floor was one I couldn't get out of my head for a long time, especially at night when I'd lie quiet. Greg would lie next to me and hear me wail with grief and sadness over the power-lessness of not being able to bring Jason back.

I read in the Bible about King David and how he lost his first child. David committed adultery with his best friend's wife, Bathsheba, and the baby they had together died. When his son was sick, David fasted as a sacrifice and prayed for God to heal his child, but God didn't. After the baby died, David praised God, and the Bible says he ate generously. David knew his son couldn't come to him; he'd have to go to his son (2 Samuel 12:22–23). I knew God couldn't bring Jason back either; in order to be reunited, I would have to go to Jason.

Greg took me to the mall to pick up something to wear for the wake and funeral. I felt like I had been hit by a Mack truck. I read later about the physical exhaustion you feel when you lose a child. The pain was hard when I lost my brother Jamie, but this was excruciating.

Before Jason passed, I'd get on my knees in the bathroom and praise God, then pray for people I cared about, and ask forgiveness for any ungodly acts I did that day. Now I was on my knees at night, crying out to God to get me through this time and to get me through Jason's funeral service in a way that honored Jason's life.

God told Joshua, in Joshua 1:9, "Have I not commanded you? Be strong and courageous. Do not be afraid; do not be discouraged, for the LORD your God will be with you wherever you go." That was one of the first stories I learned at Bible study as a young born-again Christian trying to learn and follow God's Word. I needed that courage desperately now.

Chapter 13

The wake was scheduled for Sunday night. I told Greg I'd like to go to church that morning to get support from other believers, which was the best thing I could have done. When we walked in, Pastor Ray asked us to come up to the altar so the congregation could pray over us. He told everyone that we had just lost our only son and asked if they could come up and "love on us," as he put it. What happened next was another message that God was with me, that he had my son, and that he was in control.

A courageous, outgoing seven-year-old boy whom I saw at church every week but never spoken to was the first person to come up. He walked up to me, when I had such grief on my face, and told me my son was in heaven like his grandfather and then hugged me. I started crying and felt like I was hugging my own little boy in heaven. I learned later that the little boy's name was Kaleb, which in Hebrew means "wholehearted" or brave. In Numbers 13:30, Caleb was one of the twelve spies who went into Canaan. When he returned to Kadesh, he said to the people before Moses, "We should go up and take possession of the land, for we can certainly do it." He was not giving any power to the giants they saw in the land that day. This young boy at church was well named. He was a courageous boy who gave encouragement to others.

That is how God works, through people who love and know him. In the months following Jason's death, Kaleb would run up and hug me during the greeting time. One day, he looked at me and gestured for me to smile. I knew again God was letting Jason speak to me through the smiley faces. After getting through the service that morning, we stopped at a coffee shop to pass some time before going to the funeral home for the wake. I was anxious at the prospect of seeing my son lying in a casket. Still, I knew nothing could be more devastating than finding Jason dead, an image that haunted my thoughts every night before I fell asleep. Only God's grace could get me through these days, along with support and love from my husband, friends, and family.

The week after Jason passed, I thought a lot about him as a baby and myself as the mother of a baby. As I was taking a shower, I looked down at my vagina, where God allowed Jason to come through me to enter this world. It was a strange feeling. I felt like God was reminding me of the privilege he had given me to carry one of his children.

I had had abortions before and after I gave birth to Jason, and although God has forgiven me for those acts, I couldn't help but regret my carelessness and the consequences those unborn babies paid. I know the children I aborted are in heaven with Jason now. He'll have siblings there to meet him, and I will see them all in heaven. I knew I had to stay close to God and in God's Word. If not, I'd be torturing myself with self-condemnation, and the Bible tells us not to engage in that. "Therefore there is now no condemnation for those who are in Christ Jesus" (Romans 8:1). The enemy, Satan, was lurking close by, and he'd feed off my weakness to keep me from God and his Word. But he wasn't going to have his way with me this time. As sad as I was and despite the pain I was in, I knew better. I'd be a great trophy for him if he led me away from God's kingdom. I had to continue on to do whatever work God planned for me in the future.

We walked into the funeral home. Jason was in the first room on the right. I hesitated a minute before walking over to the casket, and then I saw his face. He looked just like himself, with his youthful round face and wavy light-brown hair. He didn't have his glasses on because I had left them in the apartment. I regretted telling the funeral director I didn't want Jason to wear the glasses since he wore them daily. That was me being controlling again. I noticed there was a little red mark on the inside of his arm. The funeral director saw it right away and took care of it. I asked him to cut a piece of Jason's hair for me. The funeral staff was very caring, and I felt safe having

Jason's service there. A little compassion goes a long way in such times.

The staff pointed out that Damian had made something for me. He was the young man from the flower shop who was collecting donations for his sex-reassignment surgery in a smiley cup. It was a smiley face made of blue carnations, with a beautiful letter attached to it. I was touched by this young man's compassion for a woman he didn't know. You never know who will be there for you.

Greg had put together an array of pictures for a video. The photos showed Jason with everyone who meant something to him. I went over to watch it and hear the songs I chose to play for background music. One was "You and Me Against the World," sung by Helen Reddy. I felt that way a lot since Jason and I had gone through so much when he got sick. Another was "The Wind Beneath My Wings," sung by Bette Midler. Jason had watched *Beaches*, the movie this song is from, shortly before he died. Jason had a lot of compassion. He stood in my kitchen, telling me how he cried his eyes out watching it. I said, "I know, Jason, those movies are sad." Since the little girl in the movie loses her mom, I wondered if he was thinking about my death and how he'd feel when I died. I know he thought I was the one who kept him going, but it was actually the opposite that was true.

These moments at my son's wake were surreal. I along with Greg, Susan, my brother-in-law Michael, and Bobby were in the receiving line next to the casket. A couple of my friends brought little tokens of comfort to give me while passing through. Next to the casket, I had placed a picture of Jason and me, taken from behind while walking on Deer Island in Winthrop the prior October. It showed the blue sky ahead of us on a sunny crisp day, with the boats in the harbor on the horizon. I told everyone it was Jason and me walking into heaven together. The photo couldn't have been more fitting for the service.

As everyone was coming and going, I was surprised I remembered all their names. Pastor Gus and Craig, the man who came to my house with the flower delivery, were there, sitting in the back of the room, being supportive Christians. A couple of people came who

I really didn't expect to see, including my ex-boyfriend Jesse's mom, Neva. She hadn't changed much since the last time I saw her. She smiled and hugged me as I introduced her to my husband. Seven years of dating Jesse meant seven years of a relationship with his family that my son was a part of. Neva smiled and said how young Jason still looked. She remembered him as a little boy, playing with his toys at her home in New Hampshire. We had been a family, something I didn't experience much as a child, but I was glad Jason did. Neva said Jesse would be at the funeral the next day. I was glad because Jason was close to Jesse growing up and was deeply affected by our breakup.

My childhood friends Lisa, Marla, and Lisa S. came with their significant others, as did Susan's family and my close friends from AA and Al-Anon. Greg's clients and mine stopped by to express their condolences. To say the least, it was an emotional and draining night, and I knew we still had the funeral service ahead of us the next day.

A few people asked about the cause of death, but I knew from talking with other people and hearing about the volume of case overloads at the coroner's office that six months could pass before I'd know. I think most people assumed Jason died from natural causes because he no longer drank or used drugs.

As the service came to an end, I spent some time alone with Jason at his casket. I rested my head on his arm while the music played, knowing our time together was ending. Soon I would no longer see his face or touch his body. The importance of being a mom, how our children are a part of our flesh in a way no one else can be, became much clearer to me. Jason had been a part of me, and now I had to let him go. "Absent from the body, present with the Lord," I reminded myself constantly.

When it was time to leave the wake, I thought how nice it was to have Jason's pictures being shown with the music playing in the background. I had felt connected to him all night, and I truly felt the Holy Spirit there among us, giving support and love to all who visited. My husband was staying close to me while dealing with his own pain. I asked God that night to give me a good night's sleep because I didn't want to be tired for Jason's farewell. Since it had been almost a week since he passed and Satan wanted to keep the image of the moment I found Jason in the forefront of my mind, I asked God for peace.

Susan prayed for all of us that evening at the house. I was praying in tongues for peace in my heart and the grace to get through the next day. I needed whatever supernatural power I could get. As Paul said, "He said to me, 'My grace is sufficient for you, for my power is made perfect in weakness.' Therefore I will boast all the more gladly in my weaknesses, so that Christ's power may rest on me" (2 Corinthians 12:9). In other words, I don't need anything to bring me relief, like drinking, eating, gambling, whatever people may do. God's grace would get me through this.

The next day would be my last day with Jason, and his funeral would be one most people wouldn't forget. They'd learn about who Jason was, our relationship with each other, and how the truth can set you free. It was my responsibility to honor Jason by witnessing what he dealt with on a daily basis, his triumphs and struggles, along with his relationship with his not-so-fearless mother. I wrote down some topics I wanted to talk about in the eulogy, but I knew I'd probably end up praying and asking God to say what he wanted me to say. Before I went to bed, I spoke to Jason. I promised him I'd be honest, not worry about what people thought, and just tell the truth.

* * *

Greg and I woke early the next day to be at the service by nine o'clock in the morning. My close friends were there once again to support us on such a sad day. My pastor came with his wife, Trish, and she sang "Amazing Grace." I was happy they were there. I needed believers around me to remind me of the hope I'd need to hold on to in the years ahead, for whatever time God allowed me to remain here on earth. When I looked up, it was nice to see Daniel, Marybeth, and Gail—people who knew Jason well from the counseling center in Cambridge. Marybeth had originally known Jason from the Castle School. Gail worked the center's front desk. She had a way of talking with Jason and "calling him on his stuff," as she worded it, which Jason found comical because he knew it was true.

My son trusted Daniel and had been visiting him for more than ten years. When Daniel walked in, I felt a love for him because he represented my son's true self. Seeing these people from Castle and the counseling center took me back to Jason's childhood. I felt close to Jason when I saw them because they had been on the road with him longer than anybody.

I had called my mother earlier in the morning, but she didn't answer her phone. She had come to the wake but left early. She sat in the front row and hadn't said anything other than that her tailbone was bothering her. When I looked at her, she looked like a child. She had nothing to offer me emotionally. Jodi had been nice enough to give Ma a ride to the wake. Now Ma was nowhere to be found. I knew she wasn't feeling her best, but I never dreamed she wouldn't come to her grandson's funeral. I learned later that she was out shopping for groceries. She could have been dead, but I couldn't worry about that; I had to concentrate on my son.

My two biological brothers, Todd and Wayne, didn't attend either. One phone call came from Wayne in North Carolina. He sounded like he had been drinking. He said, "We're not supposed to bury our kids," or something of that nature and a few more things. I don't remember what they were. I didn't want to talk with him, as I sensed he was feeling good. I was polite, but I said, "Thank you, Wayne, for calling. I have to go." I never heard from him or his wife again. But who am I to judge? Who knows what I would have done if I hadn't gotten sober and had not found God?

Maya Angelou says, "When people show you who they are, believe them the first time." I learned a version of that saying from a friend, but the "first time" part I didn't know and I had to learn. The important truth is to believe what you are experiencing, not what you'd like to see happen.

What did I expect? Alcoholism and narcissism run deep in my family, so needless to say, I had no immediate family at the funeral. As a matter of fact, I had no blood relatives there. I would have to forgive my mother and my brothers, but I can tell you, it was very hard to understand. I've come to accept there was no love in our family. How can you know love when you don't know God? I used to tell Jason all the time God is love. He and I had love, and we both had God.

We decided that Daniel would speak first, then Susan, followed by Greg, and I'd be last. The room was filled with many kind faces. I felt the Holy Spirit there and the pure love of God. Jason had people there who truly loved him. Pastor Ray got up and said a few words and then introduced Daniel. It touched me to see Daniel standing there next to Jason's casket—a man Jason spoke with every week, who Jason considered his friend. My heart melted when he spoke of Jason because he knew my son well.

Daniel said Jason had great insight, which he did. He spoke of Jason's relationship with his illness and the day-to-day struggles he had to overcome. He said Jason was happy, which was all I ever wanted for him. Daniel talked about the time he spent with Jason each week and how Jason loved to stop by the local pizza shop in Cambridge and order his Cuban sandwich. As Daniel and Jason bonded, they talked about video games, movies, and other fun things; but most importantly, Daniel validated Jason's emotions. I never dreamed I'd see Daniel speaking at Jason's funeral, never in a million years. But I was grateful.

Next was Susan, my friend of over forty years. As Jason's god-mother, Susan had spoken with Jason the year before, when I called to tell her Jason just gave his life to Christ in church. Now Susan told the story of my boiling Jason's clothes when he was a baby. It brought back the years when Susan and I were young mothers finding our way through life. I realized then how much I appreciated her having that history with me. She talked about all that Jason and I went through, how we had gotten him help, and how well he did.

Next to speak was Greg. He prepared himself, as he always does. He had his piece of paper and spoke about when he first started dating me and the first time he met Jason. It had been eleven years ago, and that would be the beginning of an actual father-and-son relationship. In his true unselfish way, he never mentioned his own pain but how difficult it must be for his wife. He said Jason never asked for much and was able to be happy with the simple things in life. He didn't get caught up in the complications that life can bring. He was humble and enjoyed his time wherever he was.

When I looked at Greg standing there talking about our son who had died, I was grateful he was the one I married to be there for Jason. He was the perfect father for him. He had the patience to deal with Jason's limitations.

Jason appreciated the way Greg broke things down for him to understand. Greg would explain how Jason could better manage his money. He'd tell him not to buy movies or HBO boxing as much as he did and to limit himself to maybe a movie a month. He'd talk with him about his hygiene. He'd tell Jason to do one thing at a time so he wouldn't get overwhelmed. He'd help him with his thinking and reminded him of the reality: he was not alone; we were here if he needed help. The two of them were close enough that Jason knew what Greg could communicate to him without speaking. Jason loved to drink iced coffee and then start talking a lot. Greg would look at him in the corner of his eye as if to say, "You're talking too much," and Jason would say, "I know, Greg. Too much coffee."

Greg was much calmer with him than I was. We both said the same things, but Greg had less emotion while I was the worried mom. When Jason was at his door, counting and pulling the knob because of his OCD, Greg would say to him calmly, "It's locked, Jason." I would say the same thing but have less patience than Greg.

Jason would say to me, "Mum, why can't you be like Greg? He doesn't get upset."

"Because I'm your mother, and I've been doing it a lot longer than he has," I'd say to him. "Mothers have a different bond with their children."

I was to speak next. I had bought a simple black dress for the funeral and wore black suede heels that were low to the ground. I was feeling free again, like God's grace was carrying me. I felt like I needed to do this for Jason. I had the eulogy written out, but as I began to speak, I felt I needed to talk freely about my son.

The first thing I wanted everyone to know was that I didn't want to be a mother at such a young age, and I was resentful over that without even knowing it. I told them Jason felt the anger and the detachment I had toward him until he got sick. I talked about thinking I had control over my child and about how selfish I was, wanting him to be just like me. I said we don't own our children; God does. They are lent to us by God, and we are given the privilege of being parents. I spoke of how I disliked Jason having a mental illness, and I wanted him not to have it because I was the one who had to deal with it, and that was selfish. I spoke of Jason becoming ill, the ups and downs we went through, and how his mental illness actually brought us together. I said it was only through the grace of God and the love I learned I had for my son that I could get Jason the help he needed. Through this crisis, I realized I truly loved my son. I spoke of our conversations and how I will miss them, of how we talked about our fears, and the obsessive thought process we both had.

I wanted people to know Jason was no dummy. He knew there was a God. He also knew that Satan existed and was trying, every day, to steal his peace from him. I told them how Jason once told me, "Mum, I think our real purpose in life is to know God." I wanted everyone to know my son had a divine purpose here, although his life was short. I talked about his daily struggles of locking his door, turning the key, and counting—all that he had to overcome every day just to get out of his building.

I spoke of how he was up and out early almost every day and how that can be difficult for a person with mental illness. About the paranoid thoughts he had to overcome, the voices he sometimes heard that were negative toward him and his life. How his mind told him someone was constantly trying to hurt him or take something from him. These were the thoughts my son battled, even on medication, just trying to have a good day. He worked hard to find peace. He took two buses and two trains to see Daniel every week in Cambridge. He was consistent with his biweekly appointments at the Clozaril clinic in Boston, where he had his blood checked. He paid his own rent and cable bill, which I gave him a hard time about every month.

Oh goodness, he and that cable bill. Jason was funny—he reminded me so much of myself. He was battling that impulse to spend money on movies every month. I spoke of how I told Jason about my compulsive behaviors too and how I struggled to say no to myself for things I wanted and couldn't afford.

Right before he passed, Jason had turned off the cable connection to his video game system, which I was shocked to hear. I said, "Jason, good for you that you don't feel you need it anymore." My heart was telling me he was growing up and finding healthier ways to spend his time. He said he didn't like the stress of playing with people he didn't know. I guess people could be sore losers on the Internet.

These were the things we talked about when we spent our time together. We talked about the progress we were both making on this journey through life. Saturday mornings, on our way to go grocery shopping, was our time to get out these real conversations of truth, I said. He was doing well, and we were a family. I felt we were okay and we had many years ahead of us, but God had another plan. I then read a poem I wrote after doing the twelve steps of AA, when I first realized how emotionally detached I'd been from him. It's titled "I Have Come to Know Him."

In his younger years, my mind was busy and I was detached.

How time slipped by, and precious moments were taken for granted.

When he wanted to play cards and I wouldn't comply.

The many quiet times when we could have connected have passed.

Darker times have come upon us, and who is this child before me?

A young man I've grown away from and do not know.

I reach to God for guidance to help us heal ourselves.

Playing cards and precious moments have returned with laughter and trust.

The light has come, and we have grown as one.

At last, I have come to know him, Jason, my son.

I told the gathered friends and family how much Jason loved his Xbox, PlayStation, basketball, boxing, and Chinese food. He knew how to enjoy himself and was pleased with how his life was going. He certainly had earned his happiness, considering all he had gone through with his mental illness.

I ended by saying that when I see Jason again, I hope he says to me, "Mum, you were right, there is a loving God after all." I then walked over to the casket and kissed him on his cheek.

When I finished speaking, I felt at ease, knowing I had told the truth. I had honored Jason and celebrated his life. I wasn't always the unselfish mom, but I did love my son. I spoke honestly and didn't care what people thought. We all have baggage, and we all live with a sinful nature every day, but God can help heal us and our relationships. I felt grateful that God had given us the time we had and for the healing that took place between us. Our relationship wasn't perfect, but it was certainly more trusting.

When I sat down, my pastor said, "Now I know where Jason got his authenticity from." It was nice to hear, but I knew it is only through God that we can have that kind of honesty. We hide nothing from our Holy Father. Pastor said a few words; then we played a song by Michael English titled, "I Bowed on My Knees and Cried Holy." Susan had introduced me to Daniel Crews's recording of the song the year before. In it, the singer asks to be brought to see Jesus in heaven along with Abraham, Jacob, and Timothy. The lyrics were a powerful reminder Jason was now with Jesus and not alone.

* * *

Greg left me alone to say my goodbyes to Jason before the casket was closed for the last time. I didn't want to let Jason go, but I knew I had to. Inside, I felt Jason was in a spiritually higher place than I was.

After all the years I talked with him about God, Jason was now with him, in a place I longed to be. As I sat in the car with Greg, a shower started to fall, causing me to think of all the conversations Jason and I had, realizing I'd never hear "I love you, Mum" again. I can't tell you how painful it was to come to that realization. Confronting the fact that I'd never hear his voice again. I knew that no matter how many days I had ahead, my life would never be the same.

The procession left the funeral home, and I asked the driver to go down Howard Street in Revere, by the house I lived in when Jason was born. It was only a short distance from the cemetery. I realized that coincidentally Jason died around the corner from the house where my parents lived in East Boston, when I was born. Now he would rest around the corner from where he spent his first days on this earth. It was painful and sad to think back to when he was little in that house. I was young and clueless about what I was doing. We overcame so much. Now there'd be no more struggling and what-ifs.

Soon we were driving down Howard Street. The procession stopped for a few seconds, and I couldn't help but think of Jason as a baby, sitting in that front living room with me while I watched the Claus von Bulow trial. I'd lay him on the crushed red velvet couch with gold wooden trim while I watched TV. That was thirty-one years ago, and now I'm burying my son.

I urge anyone reading this: do not waste time in this life. Anything can happen at any time, so we must make the best of each and every day. We need to tell those we love that we love them and demonstrate that love as much as we can. One thing you cannot do is bring back time.

We arrived at the cemetery, and as we approached the grave, my pastor mentioned that the rain was stopping and the sun was coming out. He spoke briefly and asked if anyone wanted to say anything about Jason. A few people did, and I loved hearing their thoughts of him. Pastor's wife Trish sang the doxology, which was moving.

I stood in front of the casket, coming to terms with the fact these were our final moments together before Jason was put into the earth. I stood there in a fog while everyone waited behind me. It seemed like no one wanted to leave. I eventually touched his casket, and people started dropping flowers to say their final goodbyes.

I saw Jay crying, and I went over to comfort him. He and Jason had become close again in the past year. They played video games online every day and talked on the phone. A year later, returning to Jason's grave on his thirty-second birthday, Nico, Jay, and others in our stepfamily would enjoy some time reminiscing about Jason. But for now, we were joined together in crying and missing him and his fun, unique personality.

The collation was at Spinelli's in East Boston, a function facility a couple of towns over from the cemetery. About fifty people came, and I appreciated the support. A couple of my clients, Steven and Barry, who I considered good friends, had closed their businesses for the day to attend the funeral with their wives and staff. This was on a Monday, which is a big day for business. Their presence meant a lot to me, and I'll never forget it.

I was also thinking of the people who hadn't shown up. At the time of the funeral, I was very angry. As I said, my mother and my two brothers didn't show. Neither did some people from the glass company, including Tom. These were people I respected and who knew what Jason and I had gone through, so I was hurt that they didn't come.

I understand that responding to the loss of a child can be scary for the people around you. Most people don't know how to handle these losses. But in today's world, sending off an e-mail is better than doing nothing at all.

Tom waited two months to call me. This was hard to understand at the time, but some people are capable of only so much. I learned a lot after losing Jason. The experience reminded me again that God, not people or my job, is my loving source. These people were showing me who they were and that our relationship wasn't what I had thought it was. I spent a lot of years putting my job and clients before myself and my son, and I have no one to blame for that but myself. We think we have so much time, and we always think we need more money. God has shown me that anything you worship above him is idolatry. God's love is consistent and safe. My heavenly

Father will never let me down. The loss forced me to grow spiritually in a way I never dreamed, and I'm grateful.

The one person whose absence I knew Jason would mind was my ex-boyfriend Jesse. Jesse's mother said at the wake that he would be there, and I was saddened that he hadn't shown up for Jason. Well, people do what they have to do. After all, I did a lot to hurt Jesse. Jason had also been difficult and defiant sometimes when Jesse was living with us. I was glad that the last time Jason saw Jesse, he made amends to him—"cleaning his side of the street," as we say in AA. Jesse responded kindly, saying, "We were all young back then," but Jason had already demonstrated he was not young anymore. Good for you, Jason, for your maturity.

I was still feeling like a truck had hit me. I was exhausted and lost. How would I go forward without Jason? When I pictured the future, I'd get overwhelmed with a feeling of loneliness and despair I can only describe as falling down a deep dark hole of emptiness inside my soul. I took the rest of the week off and decided to go back to work on Monday. That day, June 10, would be the twenty-fifth anniversary of my sobriety, but that didn't mean much to me now. I just needed to get through the day.

Chapter 14

We had until the end of June to clean out Jason's apartment. I wasn't looking forward to it, but I didn't want someone else to do it if I wasn't there. Greg and I decided on a Saturday, and Jodi and Bobby came to help. We put Jason's clothes in four green trash bags, along with a few items I wanted to keep: his wallet, a jacket he wore a lot, his eyeglasses, his stereo, and a television we bought him for Christmas. Greg and Bobby cleaned the kitchen and bathroom while Jodi and I did the bedroom and living room. Jodi and Bobby cleaned the apartment as if their own child lived there. I thought of how guarded Jason was with his belongings and how he would have had a fit if he knew we were touching his stuff. We gave the furnishings to friends and family so they didn't get thrown out. Before we left, I took a moment to lie down in the exact spot on the bedroom floor where my son died. I wanted to be where he was lying when he was taken to heaven to be with Jesus.

I went to the cemetery every day to visit with Jason. Although I knew his spirit wasn't there, I needed to be near his body to feel closer to him. I knew God was with him and he wasn't alone. Driving there by myself and having the wave of heavy grief weighing on me was like nothing I had ever experienced. Being alone caused the memories of him to flood back.

Some of them I didn't want to remember, and I knew the enemy was doing his best to condemn me. Satan wanted me to blame God. He'd whisper, "See, you really can't trust God." He wanted to destroy me to keep me from my purpose, which is to glorify God. I had to continue looking to God and, most importantly, be in his Word.

The Wednesday after the funeral, I made it my business to go to Bible study. I don't know how I did it, but I knew I had to be there. I didn't want to stray too far from my brothers and sisters in Christ. Listening to my pastor, I realized that life goes on, even when your child dies. Now I'd have to lean on God more than ever, and I was okay with that. The whole experience made me feel closer to God and allowed me to realize I was getting through it with him. I didn't have to drink or do anything harmful to relieve the pain. Bereavement books describe this process as "leaning into the grief," which I knew I had to do to survive my life ahead.

I'd wake every morning with Jason on my mind. I thought of him standing in my kitchen, chuckling for no particular reason, which he was prone to do. I knew this phase was only the beginning, realizing and accepting I'd never see him again here on earth or hear him say he loved me. Every day I felt more and more like I wanted to jump out of my skin. I felt trapped because there was nowhere to go with the pain. It's hard to describe the feeling you have when you want your son back, but you know that even God can't do that for you. I knew only those who had a lost a child could truly understand. I couldn't yet think of him and smile. That would come in the later months, when I'd fall into my intimate time with him, particularly before bed.

Although my mother didn't make the funeral, I knew I had to forgive her and move on. She had an appointment at Boston Medical Center the following Thursday, so I thought I'd meet her there. I really was trying to do the right thing, and I felt God would want me to. When I arrived at the hospital, she sat next to me, and all she could talk about was her upcoming appointments and her port for her chemo. I had just buried my son on Monday, and all she talked about was herself. She never bothered to ask where he was buried or how the service went. No, it was all about her. I texted Greg that I was struggling, sitting there listening to her.

As she was looking down at her paperwork, I watched her with pity and realized that my mother was mentally ill. She just couldn't do any better. The realization was very sad, and it made me grateful for the relationship Jason and I had. We had talked about our feelings and were willing to admit when we weren't honest with each other. I praised God for our healing once again.

On the drive home, finally after all these years, I let Ma know exactly how I felt. I had never spoken up to her before because she always made me feel like she was the victim and I was doing something wrong. If I did speak up, I'd always feel guilty afterward.

I lay into her in the car. She had nowhere to go and was a captive audience, so she had to just stay there and take it all in. The ride home was about fifteen minutes, and I made good use of it.

I said, "How could you not ask me about Jason's service? And how could you have thought it was a good idea to go grocery shopping rather than attend your own grandson's funeral?"

She said, "I didn't want to bring it up to make you feel bad."

Another lie. I let her know that I knew she was envious of me and that she did everything she could to make me feel miserable about myself. I told her that she and my father had abandoned their children and that I was a much better mother than she ever could have been. I told her she needed to go to God with her sins and ask his forgiveness as she was in her final years. I let her know we are all sinners, but we need to repent to receive forgiveness.

I wanted her to feel trapped, like I did when my brother was molesting me and she allowed it. I started telling her that while growing up my brother was always trying to peek at me and that he acted inappropriately toward me. I finally said the word *molest*. I told her he was molesting me, and she knew it was going on but did nothing to stop it. She didn't act surprised at all. She sat in the car and didn't say a word. Not one word. That's how she was when we were growing up—she kept a lot of secrets.

I felt a release. I felt better after telling the truth of what went on in my childhood. I remembered Jason being at our house on my fiftieth birthday, how he cried about feeling unwanted, and how good he felt getting it all out with no one denying his feelings. I guess that came full circle, to me telling my truth with my mother and feeling free about it. Unfortunately, in my case, my mother continued to live in the lie.

Two days later, I received a letter from her in the mail. She wrote that I didn't need to pick her up at the hospital that day. She hadn't asked me to come and get her. That was the best she could do. No reaction to my telling her my brother was molesting me. No "I'm sorry that was happening." No "I didn't know." No mention at all. The denial in an alcoholic, abusive, or narcissistic family system is so deep it's sickening. There is no mention of reality or emotions in these family units. Instead, the family steals your reality from you. This is why I doubted myself for so long and wasn't sure of my perception of things. Jason's and my thought processes were not far from each other. I continued to visit her and walk her dog in the coming months. But why? I wasn't even sure anymore if this was what God wanted me to do.

* * *

On my first day back to work, I attended a company-sponsored golf tournament in Ipswich. I thought it would be an easy day to return, but it turned out to be difficult. I had mixed emotions, including some anger. Forgiving the people who didn't come to Jason's service took some time. But the coworkers who did stand by me were there, and I couldn't have appreciated them more. My husband was with me since he was golfing in the tournament, which helped tremendously. I was still in a fog. The best I can say is I somehow made it through the first day.

My new manager was very gracious, letting me acclimate slowly. I really couldn't do much more. I have about one hundred seventy-five clients I visit monthly. The ones who didn't know of my loss I would tell on my next sales call. Well, the truth is I didn't have to tell them—from my demeanor, they could see I wasn't myself. The next two months on the road were draining, to say the least.

Stacey, my sponsor, asked me one day, "How are you getting through this, Karen?"

I said, "It's by God's grace because I feel like I want to jump off a building."

I told her I did my crying and wailing at home and while driving in my car. Some days I'd need to drive thirty miles away, and I'd be a little afraid of being alone since that's when all my feelings came up. I'd be driving along and just break down, with unbelievable wailing coming from the deepest part of my being. I wasn't afraid of it because I knew the grief had to come out somehow. With the pain I was feeling, I had nowhere else to go but to Jesus. My Bible reminded me I was okay in these times of being alone because he was with me.

My boss Tom reached out to me a couple of months after Jason passed. He called one afternoon to ask me to meet for lunch. I didn't hold back when he called. I told him how disappointed I was that it took him two months to call after missing the services. To be honest, if I hadn't cared about my relationship with him, I wouldn't have said anything.

We met for lunch, and he expressed his regret. He said he'd hurt himself playing basketball and was wrapped up in his own self-pity. He said he knew better than to make excuses, which I appreciated. He mentioned the amend I had made to him years before and said he told that story to his daughter to teach her the importance of good character. I started crying when he brought it up. I think he was asking for forgiveness in exchange for the forgiveness he had given me, but my hurt was still very raw. My loyalty and my heart were with Jason. It would take some time for me to heal.

The one true gift God gave me after Jason passed was the smiley faces. Oh my goodness, I saw them everywhere. One day, I was driving through Swampscott when I looked over at the florist shop and noticed a big smiley face made of concrete, sitting on a pedestal, facing me. Really, a smiley face statue? Maybe a boat or a mermaid but a smiley face? I pulled over and told the florist about Jason. She became teary-eyed but was happy she had played a part in connecting me with him. Telling others about the smiley faces was another way to praise God, to show someone how loving God really is.

Another time God helped me through a difficult moment was when I went to the bank. It was the one I stopped into the day I found Jason. I asked God for help walking into the bank, which is located in a supermarket. As I was withdrawing my cash, the Holy

Spirit prompted me to look over my right shoulder. I noticed a woman standing by her shopping cart with a smiley face balloon tied to the handrail. As I turned back to the ATM, the woman rolled her cart behind me. I walked out of the store crying. I felt that Jason walked by me through that woman, to let me know he was with me. I praise God for that power because it is only God who allows these circumstances to happen.

* * *

About a month after Jason's passing, Greg and I saw a TV interview with a woman from the Compassionate Friends, an organization for parents who have lost a child and siblings who have lost a brother or sister. They would be holding their conference in Boston that year, over the Independence Day weekend.

I said to Greg, "We need to go to that conference. God is trying to help us."

God bless my husband. He said, "Whatever you want to do Sweetie." He was willing to do whatever he could to help us heal from this tremendous loss.

I went online and saw a couple of sessions we could attend: one for parents who have lost their only child and one for people interested in writing a book. We arrived early Saturday morning, and I can tell you, just walking in and realizing that we were all there for the same reason was overwhelming. Pictures of the children who had passed away were being displayed for all to see. I felt bad for everyone attending.

Greg and I went to a session for parents who have lost their only child. I said that I had lost my son just a month ago, that I knew God was with him, and that I was grateful we had such a close relationship and I had my faith. The reception was good, and I could see the majority of people still held on to the rawness of their loss many years later. I had no idea of the road ahead. I was still in shock and didn't even know it.

During the lunch break, we took a walk down Newbury Street and looked at the salons and quaint little shops. I thought, "How can

I buy anything? My son is dead." I knew I had to keep going, or I'd completely fall apart.

We stopped in a boutique, where I tried on dresses since we had a wedding coming up later that month. I chose a pretty coral dress. When I got to the counter, there was a smiley face tucked into a corner behind the register. The sign said to smile because you were being filmed in case you decided to shoplift. I explained to the shopkeeper what we were doing in Boston and what the smiley face represented. We went back to the convention with a little more hope that we could get through our second class.

Speaking at the session were several authors and article writers who had also lost a child. One of the authors, who had written a few books and appeared on *The Phil Donahue Show* years before, told how he lost his beautiful daughter and how it affected his life. He said when you write a book, write from the heart and don't overthink it. I appreciated that because I really didn't want to take writing classes. I left there, feeling hopeful that I could write this book and that God would lead me where I needed to go.

Greg and I headed home from the conference, exhausted. It had been inspirational to see all these people who had lost a child, like we did, knowing we were not alone in our grief. They were offering hope. Hope is something you need to have. Without it, you will perish. I thought back to the letter I received from my brother Jamie a year and half before he died. In the abyss of his alcoholism, he wrote, "Sometimes all a person has is hope." He was losing it himself as the days turned into months before he eventually drank himself to death.

One day while I was out making my rounds for work, I was visiting an agency in Arlington. I was telling the women there about Jason and his smiley faces. One woman who worked there told me she had lost her daughter. My heart broke for her too, but as I was learning, there are more of us than I realized. I got on the elevator with a little boy and his mom. I told him how I liked the trucks on his shirt.

Then to my surprise, he said, "Do you want to see my sticker?"

I said, "Sure." It wasn't a truck or a dinosaur but a smiley face sticker that the dentist gave him. I started to cry a little, but I didn't want to upset the boy. I whispered to his mother about Jason, and she became emotional and said her friend had just lost a child. I expressed my condolences for her friend and said, "Your son just made my day. Thank you."

The smiley faces became a way of recognizing Jason for a lot of people. Greg texted me a picture of a plastic bag his cigars were mailed in. On the front of the bag was a smiley face. Jason loved being in the cigar shop with Greg and the crew there, so it made sense that Greg would get a smiley face on the cigar bag. Susan and my work friend Kim T. texted me smiley faces too. It made me feel good that people remembered Jason that way.

I had to keep moving forward, no matter how I was feeling. In July was the wedding of one of Greg's brother's friends, who had been part of the family for years. It's difficult to enjoy yourself after the death of your child, but I said we'd be there, and we honored that. It was a beautiful event, held in a familiar hall a little north of Boston. I pushed myself to get up and dance. At first, it was like before Jason had died, but then the reality hit me, and I remembered he was gone. I was trying to live, but I was just going through the outward motions; inwardly, I was still in shock. As my sister-in-law Roseanne, who lost her daughter, said, "It's like being in a movie." After losing a child, you feel like you're not in your own body and you're watching the events of someone else's life unfold, not your own. The pain is so great that you detach. I guess it's a form of disassociation.

The grief I was experiencing was heavy and thick in my spirit. I'd get the sleep I needed the night before and then wake up feeling like I hadn't slept at all. Resting my head at night was very difficult. I'd be weeping, thinking of Jason, my beautiful son. I could envision him walking down the aisle of Market Basket in Middleton on a Saturday, looking for his mom to put his cold cuts in the carriage. What I wouldn't give to have one moment with him now. Just to touch his face and put my cheek on his. That would never happen again, and every day this realization became harder to bear, not easier. I knew God wasn't bringing him back.

I stayed in God's Word every day, continued to go to church, attended my AA meeting, and met every week with the woman I sponsored. Helping her was keeping me from succumbing to self-pity. I learned enough over the years to stay out of self, and that self, not alcohol or anything else, was my problem. I knew Satan was just waiting for me to fall into despair and do something stupid to hurt myself or my husband. Satan hates marriage or any biblical principle. I knew I had to protect myself from falling into old traps—the traps that kept me in bondage, which could be anything from overspending and overeating to cheating and being dishonest. I was married now; I respected my marriage, and I had no intention of hurting the one person who had been through all this with me. In the months that followed, several friends supported me. I felt like I drove my coworker Karen crazy. She'd always been a sounding board for me, and she continued to listen after Jason passed. She couldn't take the pain away, but she did her best to be there while I dealt with losing Jason and the disappointment I felt when Tom and some of the managers didn't show up for Jason's funeral. My sponsor Stacey, a gifted listener, was a constant support of love and spiritual nourishment. She never said anything foolish or out of line. Having no children of her own but being a terrific aunt, she did an outstanding job keeping me on the path. My good friend Ketna, my massage therapist, continued to be there for me. Our friendship has been a blessing for me since the day we met.

Susan was there with her godly messages and little gifts she'd send in the mail. Her sister Jodi was also a source of constant support. Without my friends and husband and Greg's family, I'd have felt very alone. Most people were kind, and the ones who weren't, I stayed away from.

* * *

Three months had gone by since Jason passed, and still, there was no sign of his autopsy report. I could hear Jason saying to me as the months passed, "Mum, aren't you wondering how I died?" I didn't call the coroner's office because I knew from talking to a few people that a report could take up to six months. To be honest, I wanted to know how he died, but I wasn't looking forward to reading my son's death certificate. I was also convinced in my faith that it was Jason's time. If I'm going to believe God is in control of everything, then I have to believe he took Jason home that day. I can't have it both ways. That was Jason's destiny, in the same way I was destined to be Jason's mom.

At times, I struggled with my anger. I was in a rough neighborhood of Boston one day and saw an addict standing on the corner, nodding. I looked over and thought to myself, "Why is he still here and my son, who straightened his life out, is dead?"

I asked God's forgiveness right away because I knew it was wrong to think that. The Bible tells me that Jason is in heaven with Jesus because he was a believer. If Jason is in heaven with Jesus, then why am I thinking this poor suffering addict is in a better place than Jason? How foolish. We are the ones who live in a world of suffering that God never intended. We were destined for paradise until the fall of Adam and Eve. Thank God, Jesus came to die on the cross to save sinners like my son and me. Jesus overcame death. What a promise we get to receive as believers. I had to remind myself of that every day.

Each day I was healing a little more, but the ache was still there. God was teaching me about myself and my relationship with my mother. I was seeing more of my mother in myself. I was grateful to have healed from some of my own narcissism in order to love my son. I never could have broken through those walls without God.

I continued to walk my mother's dog around Admiral's Hill in Chelsea. These walks were helpful since they got me out of myself. My mother started her chemo treatments, and they initially worked very well. She lost her voice for a while due to the tumor in her throat, but now she could talk again. I persuaded her to let a visiting nurse into her home to check on her periodically. Having a professional take care of her gave me some reassurance.

The last three weeks of August, Susan came to visit. While she was here, we returned to our old neighborhood on Watts Street. I stopped to ask a man if he knew any of our old neighbors who might still live there. Very few were left, but it was nice to reminisce. I had a vivid sense of what my life was like before Jason was born and what my life may have been like had I not become pregnant with him at eighteen. I cry as I write this now because Jason and I really did grow up together. I believe that if I hadn't become a mother, I may have continued to be an alcoholic and to self-destruct. I also might never have come to make Jesus Christ my Savior and be destined for an eternity separated from God and my loved ones. Jason gave me a reason to live and become sober. He gave me a reason to get up every day. Having Jason kept me on track to do the right thing and become the person I am today. I'm sorry I hadn't felt that way at first. Back then, all I could feel was hurt and alone and lacking support. Now I wouldn't have changed my time as a mother for anything in the world.

I thought back to being a child and how my childhood and Jason's mirrored each other. He was a lot like me, just a sensitive kid trying to make his mother happy. A mother's love is so important to a child; without it, he or she feels insecure and will look to others for that security. That day on Watts Street, I was grateful my story with Jason was different than mine with my mother and father.

I decided to have four of my other friends from Watts Street come to my house for dinner while Susan was here. We had a wonderful time talking about growing up in Chelsea. We talked about how hard it was starting junior high in a different school across town. Amy remembered asking a teacher to walk Lisa and her home because they were afraid of a tough girl at school. As she spoke, I thought how I never would have asked for help as a child. Good for them for telling someone they were afraid.

My friends seemed to remember a lot of good times during the years when we started high school, though for me they were the worst. These friends had no idea of the tragedies that were going in my world. My parents never being home, me being so promiscuous with older men, my drinking. They had no idea I went to junior high without washing my hair for days because we had no heat or hot water. I realize their lives weren't perfect, but they were able to move forward without the addictions and unhealthy coping skills I had to acquire early in life to survive. We had so much fun that night and many laughs, but the pain I felt for Jason was lurking nearby.

* * *

August 11 would have been the thirty-third birthday of my husband's niece Adrianna. Her parents were having a party in her name. It was a beautiful summer day for a beautiful young woman who left us so early in life, like Jason. Susan came, and I was glad because I was struggling to stay calm. No one was asking for anything from me, but it was hard to smile and pretend. I felt like I was doing what I always did as a child—hide my pain from others. At one point, I broke down. I didn't want to make a scene, so I tried to be as discreet as I could. I turned my back and looked out at the water to hide my tears from everyone sitting on the porch. Susan put her arm around me and said, "It's okay."

I wanted to run, but there was nowhere to go, and I knew it. I had to sit in it until I healed a little more. Roseanne said she felt bad for where I was. For her, the early days had been the hardest.

In September, we took a weekend trip to New Hampshire with Greg's family. The trip was difficult because I was beginning to realize I no longer had a biological family. Jamie and Jason, the two people I truly loved who were my flesh and blood, were gone. We had looked out for one another. Although my mother and two remaining brothers were still alive, I didn't have the same connection to them. I believe, judging by their conduct, that my remaining family couldn't love me either. They just weren't capable. I've accepted that. I feel for all the members of my family and what we lost with one another. God is love, and only he can teach us what true love is. Without God, I am an extremely selfish person. The Bible teaches us we have to daily "die of self" (Luke 9:23: "If anyone would come after me, let him deny himself and take up his cross daily and follow me"). That's a tall order, and it can be hard to do, but my Bible readings and AA's twelve steps keep me on track. I fall short every day, as we all do.

I was hoping that going away with Greg's family would get me out of self. We headed up to Portsmouth, a beautiful coastal town with lots of quaint little shops. I was doing my best to be in the moment, but I can assure you it wasn't easy. While driving in the car with Greg, I couldn't bear the grief. I felt trapped, and I wanted to jump out onto the highway. I was feeling the powerlessness of losing my son, and my feelings were unbearable. I couldn't drink to make them go away, so I was left feeling raw, with this sad emotion I couldn't control.

We went shopping and ate in a modest-looking seafood restaurant that had great food. Some of the time, it was too cold to walk around outside, so we hung out in our hotel rooms, eating chips and other snacks, and conversed. It was nice to be around people who cared, but I couldn't pretend I was happy. Adrianna's father, John, was a great help. At dinner one night, he sat next to me, and we talked. He understood what it felt like to have such raw emotions.

At one point in the weekend, I got upset with Greg. I wasn't feeling emotionally connected to him. I was feeling alone. After all, here I am with eight members of his family while the family I knew and loved was gone. We stopped at the outlets in Kittery, Maine, and Greg and the guys wanted to find a wallet or something. Greg wanted to go off with his cousins and leave me to shop with the girls, which any other time would have been fine, but not now.

The men started walking off together, but I felt like Greg was moving on, and I was alone in my heartbreak. I was hurting so bad I wanted to scream my anguish out loud in the middle of the parking lot. Nothing was making sense to me. I looked around at people shopping at outlet stores. They don't know my son just died. Their world doesn't stop because my son died. But mine did.

I stood in the parking lot, staring at Greg and feeling numb. I said, "I can't do this. I'm having a hard time."

He said, "I'll stay with you," but by then, I felt again like I wanted to run away. I was angry and told Greg to go with his cousins. Oh my goodness, it was tough. I was questioning why I went along on the trip at all.

I think I wanted Greg to fix my pain, but he couldn't. At the end of the weekend, I cried all the way home in the car. I was letting out all the grief I had held in just to get through the weekend. Greg's family are wonderful people, and I knew they wanted to support us. Although it was hard and I had all these emotions going on, I was still glad they were there.

Chapter 15

We all have multigenerational curses in our families. Fear, narcissism, alcoholism, mental illness, and agoraphobia are just some of my family's curses. I know with prayer and God's help, they can be overcome.

I brought my mother to a few more of her appointments, but my heart was not in it. When she refused to come to Jason's funeral, I knew my mother had no love for me. I had spent all my life trying to get something from her that she didn't possess. Although I denied it for years, I was beginning to understand my mother's lack of feeling toward my siblings and me. I was getting a clearer picture of her mental illness.

She had many unresolved issues within her spirit. She lived with a lot of secrets and her own pain from the past. She was afraid of people. I never knew my mother to have a friend, or even mention one, during my entire life. I understood what that felt like, and so did Jason.

There was a lot of mistrust in her life, especially between us. I was a threat to her relationship with my father because I was the only daughter. When she became involved with her lost love, that caused me to mistrust her again.

It was sad that in her lifetime, she never received the most important love a person truly deserves. She didn't love herself.

Mental illness often involves a denial of reality. I lived in that denial most of my life, so I knew it well. Truth is the most powerful weapon against Satan. Satan wants us to live in deception and doubt God's love for us. It was taking years, but I was finally beginning to come to terms with my own truth. I was gaining more insight into the anxiety I often experienced while driving.

Looking back, I began to understand that I hadn't been trusting in God completely with my life and Jason's. After I read my fifth step to my sponsor, I was immediately thrown into a crisis with Jason's mental illness. Dealing with Jason's illness triggered the same response I had from taking care of Jamie when I was a child with limited knowledge and resources. Although I knew God was there, I felt I had to take care of everything myself. I was trying to control something I couldn't control.

My anxiety also stemmed from anger toward God for putting another mentally ill person in my life. I see clearly now that Jason's illness and behaviors brought up my feelings and anxieties from being trapped in a house with Todd. Like Todd, Jason was sometimes either explosively angry or paranoid that someone was conspiring against him. I was afraid I was going to be trapped again in a situation with someone I couldn't protect myself from. I was reacting the way I had as a child—scared and unprotected. But I was an adult now, and Jason was my son. I didn't have to put up with abusive behavior anymore or try to make Jason happy all the time to keep the anger at bay, the way I had with my brother.

The Holy Spirit was making things clearer, letting me know God was with me. I didn't need to trust in anyone or anything but him. Through all the pain, God was breaking more strongholds in me. God was taking away more chains of bondage and setting me free. That's what God does when you confess your sin to him and are willing to let go of people or things you think you need to hold on to, to survive. The survival skills I once used so effectively no longer worked, and I no longer needed them. It's in the letting go, not the holding on, that we are set free.

* * *

One day in September 2014, I stopped at my mother's house. I walked in and said, "Ma, what the heck is going on?"

She had been having trouble moving her bowels, so she took a Colace pill, but she didn't realize what could happen. Now she couldn't control herself. Her feces were all over the apartment. Looking around, I was overwhelmed by the smell, and the first thing I wanted to do was clean the apartment. As an adult child, that's what I did: I reverted to childhood behaviors to get rid of the anxiety.

I filled the bathtub a few inches and helped her into it so I could wash her. I never imagined seeing my mother naked and washing her genitals since she was always so private with herself. I'm really not good at providing personal care for others, but you do what you have to in a crisis. God's grace must have been helping me empathize since Ma had not supported me when Jason died. I ran down to a nearby Market Basket to buy here some Depends. By the time I got back, her feces were everywhere again. The poor thing. I didn't know what to do.

I said, "Ma, please don't take that pill again." Todd eventually came and cleaned the apartment, including the rug. He did a great job straightening it out. I was just grateful I didn't have to do it. From that day on, it would be one issue after another with her.

I continued to check in on my mother and walk Candy. At one point, Ma hurt her knee and was bedridden for three weeks. I kept encouraging her not to miss her radiation appointments, but she refused to go. This was her decision, but I knew deep down her cancer was not going away. I couldn't force her to continue her treatments, so I kept praying for her.

During this time, I decided to become the coffee maker at my AA meeting. Taking on this role is a commitment to be there every week. It gets you there early for the meeting, and serving others gets you out of yourself and away from self-pity. I'd bake cookies for the meeting, which the people in my group loved. I was also meeting with my "sponsee," and I continued to go to Al-Anon on Saturday afternoons with some of the most loving people I have encountered in the program. Every week, they listened to me share my story, where I was with my walk with God, and my tears of grief. I was grateful to everyone in both programs.

Greg knew I loved Bermuda, so he booked a trip for September with Bobby and his wife Danielle. Bobby and Danielle usually took their kids on vacation, but this time, they left them at home. I was doing my best to look forward to the trip. I had loved Bermuda ever since my first visit in 1993. This would be my tenth. But this visit, something would be different: I wouldn't have Jason to come home to.

We stayed at the Hamilton Princess Hotel, which is situated on a hill and has a beautiful, sprawling golf course. We shopped downtown and visited the caves on a rainy day. We had lunch on the outside terrace overlooking the hotel's beach, with a large rock formation in the middle of the water. One day, I was swimming in the ocean and having a moment of fun until I was suddenly overwhelmed with being reminded Jason was dead.

"How could you be having fun?" I asked myself. I knew it was okay to be swimming and I wasn't doing anything wrong, but it was still very hard. I sat back in my beach chair with tears streaming down my face while I fell into deep thoughts of my son.

That's how it went every day, as I fell in and out of time with him in my mind. I still felt a close relationship with Jason, but it was different now. I could feel his love, and sometimes it felt deeper than when he was on earth. I thought about the time I went to Bermuda before Jason got diagnosed, when I had no business leaving him alone at fifteen, knowing he had issues. Now that he was gone, I was feeling remorse for that behavior. I had to keep going to God to remind me he had forgiven me. Satan was waiting in the wings to condemn me; I had to stay on guard. I read my Bible every day to protect my mind from his schemes. Jason liked to say, "An idle mind is the devil's playground." Jason knew you had to be purposeful in your thinking, or you'd be deceived.

On the day we flew home, the sky was dark and gloomy. I don't like to fly, so I started obsessing about turbulence. Well, my gut was right unfortunately. We had a very bumpy ride. Greg is always calm on plane rides and often falls asleep, but even he admitted the turbulence was bad. All I could do was say the Our Father over and over again. When you think all you can do is pray, that's all you need. I was even thinking that maybe Jason passed so young because God had planned that I would die that day. I thought that if I died, at least I'd be with Jesus and Jason. How self-centered can you be?

We got home safely, but I thought about my fear of death. I had to question my faith at that point. If I really believed I'd go to heaven to be with Jesus and Jason and that heaven was a better place, why was I afraid? I came to understand that I had been trying to control my death my entire life. I had feared so many things, even after being saved. I was slowly realizing that I needed to keep my conviction because God had a destiny for me.

God was allowing me to mature spiritually through this huge loss.

* * *

Halloween was coming up. When I was a child, I loved Halloween, not because of the goblins but because I could be anyone I wanted to be. I wasn't comfortable in my own skin, so hiding behind a mask or costume somehow gave me the freedom to be myself.

For the previous two years, Greg and I had volunteered at Trunks for Treats at church. It's a fun way to have children from the church and the community visit decorated car trunks in a safe environment—the church parking lot. I needed to continue to get out of myself and be of service somehow, or I'd fall into self-pity. I dressed as a clown, and we spent an hour and a half entertaining the kids. We had a good time, and I was able to enjoy someone else's children for a night.

Our first holiday season without Jason was approaching, and Greg and I were thinking of how to spend it. The grief books say that when you lose a child, you have to do what's best for you. Since Greg and I married, Thanksgiving and Christmas were spent at our house. Greg's family always came, and the one person on my side of the family was Jason. My mother was invited but chose not to come because we didn't serve alcohol. Now Jason wouldn't be there either. How could I possibly cook for the holidays without him? Hosting our usual Thanksgiving without my son sitting at his place next to my husband just wasn't going to happen. I wouldn't be able to handle it.

We decided to have Thanksgiving dinner with Greg's family at the Boston Harbor Hotel overlooking Rowes Wharf. The room was full with about a hundred people. We were seated at a round table in the middle of the floor, feeling a little squeezed in. An adjacent room had food stations with turkey, pork loin, and all the sides you can think of. On the end of one of the tables was a display of crab legs and shrimp, which I usually loved but found hard to enjoy that day. I couldn't care less where we were. I just knew I had to keep moving forward. I gave thanks for having Jason all the years I did. I did my best to get through the day, but it was lonely for me. I looked around at Greg's family, all connected by their flesh, and I no longer had a part of me, my son. Accepting that was devastating. I was envious and felt hurt and lonely.

At my house the year before, an in-law on Greg's side, told me she had lost her son when he was seven. I sat with her that day to comfort her and told her how sorry I was. Who would have thought that I would lose my son six months later? I looked over at her this day and said, "I don't mind talking about Jason. In fact, I like to because I don't want people to forget him." I expressed sorrow for the loss of her son too. I sensed she may not have wanted to talk about her loss, so I didn't push the issue. Before going home, we stopped to see Roseanne and John. I needed to see Roseanne since she knew as a mother what I was going through. My heart broke for them too. I was grateful to be able to talk with them about our love for our children.

* * *

I was still walking Candy on Admiral's Hill and checking on Ma. Todd also came by periodically to check on her, but he had a four-hour drive from New Hampshire while I was just two towns away. I was getting to know the other residents in my mother's building. Her neighbors continuously asked how she was doing. I was beginning to feel like I lived there.

My mom was getting weaker, and I began to realize she'd probably die soon if she didn't start back on her radiation treatments. As with my dad, I was starting the grieving process by accepting that her death could be near. Right before Christmas, she landed back in the hospital. Thirteen months had passed since her diagnosis. Her heart was weak, and her blood pressure was very low. She was in rehab for a while, but she wanted to go home for Christmas.

Todd took her home to be with the dog. He dug out her Christmas items and put up her tree. She had her green artificial tree for over twenty years and always put those silver icicles on it. She also had a wreath she had made from a wire hanger and sandwich bags, which Todd hung outside her door. I was glad he was there to do that for her. Whenever Todd was with my mother, he did whatever she wanted, and I became the outsider, but I was learning to accept that. I felt for her during this time, but I was also trying to get through my own nightmare of losing Jason.

I see now that Ma had difficulty expressing her feelings. That's why she drank, to stay numb, like I did. I was trying to learn more about my mother's childhood experiences. Like me as a child, I think she told her own story in her mind about what went on in her family. I believe we do this to protect ourselves. When our parents aren't in the home to provide food, shelter, and emotional support, the truth is too painful to face, so we create our own version of events. I refused to believe, regardless of what my parents were demonstrating, that they didn't love us or care what was happening to us.

Greg and I decided to go to Portland, Maine, for Christmas. I didn't want to be home and be around everyone, and we had never been to Portland, so it was a new place to spend the holiday. We hid out at a hotel in the downtown area and ate dinner at an Italian restaurant on Christmas Eve. The place was busy, so we sat at the bar. Christmas music was playing, and everyone looked like they were having fun, and I was thinking, "My son is dead." No matter what, I couldn't get relief from the grief. It was raining a little and very cold as Greg and I walked around aimlessly, window shopping. On Christmas Day, we ate at the Danforth Inn, a Federal-style brick mansion. I started writing this book in August, two months after Jason passed, and I brought my laptop so I could continue to write during our stay. It was a lonely weekend, and I can't imagine how I would have made it through that first Christmas if Greg wasn't with me.

Waking up in a hotel room on Christmas morning was an odd feeling. I thought back to my Christmas mornings with Jason when he was young. We'd usually be alone in those days since my ex-boyfriend Jesse would be with his parents in New Hampshire. Jason would wake up, come into my room, and ask if he could open his presents. I'd get up and sit with Jason while he opened everything.

I can still see myself collecting his wrapping paper to throw away. God forbid that, being a clean freak, I'd let him throw the paper on the floor. Jason would look up at me and feel bad and say, "Mum, open yours." Jason didn't buy me gifts or cards until later, when Jesse and Greg prompted him. He had no money other than what I gave him for himself. I suppose he could have saved some of it to get me something, but I didn't expect anything from him. Jesse eventually gave him money to buy me something on holidays. When Jason was little, I'd get presents later in the day from my boyfriend, parents, or friends.

I used to feel bad that we were alone on Christmas mornings, but now I look back and am grateful for having the memory of only the two of us. I didn't have a lot early on, but after I got sober, I did all I could to give him whatever he wanted. He didn't ask for much, but he always enjoyed his Nintendo or Xbox games. Although he got worked up over the games when he was younger, I believe they gave him some type of security and peace and shielded him from the detachment and pain he felt from me. I guess psychologists would call that *disassociation*. I did the same as a child with my compulsive cleaning.

The games were my babysitter, and Jason played them more than was healthy, but I would have to let that go now that he was gone. I'm a mother who wasn't perfect, like every other mother out there. I had to learn about forgiving myself and loving him more. These were my thoughts on our first Christmas without him.

* * *

The first Thanksgiving and Christmas were behind Greg and me now, and I was glad. With New Year's coming, I thought about a woman in one of the grieving books who, after her child died, felt bad moving into the next year because it was a year her child didn't live in. But I knew, as she wrote, we bring our child into the next year through our memories. My son will never leave my heart until the day I die. He will always be with me. I'll continue to love him until we meet again in heaven on those streets of gold. My faith will strengthen me, remembering Jason is with the King of kings and the Lord of lords.

My birthday was also approaching in March, and I wanted nothing to do with it. I was remembering my fiftieth, the year before, when I got upset with Jason about the binder clip on his pants. I didn't want to beat myself up for not having more patience with his mental illness. When my birthday came, I thought about Jason not getting to celebrate his thirty-first and go out for sushi. How could I be happy on my birthday when my only child was not here to celebrate his?

I had to keep my eyes on the prize, knowing that he was in heaven. I'm human, and my flesh longs for Jason, but my spirit knows he is with Jesus, celebrating more than I could ever imagine. I got through the day by taking care of myself the best I could and not letting negative thoughts from the past own me. Instead, I woke and did my prayer and meditation for about an hour; then I went to the cemetery to visit Jason. I went to an Al-Anon meeting; I got a massage, and Greg took me to dinner at 9 Park Street in Boston.

My mother was getting weaker, and her cancer was not being treated. Her voice became a whisper again. From January to May of 2014, she was in and out of hospitals and rehabs. She was stubborn, like most elderly people can be when they want to stay independent but know they can't anymore. One day in early May, I went over to walk the dog and check on her. Ma was talking to me through the door. She couldn't let me in because she was too weak to get out of bed. I was looking for the maintenance man to let me in. I also called the home health care agency to send a nurse to check Ma's vital signs to see if she needed to go back to the hospital. The nurse drove up from Rockland, about twenty miles away, to help her. After she arrived, I realized I had a key in my pocketbook. I was such a wreck I had forgotten it was there.

Ma got upset with me when I gave her other living options, but the uncertainty was becoming too much for me. I was the only one of her children who lived nearby, but it hadn't even been a year since I found my son dead in his apartment, and I didn't want to find my mother dead in hers. I was hoping the nurse would tell me Ma had to be admitted.

That was the last day Ma spent in her apartment. Greg and I received a call telling us she was at the Whidden Hospital in Everett. When we went there and the staff wheeled her by us, she was unconscious, and her head was the size of a soccer ball. I thought for sure she was going to die, but she wanted to be resuscitated. The doctor told us clearly that Ma's quality of life, if and when she woke, would be uncertain. Todd, as her health care proxy, asked Greg what he should do, and Greg told him, "I wouldn't want to be resuscitated, but your mother does, and I would honor her wishes." I knew this was between Ma and God. If God wanted to take my mother that day, he would.

We returned to the intensive care unit the next day, not knowing what to expect. I walked in, and there was my mother, the fighter she was, looking great like nothing had ever happened. Her head was no longer swollen. God bless the doctors and nurses—Ma was getting good care at a hospital that didn't always have a good reputation. My dad had died at the same hospital nine years before, in what may have been in the same room. My mother wasn't ready to go, and God wasn't ready to take her. She stayed a few days and went back to rehab.

It was during one of Ma's hospital stays that I confronted Todd about the sexual abuse. I said, "Todd, you molested me when we were kids."

He said, "What are you talking about, Karen? I always protected you. Remember the time some kids were teasing you and I had them beat up?"

I asked him, "What does that have to do with you touching me and kissing me in Ma and Dad's bedroom and pimping me off to your friends?"

Todd just walked away. He's a master at deflecting and twisting the truth. That's what he did when we were growing up. He would try to steal my reality by making me feel bad because he did something to help me; meanwhile, he refused to own the hurt he had caused.

It had been awhile since I'd seen the doctor for my anxiety. I had been thinking about him since Jason passed while walking my mother's dog on Admiral's Hill in Chelsea. I hadn't talked with him in almost a year as a client, due to financial reasons.

I e-mailed the doctor about making an appointment. When I returned home, I opened my mail and found an envelope from Joyce Meyer, the author and Bible teacher. It contained a flyer that said, "It's not too late for you," with a smiley face and a black binder clip, just like the one Jason fastened to his pants the day I got upset with him. I felt that God was saying, "You can change who you are and what you believe about yourself and become more like Christ." This was a reminder that, although I hadn't always had patience with Jason and his mental illness, God was not giving up on me. God was letting me know I was on the right track.

Chapter 16

Almost a year had passed, and we still didn't know the cause of Jason's death. I called the medical examiner's office occasionally and learned we weren't the only family waiting for results from an autopsy. I knew the office had budget and staff issues, but I was disgusted with the whole situation. Mother's Day was approaching, and I didn't want to find out my son's cause of death near that day. I hoped the report would come later in the month.

I couldn't believe I had made it this far without giving up on life completely. Every Saturday, I went to the cemetery to visit a grave I knew Jason was not in. I brought him flowers, which I know he couldn't care less about. I wanted the flowers to look perfect in front of his stone, and I could hear him say, "Mum, don't worry about it. It's no big deal." Jason didn't sweat the small stuff. Saturday was our day together and always will be.

I kept every card Jason gave me, and his last Mother's Day card was no different. I kept it on the counter all year. It sat next to a picture of the two of us, and I reread it frequently to remind myself of Jason's love for me. It's a tall triangular card with a thin silver ribbon on the inside crease. In the corner of the front cover is a small silver vase with pink roses.

The cover says, "Mum, you might not always know exactly when or how you're making a difference in my life, but believe me— even when you don't realize it, you are. Some days, it's the help or advice you give, but more often, it's simply the way you love me and believe in me—no matter what."

Inside, it reads, "It means the world to have you in my life. You really are the best. Happy Mother's Day."

Underneath, Jason wrote, "Happy Mother's Day, Mum. I love you." He added the smiley face like he always did: two straight lines for the eyes, one for the nose, and the smiley mouth. He didn't put the circle around this one.

I decided not to go to church on Mother's Day. It would be too emotional to see all the sons with their mothers. My pastor has the mothers come up for prayer, and I love that he does that, but I couldn't watch it without falling apart. I needed to be at home with my grief on this first Mother's Day without Jason. I prayed and meditated in the morning, read my Bible, and thought of my son. I knew God would be okay with that. It actually turned out to be a good day. I visited his grave and thought of all the struggles he had and how we grew up together. I let go and gave him to God without feeling the burden of sadness I usually feel.

I also visited my mother because I felt it was the right thing to do. But I thought of our relationship and how I really didn't know her. There was no relationship at all. It wasn't just that she didn't love me; I also didn't know how to love her because I was too busy trying to seek her approval. I'd always buy her nice things for holidays and birthdays, hoping I'd get the acceptance and unconditional love you get from a mother. It wasn't there; she wasn't capable of giving it. I was finally accepting that and doing what I needed to help her in her last days, as my compassion toward the both of us grew.

Ma missed out on so much with our family. I'd invite her to our home for dinners and the holidays, but she never came. The last time she was at my house was Jason's twenty-fifth birthday. I asked her to leave the alcohol she brought in the front hall.

She did so, but only reluctantly, saying, "Oh, all right."

I said, "Ma, I told you we don't have alcohol in our house." Greg had given up drinking a year after we met, and Jason no longer used drugs or alcohol.

That was another demonstration of not honoring my boundaries. She never came to my house again. She never wanted to be anywhere unless alcohol was served. She couldn't cope without it.

My parents didn't have a relationship with Jason or any of their other grandchildren. How sad that they missed out on a wonderful relationship with a young man like him. What a loss that they didn't get to know him in a personal way. They came to my house for his birthdays and some other events in his life, but neither of them spent time with him alone. Jason once said to me, "Mum, Papa and Grandma never did anything with me." He wasn't angry about it, but as he got older, he realized that an important relationship was missing. Jason was no dummy. He knew who was safe and who wasn't. Fortunately, he had other people in his life he felt he could trust.

Two weeks before the anniversary of Jason's death, I received the call I was waiting for from the coroner's office. The report stated "probable cardiac dysrhythmia due to a seizure of unknown etiology." I looked up the word *etiology*, which meant "origin." Jason had a seizure the night he died, but the coroner's office wasn't sure why.

I believe the seizure was caused by one of his medications. He took only two meds: Abilify and Clozaril, both antipsychotics. Abilify has been known to cause seizures. Learning Jason died of a seizure didn't provide any "closure," as some people around me suggested. There is no "closure" when you lose a child. It's not a chapter in a book that you can close. In fact, I don't believe you get closure with the loss of *any* person you've loved and lost. Love lasts forever. It doesn't close up shop now that the person is no longer here.

I cried after I hung up the phone. I thought of what my son would say if he found out the results of his death. When Jason was here, we talked about his meds, and he'd say, "Mum, I couldn't function without them." I had to believe that God took Jason home because his time here was complete. The coroner's office also said that Jason didn't suffer. I hope he didn't even realize what happened when God took him home that night. So many people, like my husband's niece Adrianna, die slow deaths, and I had to thank God my son didn't. Adrianna suffered with cancer for almost two years, and it was hard to witness.

On the one-year anniversary of Jason's death, May 28, 2014, I stayed home from work. It was a solemn day for me, but I did my best with it. I went to the cemetery, and I'd like to say I spent time with him, but I'm always spending time with him in my heart and my mind. I wanted to get through this day in peace, but that night, my mother was taken again from rehab to the hospital. I couldn't believe it. I felt like I couldn't get a break. My mother's situation was becoming a roller-coaster ride, and quite frankly, I was getting tired. This was starting to feel like when I was child and I never had time to worry about taking care of myself. There was always a crisis in the house that I was left to fix. I was the one trying to keep it together. I know it may sound selfish, but here was a woman who went food shopping the day of my son's funeral, and now I was supposed to be there for her.

I was starting to see that in some of my relationships, I was still allowing others to victimize me. As a child, I had no other choice; I was trapped in a situation I was powerless over. Now, as an adult, I could make choices to protect myself, and I didn't have to let anyone take my life away from me. Ma didn't plan to be hospitalized on Jason's anniversary; it wasn't her fault, but I felt I needed to have this day for myself.

My husband and I went to see Ma in the ICU late that afternoon. The wall calendar in her room was flipped around so you couldn't see the date, and I told Greg that God was protecting me from looking at it because I had to get out of myself and any self-pity I might have been feeling. Although it was tough, I was kind toward my mother during our visit. She gave me her disdainful, dirty look when I explained I couldn't understand her whisper. I wanted to explode, but I kept my mouth shut. Greg was able to understand her. She said she missed going to the beach. I felt bad because I knew this was the beginning of the end for my mother; she'd never be at the beach again.

The doctors told Ma that because the tumor in her throat had grown, she couldn't have a breathing tube put down her throat. She had two options: to take a chance, never be resuscitated again and go naturally, or to breathe through an incision in her throat, a tracheostomy. Ma decided to have the trach put in, along with a feeding tube. Greg and I went to see her after the procedure, and she looked great—God bless her—sitting up, alert, and smiling, like a person who didn't realize she was dying. Her complexion was fair but not pale. I said, "Ma, you look great," but she responded with her usual look of disappointment. What can I say? I couldn't win. If I was positive, I got the look, and if I was negative, I got the same look. I tried to be the encouraging daughter, but she didn't want any of it.

Ma wouldn't be going home, so Greg and I decided to take in Candy. I had grown attached to her over the past year while walking her every day, which had helped me through Jason's death.

She would have to sleep in our basement while getting acclimated to Wednesday, Jason's cat.

Greg, in his flexible way, got all kinds of toys and treats for her, dog food, a new leash, and built a barrier in the house to keep the cat and dog separate. I took Candy out every morning, and Greg came home at lunchtime to spend time with her while he smoked a cigar with his partner, Ralph. We hired a trainer to help bring Wednesday and Candy together, but after the first lesson, when I went to move Candy from the couch, she nipped at me.

I have to admit that I was having a difficult time with the responsibility of keeping her. The situation was reminded me of when I gave birth to Jason, when I didn't know what to do or ask for help. Once again, I was feeling trapped, doing something I wasn't ready to do. I could feel her neediness, and I didn't want it. Since I was abandoned and neglected as a child, I had trouble abandoning anyone. Eventually, Greg and I decided we had to find another home for her.

Of course, we weren't going to give her to just anyone. Ralph had a sister-in-law who just said goodbye to her own dog. She saw pictures of Candy and came by the house to meet her. As soon as Rhonda walked into our house, she picked up Candy and held her in her arms as if she was already her own. A match made in heaven. Greg and I packed up Candy's goodies, and she was off in Rhonda's new Volkswagen Beetle, which was a shade of gray that matched Candy's coat. I started crying after they drove away because this was another goodbye to a life I helped take care of. But Candy had a good home, and I didn't have to worry about her.

There was no way I was going to tell my mother Candy was no longer living with us. She was in her last days, and I didn't need to give her something else to worry about or hurt her feelings. Although I never received this type of consideration from her, it was the right thing to do. We let Todd in on our plans, and he was okay with our decision. We certainly didn't want any issues with him about the dog.

* * *

The night of my mother's first resuscitation, I lost my phone at the hospital. I wasn't upset about the phone itself but about the loss of a short video of Jason I had from a basketball game we went to a few months before he passed. I couldn't shut the video off during the game, and I pointed the phone at Jason for about three seconds so he could help me. It was the only video and audio I had of him.

We had a good time at that game. I remember feeling happy we were doing something he loved. We were having fun, and I wasn't driving him crazy. I was just happy to be in his company. I know this is not biblical to say, but because Jason was a Gemini and I am an Aries, we got along great. Aries and Gemini are supposedly stimulated by the mind and feed off each other. We both loved to share our ideas and have philosophical debates, and we both got bored easily. Astrology isn't something I live by, but I think some of the characteristics are intriguing.

On August 18, Bobby and his family were going to Disney World and invited Greg and me, thinking we could have a little fun. My mother was in grave condition, so we visited her before we left. She made it clear that she didn't like where she was—a hospice in North Reading, a converted house on a main road surrounded by woods, next to a Catholic Church. The staff was kind and compassionate, knowing Ma was in her last days. I know she didn't want to die; none of us do. But I also kept in mind that she got to live fifty years more than Jason, and that was a long time.

I talked with her as gently as I could about repenting for her sins and asking God and Jesus for forgiveness in her last days. I told her that God was not mad at her—he loved her, but it is only through him we can be forgiven. She wanted no part of Jesus, but I continued to pray for her.

Ma had asked me to bring an eye pencil, hairbrush, and bobby pins to her in the hospice, which I did. Of course, she asked for the one thing I forgot to pick up, which was a pair of drugstore reading glasses. I felt bad I fell short again, but I didn't beat myself up over it, which was growth for me. Todd was there, and he could run down the street and buy her a pair.

Afterward, while in the car with Greg, I said, "That was the best my mother could do? Ask for her makeup?" She hadn't eaten in three months and weighed about seventy pounds, but she wanted an eye pencil. She was holding on to living and didn't want to die. Who could blame her? It was still about what she looked like, and she didn't care one bit about how she felt. I wanted to tell her, "God is waiting for you. How about being prepared for him in your spirit and not in your flesh?" I felt sad that she hadn't experienced a relationship with God in her life. I truly believe a relationship with Jesus could have helped her be healed from her own childhood wounds.

As usual, she offered me no conversation about our lives. Realizing she could die while we were in Florida and that I might not see her again, I told Ma that I was a good daughter to her. I had to say it since she always made me feel like I wasn't good enough. Considering all the neglect, abuse, and denial, I had done a lot to help her. Another daughter may not have been there at all. Maybe I could have thanked her for being my mother, but I didn't, and I don't regret not saying that to her. I'm grateful to some extent since I wouldn't be here if it weren't for her, but my gratitude goes mostly to God. I am what I am in spite of her, not because of her.

When you grow up not feeling loved, as I did and as I believe she did, you can't possibly know how to give love apart from God's grace and knowing him. Yes, we can go through the motions of life robotically, but to really feel love and unselfishness only comes through his grace.

This past year, I gained a lot of understanding about my own shortcomings and how my relationship with my parents affected all my other relationships. Most people I met I wanted to change because I couldn't change my parents. These people wore many faces but had the personalities of my family. I continued to try to please them and win their love, to no avail. My mind told me I had the power to change people, but none of us do. I didn't want to believe my parents didn't love me, but they didn't, and I finally allowed myself to accept that.

Praise God, I was able, by the grace of God, to change my relationship with my son. Through our trials, Jason saw me stand by him, no matter what. Isn't that true love? To be there for someone and love them through anything they need to get through? I certainly wouldn't have been capable of that without my relationship with God. I'm way too selfish to do that on my own. My mother used people, but so did I, and I might still be doing that today if I wasn't trusting and relying on God. I no longer want to seek out people who I need something from. I want to be open for who God wants to put in my life, not who I think I need.

Ma's boyfriend Andy never came to see her during her last days. He stayed in Virginia with his wife. Her health was also failing, and he was taking care of her. Ma didn't mind. She didn't want him to come up anymore.

She said, "I don't want him to see me like this."

I said, "Ma, if he loves you, he's not going to care."

He called once when she was at Melrose hospital. It was on his birthday—I think August 10.

I said, "She can't talk. I'll put the phone to her ear." I don't know what he said to her.

Did my mother love Andy? I believe she cared for him, but I don't believe she loved him in the way we know it. Did he love her? He certainly didn't leave his wife for her. Staying with her during Ma's last days was the right thing to do.

* * *

I realized my mother could die while we were away in Florida, but I decided to go anyway. I knew Todd would be on hand to help her. I was anxious about flying, as always, but I was hoping we could have a nice break. My brother Bobby is a joyful and loving human being, and his two teen boys are well-behaved and easy to be around. We checked into the Wilderness Lodge, a hotel on the Disney World grounds. I had never stayed on the Disney property before.

Other than that, I felt nostalgic because I took Jason to Disney World three or four times, and I took Bobby on his first visit there when he and Jason were young. Bobby and I have known each other for over thirty years, which I appreciate more and more as time goes by without Jason. History with the people around you is so important because it allows you to share memories of people who have passed.

Together, Bobby and I had memories of Jason from before I met Greg. That connection was becoming more evident as the months moved forward without him.

I was wishing the three of us were back in time, when we were young. I would have given anything to live those years without my untreated alcoholism. I was grateful, looking back, that I was able to bring Jason to Florida, even when we were living on our own and I made eight dollars an hour. Thank God, Fred lived in Florida, which gave us a place to stay for free and I didn't have to give myself up for it. I think Jason was four or five the first time I brought him to Disney World. He loved the rides and the games. We went on Magic Mountain, and I have a picture from Splash Mountain. The song from the "It's a Small World" ride drove him crazy.

The first morning of the trip with Greg and Bobby, I woke up and sat out on the balcony to do my prayer and meditation. I invited God into my day, as I do every morning. It only makes sense since he holds my life in his hands. Prayer and meditation had already helped me through the first year without Jason. That morning, I thought about my fear of flying and how tired I was of trying to control my life. Alcoholics are driven by fear, rooted in our own selfishness of needing to be in control. We want to control everything, even our death. I offered my life up to God that morning and asked him to give me peace in my spirit. The days ahead would be trying, with reminders of Jason everywhere. I was determined to enjoy myself with the few close family members I had left.

One morning, Greg and I were sitting at the pool when I noticed a plane writing a message in the sky. I thought the skywriting was probably an advertisement. To my surprise, Greg looked up and said, "Look Sweetie, it's a smiley face." The skywriter had written "Trust in God," with a smiley face at the end of the message. My eyes filled up with gratitude that God was letting me know Jason was with me. Through the past year, he had shown me many smiley faces during the darkest days of my grief. There is a difference between simply believing in God and believing in God and his promises through all the good and the bad times of life. My faith has been challenged since Jason's passing, but I have learned to keep my eye on Christ and to always remember that eternity is awaiting me.

Getting through the rest of the week at Disney World was a challenge. I couldn't help but think of Jason when he was little. My mind went back and forth between the happy times and the stress I'd felt as a young parent. I'd get so worked up over the littlest things, like if he spilled his milk or didn't clean his room to my expectations. I remembered the times I went out at night with clients, making my job more important than him. He'd ask me to play cards, and I'd tell him I had to cook supper.

But it's the little things like playing cards at a kitchen table, being in the moment instead of obsessing about work, that are meaningful. I was constantly looking for love in men and in my job. I couldn't enjoy Jason because I was too busy trying to get love. I realize now that love was right in front of me with him. Satan dogs me every day to beat myself up and to hate myself for my sins. I have to continuously go to God over this.

I was thinking of Jason while riding the Disney buses to the different parks all week, seeing the little boys with their moms. My eyes filled with tears when I remembered him at that age. At moments, I just wanted to cry out loud, but I had to compose myself.

Bobby, Danielle, and the kids had a great time; and Greg and I were glad to be a part of it, but I decided to call it quits after the fourth day. Seeing all the children around with their parents while knowing I'd never be a parent to Jason here on earth saddened me. I had done my best to keep up with a cheerful spirit, but I was ready to go home.

Greg and I returned home on a Saturday night in late August. My mother was still in hospice, and I wasn't sure when I'd be able to visit. Ma had always believed she'd die on a Sunday. Well, another Sunday passed and she was still with us. I went to bed on Sunday night, only to be awakened by a call at two o'clock in the morning. The nurse told me Ma was unresponsive and asked if I would be coming because she didn't think it would be long. I said, "Yes, in a couple of hours." For some reason, I went back to bed and slept like a baby. I was awakened again by another call informing me that my mother had passed at three fifty-five in the morning. The nurse asked again if I'd be coming by, and this time I said no.

I got out of bed and felt a little guilty that Ma died alone, but my guilt didn't last long. If I had left at two o'clock, I would have been beside her while she passed, but I knew she wouldn't have wanted me there. My mother would have been irritated if I sat by her bedside, offering loving words of comfort that I was more than happy to provide. For once, I honored her wishes, which was to be alone.

You may be thinking I sound cold, but when a person doesn't want you, why would you keep going back to them? If I could have given my mother one more day to live, I would have, but it was in God's hands. I was finally done lying to myself that I had a relationship that didn't exist. Of course, I felt bad she was gone, but not as bad as I felt that Jason, who I loved and who loved me, was gone. For Ma, the tears were few, and I understood why as the days went on. You can't grieve for someone you don't know or love. I realized that all the years I spent trying to earn my mother's love, as opposed to actually loving her, didn't work. I didn't feel loved by my mother. Therefore, I didn't love her either.

I've learned a great deal about growing up in a family without love. The book *The Loveless Family* by Jon Bloch validated a lot for me about the family I grew up in. People have said to me, "Oh, that's just their way. They didn't know any better." This can be true, but that's no excuse. Love isn't putting your children down or leaving them. Love isn't putting your career or your boyfriend or girlfriend first. Love isn't letting someone else raise your children. We live in a "me first" world, and love is very scarce. Love is a self-sacrificing relationship, where you want the best for the other person's life. Love is giving up self to be there for someone else and not trying to control them. So mine remains, for me, a family without love.

Todd made all the funeral arrangements for my mother. Most of the insurance policies were in his name, so it only made sense for him to make the decisions. He had her cremated and selected the urn for her remains. I prayed for God to have mercy on my mother and her sins of the past, the sins that she wouldn't talk about to anyone. As Pastor Gus said at my church, "We don't know what a human being can do in their last moments before death." Maybe my mother did turn to God and ask his forgiveness. I can only cling onto that small glimmer of hope.

Before the service, Todd came by my house to pick up my mother's bank card since he was the beneficiary. He had a stack of papers with him.

"Here, Karen," he said. "I wanted to show you something."

"What is it?" I asked.

"This will tell you what they told Ma I had."

He wanted me to read a few pages of an interview that was done in the early seventies between my mother and a caseworker from Massachusetts General Hospital in Boston in regard to Todd and his behavior in school. My mother gave Todd a copy of this interview, and he kept it at his house.

My other two brothers and I always knew there was something psychologically wrong with Todd, but we never knew what it was. Glancing at the interview, I learned that Todd had been diagnosed with Klinefelter syndrome, also called XXY syndrome. Todd left quickly after getting the bank card, and I was glad. I didn't feel safe being alone in my house with him, and I was sorry I let him come over. I was afraid he'd do something like walk by me and touch my butt because he was always pushing my boundaries. I didn't read more about his diagnosis until he left.

Klinefelter syndrome is a genetic condition that occurs when a male is born with an extra X chromosome. The primary feature is sterility. A person affected may have weaker muscles, greater height, poor coordination, less body hair, smaller genitals, breast growth, and less interest in sex. Intelligence is usually normal; however, reading difficulties and problems with speech are common. Only about two hundred thousand cases occur in the US per year, so it's very rare. I have also read that teen boys with this condition can suffer from depression, attention deficit disorder, alcoholism, and schizophrenia. So not only do they have body image issues; they may also have psychological issues.

Todd fit the description to a tee. When he was in his twenties, he told us he was sterile (he was married for seven or eight years in the mid-eighties, and the marriage produced no children). He was tall for his age and had sparse facial hair and poor impulse control. He had learning difficulties; maybe his frustration over this was what made him so explosive. Todd did not get the help he needed in those days, which was unfortunate for him and our family. I later learned that a disproportionate number of individuals with Klinefelter syndrome end up in the prison system. That researcher attributed this to the perception that Klinefelter syndrome was associated with criminality, which was later refuted. The researchers should have interviewed Todd.

I'm not sure why Todd showed me the interview. He clearly wanted me to know he had an actual diagnosis. I think he wanted me to feel sorry for him, and this may have been his way of blaming the sexual abuse on his illness. After reading the symptoms, it all made sense to me.

In the report, the caseworker asked my mother about her relationship with my father and Todd's relationship with his father and his siblings. My mother told the caseworker that Todd was a sickly child and she spoiled him due to his fragility. She also told her she felt the marriage declined after I was born. My mother didn't tell the interviewer Todd was conceived outside the marriage; she put the blame on me, the one daughter in the family, who was born right after Todd. This is when I became the "scapegoat" in the family. The one the narcissist puts all the blame on. That's why I always felt like I was doing something wrong. She and Todd (the golden child) were abusing me that's why I never felt safe. Just as Dad had told me, he gave me extra attention as the only daughter when I was a child, and my mother was jealous. I was beginning to understand the co-dependent relationship with the narcissist. That's why I was drawn to these unemotionally abusive people. I'm so grateful for the healing Jesus has given me.

God's grace allowed me to better understand my mother through something else she stated in the interview: that she felt "not wanted." That revelation gave me a much better understanding of why she was the way she was. I remembered her saying she was a "change of life" baby. I think she needed to say that because it made her feel special. It might have been what her mom or dad said too, but most likely, they said it in a derogatory way. I don't know for sure, but in my heart, I believe that's what happened. Both our lives were mirror images of each other regarding our being neglected, believing we were unlovable, turning to men for sex, and having a child we felt ashamed of.

As I continued to read the report, I discovered even more ways I was like my mother, including being overprotective of my son. The lie my mother told herself at an early age was that she wasn't good enough, and I told myself the same lie. Unfortunately, we both allowed this falsehood to affect our relationships with our children. I always felt I needed to protect Jason because people would think he was "less than," just like I felt less than myself. I had to prove to the world that Jason and I were important enough and good enough, just as Bill W., cofounder of AA, navigated his way through life trying to prove himself.

My mother and I were both desperate to protect our children and ourselves from hurtful people in this world. The sad part is instead we were drawn to people similar to those who hurt us when we were children. She was drawn to what was familiar, and so was I. We both continued to revictimize ourselves through life. I also realized that Todd was the "golden child" Danu Morrigan writes about in *Daughters of Narcissistic Mothers*—the child the narcissist needs to feed their ego and sides with them, no matter what.

After reading the interview, I connected with my mother in a way I never dreamed I would: through our sons. It was a healing moment for me. This was the closure I needed to better understand a woman I called Ma but never really knew.

It still saddens me that Ma didn't get to know how much God loved her and that he wanted so much better for her as his daughter. My mother was a survivor, but unfortunately, she never felt worthy of love. I was only just starting to understand how to accept love in my own life, the love I have with my husband and Jason. Only the power of God's grace can change people's hearts. We need to be broken down, become children again, so we know who our Father is and that we can trust him to guide and protect us. We are born with a selfish nature into families that are lost, but we can be transformed by his love. He wants a better life for all of us and gives us specific instructions on how to live it in his Word. The purpose of God's Word is not to keep us from enjoying life, as Ma may have feared, but to protect us from ourselves.

My mother's wake and funeral were both the same night. She was already cremated, which she would have preferred. She didn't feel comfortable around people and wouldn't have wanted to be laid out in front for everyone to see. I suggested that Todd have her service there at Vazza's, where we had Jason's. When I arrived at the funeral home, Todd was already there with a friend. I was glad he had someone there for him. The urn he chose was quite elegant—a flowery design with multiple soft colors, very feminine looking. People were coming in to pay their respects, and it felt odd to be there again only fourteen months after Jason's service. My mother had only two flower arrangements: one from Greg and me and the other from Greg's family. I thought that was appropriate since my mother always said, "You can't smell flowers when you're dead."

Todd asked for my help finding a minister, so I asked Pastor Ray. He was unable to make it so he asked Pastor Gus who ended up coming along with a couple of friends from church to support us. He said a few words, and then Todd got up to speak. Todd fell apart quickly, and I felt sorry for him. I thought of how close Jason and I had been, then of the close relationship the two of them shared. I said a few words after Todd spoke. I let Todd know he was a good son to my mother. I said my mother and I weren't close, but I was sorry she wasn't able to stay with us longer since she wanted to live. I looked toward her urn to let her know we had found a good home for Candy. I thanked her for being my mother since I wouldn't be here if it weren't for her.

Todd went on to acknowledge everyone he could by name and shared my mother's feelings toward them, and then, as far as I was concerned, the family unit was finally over. That chapter was closed for me now, and I knew I'd probably never hear from Todd again.

Wayne didn't get to the service; he told Todd he had just started a new job and couldn't come. I wasn't surprised since the last time he stayed at my mother's he said he wouldn't go to her funeral because of the way he was treated. Well, I guess it worked out just the way he wanted. I hadn't heard from him at all. The last time I talked to him was the one time he phoned when Jason died. I was okay with that now at this stage in my life. Losing Jamie and Jason had been the ultimate hurt for me. I was okay not dealing with the untreated alcoholism anymore. I was tired of it, to be quite honest. Disease is exhausting to be around when left untreated. I had been directly affected by alcoholism for too long. The days of spending time with alcoholic family members were now behind me.

The past never totally leaves you, but you can be healed from it, and it doesn't have to define your life. Your story can change if you seek help from God as to what happens in your future. The story of my life has certainly changed quite a bit since we—Ma, Dad, Wayne, Todd, Jamie, and I—were all a family. Truth is a powerful experience when you are open to it. Sometimes you just have to find out what the truth is.

* * *

I was determined to get to that moment of truth the doctor writes about in his book. The anxiety I was still experiencing took some time to figure out and heal from. The doctor mentioned a theory which I later found to be true. I knew I was not just stuck emotionally but physically. I was still anxious driving far from home, and I still struggle on the highway with moments of crippling fear. I was becoming desperately close to going on medication. I needed more help.

The physical trauma from the effects of my childhood remained stuck inside me, fighting to come out. I found a therapist who uses a treatment called eye movement desensitization and processing therapy or EMDR. It was originally designed to alleviate distress associated with traumatic memories and help the mind heal. As an analogy, when you have a splinter, it can cause pain and infection, but once it's removed, the body can heal naturally. The same is true with the mind and past trauma. My therapist Laurie gave me headphones with bilateral sounds and a handheld device that vibrated alternately. She instructed me to follow the light on a bar that was moving left to right. During a couple of sessions, I returned to my childhood and teen years, when I felt alone and trapped. After my second session, memories were coming back in pieces. Not new memories, just connections showing how the past trauma was playing out in the present. The answer had been right in front of me, but I couldn't see it.

I know today the feeling of uneasiness that I felt in 2001 driving out to visit Jason's school was me facing the pain of abuse I never faced in my own childhood. Fear of telling Jason the truth about why I was distant from him and why he felt unwanted. God was trying to heal me and let me know I could let go of that pain from my past I was still holding on to. I could face my truth but I wasn't quite ready and I continued to hide from it. I'm grateful God gave me the opportunity to talk with Jason before he died. Since Jason's passing I have slowly faced the physical and emotional pain of a lost childhood and the loss of having parents who were unable to love me.

While driving out to see a client in 2003 shortly after dating Greg, I was suddenly gripped with fear and I couldn't move the steering wheel. I rushed to get off the highway. At the time, I was feeling like I couldn't speak up for myself in my relationship with Greg. I hadn't realized that, unlikely as it was, Greg reminded me in some ways of Rob. Rob had gray hair, lived in East Boston, and liked to gamble, particularly on the horses, and played cards. Greg has salt-and-pepper hair, grew up in East Boston, and liked to bet the horses and played cards. Shortly after I met Greg, he got a tattoo on his shoulder showing two horses with jockeys at the finish line. Unlike

Rob, however, his enjoyment of gambling hasn't caused him financial trouble since I've known him. He's very good with money.

I also learned that a piece of Greg's personality reminded me of both Rob and Todd: he didn't like my setting boundaries or confronting him about something he did that I didn't like. Fortunately, with the help of a therapist, Greg and I worked on our communication issues together. My therapist Laurie has helped me to heal from the childhood trauma I experienced all those years ago. The memories I have of the abuse and neglect I didn't process are stored in my body and need to come out. There are times at night my body will shake and tremble letting out the fear I held in for so long.

When characteristics in people or places trigger my abuse, I can feel trapped and in a disassociated state. It can come from sex, intimacy or just being close to someone emotionally again. If I'm with someone I know is unsafe, it can trigger feelings of helplessness, powerlessness or vulnerability. I know now when I'm being triggered and have learned to respond from the adult in me not the child. Today I know I can protect the adult and child within me. I have learned to nurture and listen to that child within whose needs were not met.

* * *

I've had to start letting go of the emotions and behaviors that held me back most of my life, the lies I told myself while growing up in a home of neglect and abuse. While writing this book, I realized that although I'm smart and made a good income all these years, I believed, like my mother, that I needed a man to survive. The survival skills I developed to get by in a home that was unsafe and unpredictable are no longer necessary. I no longer define myself by what happened to me but by what God's Word says of me. I am the daughter of the Most High King; and I am being loved, cared for, and protected by him. Through my relationship with him and the people he's brought into my life, God has made my past clear as glass.

I continue to move forward with my loving husband, Greg. I live every day with the memories of Jason and Jamie. I'm still with the auto glass company, now in my thirty-second year. Some days, I drive on the highway to see my clients, bearing the heaviness of grief and cry on the way. I spend a lot of time alone in the car, which can be tough some days, but it has strengthened me and my relationship with Jesus.

When I clean the toilet, wash my dishes, or change my shower curtain, I think of Jason. These were things we did in his apartment while I drove him nuts with my cleaning. I know this might sound crude, but when I cut my nose hairs, I think of Jason because I also did that for him. When I drive by the smoke shop in East Boston, I can almost see him walking out with his head down, carrying his bag of tobacco. I stop at the traffic light in front of the store regularly, and I can see the shadow of him walking toward me. What I wouldn't give to see him again.

Jason would have been ecstatic that Lebron James went back to Cleveland. Jason felt he betrayed his fans when he left, and he predicted Lebron would go back. I left a newspaper article at Jason's grave one day to let him know. I'm sure Jason already knew because he has a lot more power than I do now.

I miss Jason's laugh and his witty way of explaining things. He knew his music; he knew his sports and his video games, but most of all, he knew he wasn't alone and that he was loved. All of us want that security, and we think we can find it in so many other material things. It is not there but in God and each other that we find the secure feeling of being home.

I know I have a home in heaven and that my son Jason is there. He waits for me while I wait to be called by God to that place where the streets are made of gold. I can see Jason taking my hand and showing me around while I listen to his clever explanations of everything I need to know. He'll bring me to Jesus, Abraham and Isaac, as sung in that beautiful song played at Jason's funeral. Jason will be there with no mental illness. My husband's niece Adrianna will also be there without cancer. I can't imagine those two beautiful souls being any more innocent than they were here on earth, but they will be. They will be healed of all the mental and physical suffering they endured and be in the loving arms of Jesus. I can't wait to be in that blissful place, feeling the love of God, and with my son, whom I now know I loved and who loved me.

SUGGESTED BOOKS
AND MOVIES

Adult Children of Alcoholics World Service, *Adult Children: Alcoholic/Dysfunctional Families* (Adult Children of Alcoholics World Service Organization, 2006).

Anonymous, *Alcoholics Anonymous: The Story of How Many Thousands of Men and Women Have Recovered from Alcoholism* ("The Big Book"), Fourth Edition (Alcoholics Anonymous World Services Inc., 2001).

Bloch, Jon P., *The Loveless Family: Getting Past Estrangement and Learning How to Love* (Praeger, 2011).

Elmore, Tim, *12 Huge Mistakes Parents Can Avoid: Leading Your Kids to Success in Life* (Harvest House Publishers, 2014).

Dayton, Tian PhD, *The ACOA Trauma Syndrome: The Impact of Childhood Pain on Adult Relationships* (Health Communications, Inc., 2012).

Forward, Susan, *Mothers Who Can't Love* (Harper, 2013).

Golomb, Elan, *Trapped in the Mirror: Adult Children of Narcissists in Their Struggle for Self* (Harper, 1992).

Horsley, Gloria and Horsley, Heidi, *Open to Hope: Inspirational Stories of Healing After Loss* (Open to Hope Foundation, 2011).

A Beautiful Mind, directed by Ron Howard (Universal Pictures, 2001).

McBride, Karyl, *Will I Ever Be Good Enough? Healing the Daughters of Narcissistic Mothers* (Atria, 2008).

Morrigan, Danu, *You're Not Crazy—It's Your Mother: Understanding and Healing for Daughters of Narcissistic Mothers* (Darton, Longman and Todd, 2012).

Peck, M. Scott, *People of the Lie: The Hope for Healing Human Evil* (Touchstone, 1998).

Rosof, Barbara D., *The Worst Loss: How Families Heal from the Death of a Child* (Holt Paperbacks, 1994).

The Aviator, directed by Martin Scorsese (Miramax, 2004).

ABOUT THE AUTHOR

Karen Sobanek Cioffi is a mother and wife who lives in the Boston area. She grew up as the only daughter of neglectful parents in Chelsea, a small city close to Boston. Karen didn't graduate from high school. She left in the ninth grade but by the grace of God was able to become an accomplished salesperson for an auto glass company in Chelsea where she grew up.

Sober for thirty years, she is active in Alcoholics Anonymous, bringing women through the twelve steps. Karen loves to cook, travel, and read in her spare time. She is a born-again Christian and is active in her local church. She loves to teach people about Jesus and the healing he has done in her life. Karen has enjoyed volunteering a few years at a local homeless shelter for families. She is a great communicator who loves to learn about people and gain insight into their lives. She is looking to make a difference in the world by her life's experiences and the wisdom God has given her. Karen is also involved in Compassionate Friends, an organization for parents who have lost children, a place she thought she'd never find herself but so grateful they were there. She loves children and animals and hopes this book will provide help for those that are most vulnerable in our world, our children.

CPSIA information can be obtained
at www.ICGtesting.com
Printed in the USA
JSHW020853101119
2340JS00003B/7